FOURTEEN FEMALE
VOICES FROM BRAZIL

FOURTEEN FEMALE
VOICES FROM BRAZIL:
interviews and works

selected and edited by Elzbieta Szoka
with an introduction by Jean Franco

HOST PUBLICATIONS, INC.
AUSTIN, TEXAS

Layout and design: Joe Bratcher III
Cover design: AdrianoFagundes from a painting by Patricia de Oliveira
Proofreading: Gretchen Maclane

Library of Congress Catalog Number: 2002114883
ISBN: 0-924047-22-4 (Hardcover)
ISBN:0-924047-23-2 (Trade Paper)

First Edition

CONTENTS

To Joe, Adam & Ian,
the men of my life
and to my mother,
Krystyna

Preface

Born and raised in Poland, during the Soviet domination of so-called Eastern Europe, I never thought of feminism as an ideology that could be taken seriously because it was too reminiscent of Marxist-Leninist doctrine of the times that failed few decades later. Nobody in Poland talked in those days about women artists and men artists. Everybody was equal and diversity was a strange notion from the "decadent West." The notion of class was slightly more complex, since the differences could not be ignored that easily. Not even during the period of Stalinist terror right after the second world war. As for race, in a country where over six million people, mostly minorities, were killed by the Nazis and by the Soviets, a state of an apparent monolithic "racial harmony" was reinforced. Therefore talking of one's racial background did not go along with the official ideology of equality and unity, although the truth was closer to *Animal Farm.* In those days of the post-Stachanov effort to build socialism and fight for peace posters of women on the tractors and the like were as common as Calvin Klein advertisements of underwear are in New York today. Of course all that propaganda met with resistance by most people of both genders and being an essential woman (preferably married, with kids and Catholic) was the safe way of saying "no" to the "equalizing" system imposed by the Soviets. These years in Poland influenced me significantly to the point that I only recently discovered that gender, race and feminism do indeed have a solid raison d'être everywhere. Including Poland. I wouldn't say that I was a closet feminist all these years. I simply disregarded this world-view, linking it exclusively with Soviet propaganda.

I owe my discovery to a great extent to a classroom experience at Columbia University, where I taught a course on the contemporary short story in Brazil to a diversified group of students from different backgrounds. Naturally, the readings were by authors of both genders, whom I selected according to their innovative contributions to the art of narrative in Brazil. To my surprise, most students, male and female, chose for their papers and presentations works written by women. Asked individually about their motivation the students explained that the female voices, puzzling and inviting at the same time, were new to them. They also said that it would have been helpful to have more "personal" information about these authors, that criticism alone did not answer all the questions that those works inspired. Such information can only be given by the author himself or herself in an interview. Hence the decision of working with living authors only... This is how the idea of the book was born.

Fourteen voices suggest some sort of a chorus and it is indeed a vocal ensemble. However, the voices included range from coloraturas to contraltos with all possible variations in between. The order in which these authors appear is motivated by the evolution of the feminist canon in Brazil, regarding various ideological perspectives and writing styles. The writers are grouped in small thematic units, when possible, and the last author in the book summarizes most of the thematic concerns. They are introduced through brief biographical sketch, an interview and a text, for the most part selected by the authors themselves. Besides providing the desired personal information, the interviews are also intended as preludes to the texts that might be hard to understand outside the specific Brazilian context. All authors responded to the same questions, 10 in most cases, which were formulated after a small survey that I conducted among my American friends and acquaintances, the potential readers of the book, who come from different social and professional backgrounds and who represent different age groups and both genders. It was quite interesting to observe how many of the questions that my potential readers suggested coincided. My hope is that they will also coincide with the interests of the readers of this volume.

As happens with anthologies, there are always authors and works that cannot be included because of time and space constraints. I conducted all the interviews in Brazil in one month, traveling between Rio de Janeiro and São Paulo, where most of these writers live, with one short stop in Belo Horizonte at a conference *Mulher Literatura* (Woman /and/ Literature). My presence at that conference was an act that my Polish friends from the years of "*Animal Farm* equality" could never have imagined back in those days. Neither could I. The conference in itself was eye-opening and contributed even further to the creation of this anthology. I "discovered" an emerging and powerful group of Afro-Brazilian authors, whose work was an object of debate at various panels. Unfortunately, working independently, I was able to rely only on those authors with whom I was able to establish contact prior to my trip to Brazil. That is why the anthology does not include Rachel de Queiroz, Heloísa Maranhão, Lya Luft, Adélia Prado, Hilda Hilst, Patricia Melo and many other authors, whose work has been disseminated in other countries and should be known in the United States as well.

I would like to thank my students from that memorable short-story class for the initial inspiration. I am also grateful to Helena Parente Cunha, whose friendship I am privileged to enjoy since my graduate-student days at the University of Texas at Austin and whose help and support made the compilation of this anthology possible. I would like to thank all the authors in this volume for their unconditional dedication to the project. I am also in debt to Jean Franco who agreed to write an

Preface

introduction for this book on very short notice. The collaboration with various translators was priceless and I would like to thank them as well. My final words of appreciation go to my friends Dave Oliphant, Joseph Slate, Susan Lesak, Dymphna Staunton, Linda Mayers, Linda Sitnick and Celina Pinto for taking the time to read through some of these texts and preparing me for the "reaction of the market." Many thanks to my family and cats, as well.

— Elzbieta Szoka
Columbia University

Introduction

In 2001, I was invited to a conference on women's writing at the national university in Belo Horizonte and was astonished to find myself in an auditorium packed with women writers of all ages and ethnic backgrounds, speaking in a variety of accents. Some of the same energy and enthusiasm, the same sense of being on the cusp of a movement can be detected in this anthology of women writers who come from towns and regions as different as Amazonas and Bahia, São Paulo and Rio. Some are Afro-Brazilians, others were born into families that emigrated from Galicia and Italy. One writer claims some indigenous ancestry. Such varied backgrounds remind us that Brazil is, after all, a huge nation, with a population bigger than that of Russia, an immense and heterogeneous territory; a nation with rich indigenous and immigrant cultures, a history of transculturation and a language, Portuguese (which is not the *only* Brazilian language) — that is spoken in four continents.

Given its importance and potential, it is surprising that Brazilian literature is not better known in the United States. Its great writer, Machado de Assis, who is one of the most original and subtle novelists of the nineteenth-century, was quite recently "rediscovered" by Susan Sontag for American readers (a statue of him is the stage prop in Jandira Martini's play, included in this anthology). Brazil was never a cultural poor relation: Macunaima, the multi-racial and multicultural protagonist of a novel by Mario de Andrade, epitomized the creative transculturation that was celebrated by the exuberant avant-garde of the last century. And this is not to speak of the rich vein of regional writing, a rich poetry tradition that includes such outstanding poets as Cabral de Melo Neto, Carlos Drummond de Andrade as well as a crossover culture of poetry and popular song. Nor is women's writing a recent development although, as has happened in many parts of the world, the feminist movement played an important part not only in encouraging women writers but also in the rediscovery and celebration of their predecessors. No less than fifty women were included in a recent anthology of nineteenth century women writers . Of course there was no need to rediscover the generation writing in the fifties and sixties that included Clarice Lispector, Rachel de Queiroz and the poet Cecilia Meireles.

Of these Clarice Lispector is the most familiar. Her writing has been translated into many other languages and has been extensively glossed by French feminists such as Julia Kristeva and Hélène Cixous. For Cixous, Lispector practices *écriture feminine,* that is to say, a writing based on the confrontation with otherness, an encounter that destabilizes the limits of consciousness. In Lispector's case, this is grounded not only in philosophy but also in confrontation with those other living creatures whether human or non-human who are not (to use a phrase of Judith Butler) 'culturally intelligible.' A daughter of Ukrainian immigrants, Lispector reflects an estrangement that was immediately sensed and appreciated by Kristeva (who is Bulgarian-French) and Cixous (who is of Greek origin).

Rachel de Queiroz, also a major figure in Brazil, is something like the polar opposite of Lispector. A regional writer who often draws on the oral traditions of the North East. Best known as a novelist , she has written two plays, *Lampião* and *Beata Maria de Egito* based on the legendary figures of her region.

While feminism has been important to many of these women writers, many of them were marked by the twenty years of military rule that began in 1964 and which introduced censorship and severe repression that made it impossible for writers to address the present directly. The poet and playwright, Renata Pallottini for instance, wrote plays that were banned; and although she participated in outdoor poetry readings, her poems had to be shown to the police beforehand. Astrid Cabral resigned from her position at the University because her advisor was accused of being a communist and fired. When Jandira Martini began her career as a playwright, "everything was done with metaphor. Words like 'strike,' 'workers,' etc. couldn't appear in any script." Oppression, she emphasizes, is not necessarily a stimulus to art.

As many of the interviews with these writers suggest, they emerged from the period of military repression with a heightened sensitivity to all forms of injustice and discrimination that in many cases was stimulated by the success of women's and feminist movements. This success has been most spectacular in the political arena. Myriam Campello points out that there is now a woman on the supreme court. The prefect of São Paulo is a woman named Marta Suplicy and Senator Benedita da Silva is the first black woman to have held such a position, but "they are merely exceptions to the rule. There is no de facto equality. And moreover we still have that rigmarole of a woman earning less than a man for the same work."

Reading their literary texts, it becomes clear that what is known in Latin America as "the feminism of equality" does not address the deeper problems of sexual difference and discrimination. This may be why many of the stories and plays in this volume reflect deep-seated alienation both within the family and in relation to society as a whole and that is often complicated by the profound social divisions between the middle class and the poor as well as by racial difference. The latter has been particularly difficult to confront in Brazil because it was always supposed that attitudes were more tolerant than in the United States. Black culture pervades society from carnival celebrations, dance and music to Afro-Brazilian religion. When discrimination occurs it was often attributed to economic rather than racial difference. Yet as the Afro-Brazilian writers in this anthology make clear, black women live substantially different lives from their white neighbors. While many of the white Brazilian writers have not suffered discrimination, Esmeralda Riberiro points out, "White women go out to struggle and I have to stay in the kitchen," underscoring the fact that many middle-class women have maids and do not need to do domestic work so that working outside the home is not a problem. So deep is the denial of the race factor that Miriam Alves tells of going to see a psychiatrist when she couldn't stand the pressures of university life and being told that if she wanted to discuss race problems she should see a sociologist. Because of their situation black writers often feel a debt to their community. As Conceição Evaristo puts it, "My great dream is to be able to give my texts back to the people who gave me their life stories."

Publishing their writing is a problem that many of these women have had to face despite the fact that conditions for women have improved in the last decades. Leilah Assumpção tells us, "Producing a play in Brazil is the most difficult thing. Succeeding is a miracle. We don't have agents or anything here." Nélida Piñon, the best-known writer included in this volume, believes that "the rules governing aesthetic evaluation for women are different from those for men." Myriam Campello claims that a woman "has to have nerves of steel and be sufficiently tenacious in her desires, in her vocation, in order to secure a minimum place in the order of things." And it is significant that Afro-Brazilian writers have relied not on mainstream publishing but on the Afro-Brazilian writers' group, Quilombhoje, that encourages and publishes black writers.

The questions asked these writers about their work and beliefs underscore class and racial differences. Middle-class writers seldom feel discrimination as strongly as writers from Afro-Brazilian or poor backgrounds. Yet there are also commonalties. Many are suspicious of a globalization that deepens the gulf between rich and poor, most of them refuse party affiliations yet feel strongly about social injustices. Perhaps the most unusual question they were asked was whether mysticism plays a role in their lives, a question that would certainly surprise writers in this country. But many of these Brazilian writers respond positively to the question and many of them have been touched by Afro-Brazilian religion.

The stories these women tell are deeply tragic even when there are touches of humor as in Esmeralda Ribeiro's "In Search of a Black Butterfly." The storyteller is a telephone operator from the "Humanitarian Center" who overhears a strange conversation in which a woman claims that a black butterfly flew out of her uterus. Clearly, the butterfly represents a loss, and indeed it turns out that she has had a miscarriage when she and her boyfriend, a Frenchmen, were beaten up by a group of black neighbors. Racial mixing, supposedly condoned in Brazil's permissive society, is here condemned by the very community that had been discriminated against. But the meaning of the story is not so simple, for what precisely does the black butterfly represent? The woman's blackness, her illusions, her desire? For all the black writers in this volume, it seems that community is problematic especially in situations of extreme poverty. The narrator of Miriam Alves's story, "Alice Is Dead," although almost destitute represents himself as Alicia's protector. She is a half-starved drunkard who he allows to share his room and even a bed, although they have no family ties and no particular commitment and their hopelessness seems to stand in the way of love and eventually of compassion. The narrator, who has become a stranger even to pity, literally dumps Alicia. After dedicating himself to the trickster god, he throws Alicia into the garbage. The bleakness of this story is unrelenting, for the reader is never told how the characters found themselves in such a situation, in a place of bare existence in which humanity is a luxury. In Conceição Evaristo's story,

"Ana Davanga" community is even more problematic. The protagonist Ana Davenga is the lover of a charismatic gang leader whom she blindly loves without wanting to know anything of his criminal life. Isolated from the rest of the gang who are jealous of her, she has invested her entire existence in her lover and in her all-absorbing sexual life which shields her from knowledge of his activities. But there is no real shield and eventually she and her unborn child are killed along with the lover during a police raid. In this story pleasure and parasitism are closely intertwined with disastrous results.

The common thread that runs through much of the writing in this anthology is solitude and separation that sees no salvation either in community or within the family. One has a sense of women beating against a cage that is sometimes a family cage, sometimes a community cage, as in Helena Parente Cunha's "Single Mother" and "Two Girls at the Window," but often this cage is something less easily defined. In "The Orchid at the Exhibition," Astrid Cabral's protagonist is an orchid cultivated in order to be exhibited and, although the comparison is never explicit, the flower can be compared to a trophy wife. The orchid is helpless, her passions are narcissism and envy and her only escape is fantasy. In Lygia Fagundes Telles' story, "The Day to say 'No!'" the woman narrator is caught in an ethical dilemma as she tries to apply Saint Augustine's discipline in a world of insecurity in which inner life is continually invaded by the phone, by politicians, by music in the cab. Her thoughts too are invaded by fantasies of violence and bloodshed, by fear of accidents and by the importuning of street vendors and beggars. As she says, "There is nowhere to escape when Misery and Violence (twin sisters) are everywhere galloping on the white horses of the Apocalypse." But though refusal ought to define her as a subject, it does not quite work that way. She has uttered a definitive "no" to one of the invaders, a crippled boy who sells perfumed notepaper and who insists that writing will bring back an errant lover. But after the taxi moves on and the boy disappears in the crowd this particular refusal disturbs her. She would like to have transformed that into an affirmative, but the opportunity cannot be repeated. The paradoxical situation is that the middle-class woman, trapped in her armor of refusal is as much a prisoner as the poor because she's unable to open herself to the world.

Family relations are poisonous. In Nélida Piñon's story, the phrase, "Oh yes, I do love my husband," follows on a litany of hate. Even best friends are treacherous. In Maria Adelaide Amaral's *Cherish Thy Mother*, the relation between mother and daughter is fraught with old resentments, jealousies and betrayals. The raw passion of lesbian love in Myriam Campello's "The Woman of Gold," cannot withstand the threat of commitment. In Leilah Assumpção's *The Passion of Miss Congeniality*, a woman recalls her childhood friendship with the now spectacularly successful Mirabel and, faced with the impossibility of reliving that friendship, she murders her. Such writing is claustrophobic; neighbors are strangers who may rouse a voyeuristic curiosity as in Sonia Coutinho's "Summer in Rio." Voyeurism depends on a distance that precludes intimacy, on the refusal or impossibility of commitment, which runs like a thread through these texts that also question the possibility of "liberation" in a world where subjectivity seems to mean separation as in Renata Pallotini's "Neighbor," in which the speaker begs to be taken into a family life that she "supposed was finished."

Marly de Oliveira's poem in praise of the panther is the perfect commentary on this dilemma. The panther "pure and beautiful" can desire freedom unconditionally.

> The freedom of a panther
> consists precisely of this
> that not even she can control
> herself and whatever happens is unforeseen.

But such freedom is forbidden for human beings.

Introduction

Given the increasing pressure of commercialization, it is encouraging to find an anthology whose contributors afford us glimpses into the unresolved and perhaps unresolvable misfit between the subject and the social.

— Jean Franco
Columbia University

Nélida Piñon

Nélida Piñon

Nélida Piñon was born in Rio de Janeiro where she currently lives and works. She is the author of 14 books translated into 20 languages. In 1996 she became the first woman president of Academia Brasileira de Letras in its 100 year history. In 1970 she inaugurated the first program in creative writing at the Federal Universiyt of Rio de Janeiro. She dedicates much of her time to teaching. She has held an endowed chair in the humanities at the University of Miami since 1990, as well as the Julio Cortázar Chair (founded by Gabriel Garcia Márquez and Carlos Fuentes) at the University of Guagalajara in Mexico. she has also taught at Columbia, Johns Hopkins, Georgetown and Harvard. Her work has received numerous awards in Brazil and abroad. She has been awarded honorary doctarates from: the University of Forida; the University of Poiters, France; the University of Santiago de Compestella, Spain; and Rutgers University.

Her major works include: Novels: *Madeira feita cruz* (1963); *Fundador* (1969) [Walmap prize]; *A casa da paixão* (1972) [Mario de Andrade prize]; *Tebas do meu coração* (1974); *A força do destino* (1977); *A República dos sonhos* [The Republic of Dreams] (1984) [APCA prize, Pen Club prize]; *A doce canção de Caetana* [Caetana's Sweet Song] (1987) [UBE, SP prize]; *A roda do vento* (juvanilia, 1996).

Stories: *Tempos das frutas* (1966); *Sala de armas* (1973); *O calor das coisas* (1980).

Nélida Piñon

What led you to become a writer?

First of all, I felt very distant from that decision, so much so that I hope you'll allow me to give several versions at the same time as regarding my passion for literature. Most of all, it is a very old love, because when I was a girl of more or less eight years old, I already proclaimed myself a writer. Although I was unaware that in the future I would have to move towards aesthetics and ethics, when I was a little girl it was literature that consumed my desires. What led me initialy to be a writer was a sense of adventure. I always had a great love for the adventure stories I had read, adventures which I found within a book. I imagined that whoever wrote such stories had to have lived them. To me, writers had a magnificent life, one of travels, surprises, challenges; they were explorers of inhospitable regions; they were Sinbads, sailors or even cowboys riding over the American prairies. You will notice that I use men as references, because the sense of adventure in this early stage of life was very much associated with men, since women were forbidden to experience such pleasures of life. Since I was not aware of prejudice against women (it took a while for me to understand this), I had broad freedom within me and a very pleasurable life around me. Thus, I invented adventures, I read adventure stories, I went to the movies, I lived in a state of exaltation with respect to the possibility of traveling from my world to another world, from my street to other streets, from my house to other houses, from my body into other bodies.

What was your childhood like and in what way did it influence your work?

I had a childhood surrounded by family members, by numerous cousins; there were family meals and the attendant aromas; there were different languages spoken because I was born in a Galician home; thus, I listened to the Galician language, which was almost the Galician spoken in the 12th century. I loved climbing trees, and spent hours in a tree just reading and thinking. Another thing that I just loved was to make tents using sheets, something very simple, and stay there in the dark imagining that I was in the Sahara and in other places. I had a very vivid sense of imagination, very potent and my games were ordinary games but they were also games that reflected my way of being and my deep impulses. The most important moment of my childhood was when my maternal grandparents and my parents, Carmen and Lino, decided that we had to go to Europe, especially Spain and more especially Galicia. I spent almost two years in the country in Spanish villages. I had an extraordinary rural experience, and my childhood imagination was enriched with reminiscences of that little Galician country, a country filled with legends, stories, supernatural elements. I believe that my childhood established certain fundamental principles for the writer that I was to become and that I am now. And particularly this: It implanted in me the postulate of imagination.

In addition to that significant trip to Galicia, have you had other travel experiences in your life and do those experiences show up in your work?

There is a book about my life that I published entitled *The Voyages of Nélida*. The title has much more meaning than travel in the general sense. Yes, the text is about travel, but it is also a text that embodies ingredients that are both Brazilian and imaginary, all taken from my many years of intellectual development, from the Hebrews, from the great ancient Greeks, from the native Indians. As I said, I always read a great deal. I have always felt a need not to hold back the details; what I do hold back from the narrative is a certain style of vocation. And all of this carries me back to Brazil and that I work and metabolize all of this experience in order to create something new. Because of this, my writing in general takes on a significant poetic and metaphoric flavor. I am a traveler and I travel with absolute naturalness. There is one more detail: I travel with lots of luggage, with many things. I have never tried, and believe that I will never try to be a light traveler. I carry presents, I carry objects, I carry and bring cheeses, food and books and anything you can imagine. I am a woman who believes in abundance, in excess, and in words that are also abundant and opulent.

Have you any interest in politics?

I am very much interested in politics, yes. And over the years I have become more interested, but at the same time over those same many years I have come to distrust politicians and their behavior; I have lost confidence in the effects of politics on individual and collective life. Politics must be, in addition to an art of the possible, a process that benefits society as a whole. But I feel that there has been a great deterioration in the political processes and that politics has become more and more distant from the humanitarian objectives which must always remain within its basic scope. I do not belong to any political party and I do not wish to be a prisoner of rigid ideologies. I have an independent mind and I am propelled by intense humanism, by compassion, by a desire to change current realities. To change means to distribute the benefits, not to concentrate them. But I also know that one must beware of one's own passions because passion is not always one's best counsel.

Nélida Piñon

What does it mean for you to be a woman in Brazil?

I believe that being a woman is not easy in any society. The same applies to those women who were born or who live in supposedly progressive societies that have laws which protect the rights of women. But even so, a woman knows that she must continue fighting for every advantage that she must have in her personal and collective life. What is more, women are never part of the major decision-making centers. A woman still is a peripheral human being. She might as an exception to the rule attain power, but she is not the decision-making core. I feel extremely good about being a woman because as a woman I am part of an emotional history that is so utterly intriguing. I like very much to believe that the fame of the woman, that underlying material, which is there within her belly, her fulcrum, is an ancient material, and that if she is alert she can use it to evaluate the present. I enjoy being a woman, and I am a vigilant woman. I am a woman with a historical content, and, therefore, I have a feminist vision of the universe. However, my feminism does not suffocate my understanding of the path of history. I believe that in order to say what it means to be a woman in Brazil, one must first determine in what social category the woman falls and in what region she lives. There is a social status, there is a cultural status, there is an intellectual status that a brave or dauntless woman can attain. However, if the woman relaxes her guard, she will always suffer and become the victim of preconceived notions. Even when her talent and brilliance are recognized, men will let her know that she is an exception. And she certainly does not want to be the exception in the species.

Is the status of the female writer in Brazil different from that of the male writer?

I believe that the situation is improving. The woman has

always been recognized as creative, special and worthy people. Yes, she has more freedom from male guardianship, but even so, she is still an exception among many. The literary medium does not accept many women. There is a selection by quota. What is more, the rules governing esthetic evaluation for women are different from those for men. The literary medium is much more complacent when it comes to male thinking and creation, as opposed to female thinking and creation. There is no doubt that it is a long-lasting preconceived notion. Even if it is a subtle preconceived notion, it is still latent.

Have you have held other jobs besides writer? Have they influenced your work?

In truth, I did not have other jobs because all I did was minor in relation to literature. I have been a full-time writer. I've done things to earn a living, to increase my income. I did some journalism, either as an ordinary cub reporter or as a literary reporter. I gave classes, but never systematically. I currently hold an endowed chair, once held by Isaac Bashevis Singer, at the University of Miami in Florida. I was director of the then Department of Culture of Rio de Janeiro. For one year I struggled with various beliefs, I struggled with the city's culture, I gave examples. After that I became President of the Brazilian Academy of Letters. The first woman to hold such a post in the history of the world's academies. I was a very diligent president. I initiated new events at the academy; I established the Memorial Center, organized parties and get-togethers, lived with writers, wrote art books, made a CD, established guided tours at the Academy. Luckily, none of this was permanent because I never wanted it to be permanent. I always made it clear that literature was my destiny and I could not turn my back on literature without having to pay a high price. I then discovered that all of these things that I had done, if on the one hand robbed me from time with literature, did on the other hand provide me with extraordinary experiences. While I may have complained at the time, it was afterward that I was able to see that all of this was very precious because I am someone who greatly enjoys both the sacred and the profane, who enjoys both the mundane and the spiritual. I can be both a solitary woman and a ballroom hostess. I am interested in the human soul, in the human physique. I am intensely curious; I want to know all about the universe. All of this has translated itself into an intense and rewarding experience that I have converted into a certain narrative knowledge.

What role does your family play in your life?

I believe that it plays a fundamental role. For me, it was fundamental to have been born into my family, to have enjoyed the blessings, the love, the quarrels, the sometimes lack of understanding that a family is capable of giving or doing. The notion of "nesting" is extraordinary; it remains with you for a lifetime. The absence of a nest makes you fly through life without wings. I was loved by my family and this made me ready for battle.

I am an armed woman and I feel this to be extraordinary! And I am also committed to love and to kindness. I feel that a world full of affection is the perfect world, and it makes me grow as an individual. Thus, the family that I had is a source of pride and happiness to me. It is now at its end, since almost all of the family members are dead, and I miss them terribly. My father died when I was very young. Three years ago I lost my mother. They were adorable beings who helped me so generously that even today when I think of them, I say, "Thank you, God." Throughout my life I learned to appreciate. I have not had to turn my back on my journey down the road of love and affection.

Nélida Piñon

What is your attitude toward mysticism?

I'm not as inclined toward mysticism as I used to be. However, my mysticism was always impregnated by a pagan vision, a vision of multiple gods. I had a Catholic upbringing in a family that was very Catholic, but at the same time I was fascinated by the Greek world. The Greek world was basic to my education. Thus, I lived with the gods, I lived with the myths. I always said that the myths ate at my table. And they still are with me, they have coffee with me. If I allowed myself to be led by a mystical rendition that would bring me to any form of fanaticism, this would only impoverish me. Thus, I had a mystical and religious relationship with reality, as well as a pantheistic relationship with reality. I feel that human complexity is of such nature that no God can explain it. And moreover, man tries to invent gods in order to confront chaos, in order to live in the environment of a suffocating or asphyxiating nature that offers little in the way of epiphany. Thus, I am a person of religious impulses, of great emotion, but at the same time I am endowed with the serenity of disbelief.

For whom do you write?

I write for others, but I do not promote the existence of any image in particular. I feel that I must write while not thinking about any image. What exists for me is a multitude of people unknown to me, people who will read my work or not read it. If I invent some kind of image or label, then I run the risk of falling into the preconceived, that is, I will have to chose a beautiful one, or an odorous one, or a perfumed one, or one with a Ph.D. and a specialization in Nélida Piñon. And I just won't do that. Once when I was in Amazonas, we were traveling in a small boat; we were close to the riverbank and I saw a young girl modestly dressed, playing with some children on the side of a shack with a Brazilian flag. Pondering this, I thought that I was looking at a very poor school. I was so overcome by emotion that my eyes filled with tears. It was the only time that I thought, "If I had to chose my readers, I would want them to be these river children for whom reading in general would constitute a necessary and essential social redemption.

What are your feelings about globalization?

First, the feeling that one gets about the concept of globalization is that it is something new, something that the Romans did not know about, something that the Chinese were ignorant of, something that the Portuguese were totally unaware of. Like we've never had spices or pottery of the Indies companies or tea from the Ceylon tea companies; like the world has always been isolated. The world is a ravenous place. Nations feed themselves from other nations. We cannot delude ourselves. Who has been ordered to undertake this so-called "integration of world interests" process? Seven or eight countries? Not even. It is a world where the market says what the moral rules are, what the ethical rules are. Now then, the market was not made to dictate moral rules or political rules. The enactment of such rules is one of the ethical duties of the citizenry. People can say what is inevitable. I feel that this crossing-over is becoming more and more inevitable, but I still believe that every nation must determine its course of direction and that if possible, the course chosen by each country must be such that it brings all countries to believe that society as a whole is responsible for people. We cannot treat the children, the aged, the needy, the impoverished, those who live in human misery, those who are unable to keep up with the pace of this ominous and cannibalistic race without understanding and social protection. I sincerely believe that society is always in transition and that nothing is cemented in stone. For example, I say: Do you believe that the Romans ever imagined over their own long history that the carpenter of Nazareth would change history?

I Love My Husband

I love my husband. From morning to night. I make him coffee first thing in the morning. He always sleeps poorly and lets out an exhausted sigh as he begins to shave. I knock three times on the bathroom door, before the coffee gets cold. He growls angrily at me while I let out an anxious yell. I don't want him to confuse my effort with the cold liquid that he will gulp down the same way he consumes me twice a week, especially on Saturdays.

I then adjust his tie, him protesting because I only take care of the smallest part of his life. I laugh to calm him down, so that he can go out and face life in the outside world, and always bring deliciously fresh bread to our home.

He says that I am too demanding. I stay at home washing the dishes and going to the store, and complaining about life. Meanwhile he builds his world of little bricks, and although some of his walls fall down in the end, his friends congratulate him for such solid and visible creation.

They also acknowledge me for taking care of a man who dreams big and makes the country fair and prosperous in his peculiar and grandiose way. And that's why I'm just a shadow of a man that everyone says I love. I let sunshine into the house, gilding the objects that we worked so hard to buy. I do this even though he doesn't show me any gratitude for these shining objects. On the contrary, sure of my love for him, he proclaims that all I do is to spend the money that he sweats so hard for. I ask him to understand my nostalgia for a land that, in the old days, was cultivated by women. But he just frowns as if I were offering a theory that will shame our family and the binding rules of our home.

What else do you want, woman, didn't we get married, and agree to joint ownership of property? And as he told me that I was part of the future that only he had the right to create, I realized that the man's generosity only put me in charge of the past, with its rules well established by our life together.

I began to think that it would be wonderful not to live only in the past, before the past tense had been dictated to me by a man that I claim to love. He was all for it. Inside the house, in the warmth of our home, it would be easy to nourish the past with herbs and porridge, so that he, calm and safe, could beget the future. He definitely could not be bothered with deciphering the essence of my womb. He wanted it to belong to him, so that he wouldn't have to smell my sex in order to see whether anybody else besides him had been there, knocking at his door, destroying his walls, with their inscriptions and dates.

My children better be mine, he confessed to his friends on the Saturday of the month when we have friends over. And my wife belongs to no one but me, not even to herself. The idea that I couldn't belong to myself, couldn't touch my sex to expurgate the excesses, provoked the first frightening rupture in my fantasy about the past in which I had been immersed until then. So in addition to having drowned me in the past, while he was free to live a life that he kept to himself, he also had to tie my hands so that they couldn't feel the delights of my own body, because they might, in a whisper, suggest that there are other bodies, as delightful and fuzzy and deprived as mine, whose salt might be licked with the tip of the tongue.

I looked in disgust at my long fingernails with purple polish on them. Tiger's claws to strengthen my identity and cry out the truth of my sex. Stroking my body, I thought, am I a woman only because of these long claws and because I cover them with gold and silver, the impulse of a bleeding animal wounded in the woods? Or is it because this man adorns me in such a fashion that when I take off this war paint, he is surprised by a face that seems alien to him, a face that he covers with mystery in order to keep from having me whole?

All of a sudden, the mirror which the man brought home to make me look beautiful became a symbol of defeat. Isn't it true that I love you, husband? I asked him, as he read newspapers to stay on top of things, while I swept away the printed words that he spat out on the floor as soon as he absorbed the news. Let me work, woman, he said. How can I talk to you about love when what's at stake are the economic alternatives for a country where men have to work like slaves — just to support their women.

So I told him, if you don't want to discuss love (which as far as we know, might be a long way from here anyway, or even behind the furniture, where I sometimes hide the dust after sweeping the house) what if, after all these years, I were to mention the future as if it were a dessert?

He put down the newspaper and insisted that I repeat what I'd said. I was a little worried as I said the word future, because I didn't want to hurt him. But I wasn't going to give up the African adventure I'd just began. Followed by a sweaty and anxious procession, I slaughtered wild boars. I made my starving canines dive into their heated jugulars, while Clark Gable, attracted by my smell and by the smell of the convulsive animal, went down on his knees to win my love. Thirsty from the effort, I slurped the water from the river, perhaps looking for a fever that was inside me, but hard to awaken. My skin burned in ecstasy as words soiled my lips for the first time. I blushed from pleasure and shame, while the medicine man saved my life with his ritual and the thick hair on his chest. I felt the breath of life blow out through my mouth, as I left Clark Gable tied to a tree, to be slowly eaten by ants. Like a jungle Wonder Woman, I went down to the river that almost robbed me of my strength, avoiding the waterfalls as I cried out for freedom, the most ancient and myriad of legacies.

Watching the word future float before his eyes as he dropped the newspaper on the floor, my husband asked, how can you reject a love nest, security, peace of mind, in short, our marvelous conjugal harmony? Do you think, husband, that you can trap conjugal harmony with chains made of fishhooks, just because I uttered the word that makes you sad? So sad that you cry in your discrete way because you are too proud to cry convulsively, the latter being reserved for my female condition? Oh, husband, if such a word has the power to blind you, sacrifice me again so that I don't have to see you suffer. I wonder if there would even be time to save you if we erased the future now.

His shiny hollows quickly absorbed the tears. He voluptuously inhaled the cigarette smoke and went back to his reading. It would be hard to find another man like him in our 18-floor building with many doormen. When I went to condominium cocktail parties, he was the only one who knew how to overcome obstacles and how to forgive those who hurt him. I reproached myself for having been so selfish as to disturb the evening of someone who deserved to rest before his next day's work.

Trying to hide my embarrassment, I brought him fresh coffee and chocolate cake. He accepted my attempts to redeem myself. He talked to me about how much we spend per month, and about the financial difficulties of his company (one should be more careful with spending). If he could count on my cooperation, he might be able to get rid of his business partner in less than a year. I was happy to participate in a project that would make us more prosperous in 12-months. Without my wholehearted commitment, he would never be able to dream so big. I discretely took up the responsibility of allowing him to dream. My husband's every dream was my charge. Having been given this right, I was paying for my life with a check that was hard to enter in the books.

He didn't have to be grateful. He achieved such a perfect level of emotional control that all he needed to do was to stay with me for it to be clear that he loved me. I was the most delicate fruit the land could bear, a tree, in the middle of our living room. He would climb that tree, conquer its fruits, caress its bark, prune its knotty excesses.

For a week I would knock only once at the bathroom door. I was ready to fix him fresh coffee, in case the first one had gotten cold, in case he'd gotten lost watching his reflection in the mirror with the same vanity that had been instilled in me since childhood, once it had been confirmed that the crying newborn was just a female, one more female. My mother's definition of being a woman was to loose oneself in time. What she meant was, who can win the battle against time in the female condition? My father totally agreed, but he added that time doesn't age a woman, but rather, keeps her mystery from being revealed to the world.

Can't you see, darling, that it is the most beautiful thing in the world, a life that nobody can see, a life that nobody can harvest, but your husband, the father of your children? My father's teachings were very profound and he would always make the word aging sound like silver. I was almost certain that if a woman's story couldn't be fulfilled, if she weren't allowed to have her own biography, she would be able to keep her youth forever.

Only people who live get old, said my father on my wedding day. Since you are going to live your husband's life, not your own, we can assure you, you will be young forever. I didn't know how to carry the joy which enveloped me and which felt heavy like a shield. I didn't know how to reach his heart, startling the purity that lies there. Or how to thank him for this state that I'd never aspired to, perhaps out of my own distraction. And this was my trophy on the night I was going to become a woman. Until then I would hear whispers that I was worth waiting for — unlike my brother who was given the glorious stigma of manhood at his baptism, long before he'd ever slept with a woman.

I was always told that a woman's soul could only manifest itself in bed, when her sex was anointed by a man. My mother sometimes implied that, before that night, our sex looked more like an oyster nourished by salty waters, vague and slippery, far from the captivating reality of land. Mother liked poetry, and her images were always fresh and warm.

My heart burned on the wedding night. I was anxiously looking forward to the new body that had been promised to me, to leaving behind the shell that had covered me in the ordinary days of the life to which I'd previously been resigned. My husband's hands would mold me until the end of my days, and how on earth to thank him for such generosity? Maybe this is why we are as happy as two people can be, when only one of them brings home the food, the hope, the faith, the family history.

He is the only one who brings life to me, although sometimes I live it only after a week's delay. It makes no difference. It is even better that way, because it has all been translated for me. I don't have to interpret facts, make mistakes, resort to distressing words that end up suffocating my freedom. The man's words are the ones I will need for the rest of my life. I don't have to assimilate a vocabulary that doesn't match my destiny and might even ruin my marriage.

So I learned that my consciousness, which serves to make me happy, is also at my husband's disposal. His function is to prune my excesses, as I am naturally inclined to be shipwrecked every now and then, to go deep under the sea, looking for sponges. Will they absorb my dreams, multiplying them in the bubbling silence of their seawater-filled labyrinths? I want a dream that can be reached with a oven mit and that sometimes turn into a chocolate pie, so that he can eat it with a sparkle in his eyes, making us both smile.

Oh, and when I feel like a warrior, ready to take up my weapon and to win a new face, I dive into golden exaltation, following nameless streets, as if with my strength I could conquer a new homeland, a new language, a body that would extort life without inhibitions. Everything inside me trembles as I watch the people who pass, with an appetite that will not shame me later. Luckily, it's a fleeting sensation, for soon I look for help on familiar streets that bear the mark of my life. The shop windows, the things, the friendly people all make me proud of my home.

All these bird like acts of mine are indeed despicable. They would hurt my husband's pride. Contrite, I ask for his forgiveness in my mind. I promise him that I will stay away from these temptations. Keeping his distance, he seems to forgive me. He approves of my submission to a happy every day life, which makes us prosper each year. I must confess that my anxiety embarrasses me. I don't know how to calm down. I don't mention it to anyone but myself. Not even the nuptial vows can stop me from loosing myself in my dreams every now and then. Vows that make my body blush, but don't leave their mark in such a way that I could show which wrinkles were inscribed by their fury.

I never mentioned these dangerous and brief gallops to my husband. He would break under the burden of such a confession, or if I told him that I had been thinking about getting a job, to have some pocket money of my own. Obviously, with these follies I'm making the best of the time I have left to me. I am a household princess, he told me on several occasions and he was absolutely right. Therefore nothing should take me away from the happiness in which I am forever immersed.

I really can't complain. Every day my husband contradicts what the mirror says. I look at myself in the mirror and my husband demands that I see a false reflection of myself. I am really not the shadows and the wrinkles that I see. Like my father, he is responsible for my eternal youth. He is very tactful. He never threw me a big birthday party, afraid that I might not be able to forget how old I am. He thinks that I don't realize. The truth is that at the end of the day I don't know how old I am.

He also avoids talking about my body that has gotten bigger with the years. I can't wear my old size. I keep my clothes in the closet, enjoying them in secret. At 7 o'clock, every evening, he opens the door, knowing that I will be on the other side, waiting for him. And while the TV displays blossoming bodies he dives into his newspaper. We are the only beings that exist in the world.

I do appreciate his effort to love me. I do my best to please him, even though I sometimes don't feel like it, or get upset by a strange face that doesn't belong to him but to someone I don't know and never want to see again. It makes my mouth dry, dry from the everyday reminder of the taste of old bread, which nourishes me day and night. Bread that he and I have been eating for all these years, without complaints, anointed by love, bound by the marriage ritual which proclaimed us husband and wife.

Oh yes, I do love my husband.

— translated by Elzbieta Szoka
with Shanna Lorenz

Lygia Fagundes Telles

Lygia Fagundes Telles

Lygia Fagundes Telles was born in São Paulo but spent her childhood in small towns in the state where her father served as district attorney, police commissioner, and a judge. This childhood experience provided the imaginative background for many of her stories. In 1969 she was awarded the *Cannes Prix International des Femmes* for her short story "Before the Green Masquerade," chosen from among the works of authors from twenty-one countries. Her works have been translated into many languages around the world.

She is an honorary member of Academia de Letras in São Paulo and was recently honored in the edition *Cadernos de Literatura Brasileira.* Instituto Moreira Salles. Number 5, March 1998. Her works include: Novels: *Ciranda de pedra* [The Marble Dance] (1954); *Verão no aquário* (1963); *As meninas* [The Girl in the Photograph] (1973); *As horas nuas* (1989).

Stories: *Antes do baile verde* (1972); *Seminário dos ratos* [Tigrela and Other Stories] (1977); *Mistérios* (1981); *A estrutura da bolha de sabão* (1991); A noite escura e mais eu (1996); *Venha ver o pôr-do-sol* (1987); *Oito contos de amor* (1997); *Invenção e memória* (2000).

Lygia Fagundes Telles

How did you become a writer?

I started "writing" before I knew how to write. I began my apprenticeship telling and hearing stories. I didn't know how to write when I was a little girl, but I liked to listen to stories and to tell stories. This tradition that was so wonderful has practically disappeared in Brazil today. With television. It was a very good tradition because it stimulates the imagination. It was a way of dealing with the imaginary, and with inventing things.

I made up stories, usually terrifying stories, fantasy stories, with horror and tormented souls and werewolves. I learned to read and to write later, but what came first was that apprenticeship where I listened to stories. I trembled with fear. Afterwards, when I started telling stories, I began to be happier because I no longer trembled. It was other people who trembled. That's the power. The power. I felt powerful.

The listeners, who were children like me, would say "Lygia, you told a different story today." I repeated my stories a lot, because children and old people like repetition. I began looking for ways of "recording" these stories so that the plot wouldn't change. That's how I started writing. Afterwards, I began reading magazines with cartoons, children's stories, and the pamphlets that are often read in small towns in the hinterland. In school, I became interested in literature at a higher level, but it was still very conventional. There were love stories, and a lot of water mixed with sugar. In law school, I began reading Dostoevsky, Tolstoy, Faulkner, and Poe. I was enthusiastic about all of them. That's when I became fascinated with world literature. Afterwards, I became fascinated with our own Brazilian literature. Machado de Assis. Romantic authors. That was after I had been fascinated with Dostoevsky or Kafka, however. I have a passion for Kafka.

What aspects of your childhood are the most significant for you and how did your childhood influence your work?

In my most recent book, *A invenção e memoria,* there are many texts that were not completely made up. Some of them are recollections of cities that I've visited. In this book, you'll see my extremely strong relationship with nature. A lot of green, mango trees, trees with fruit, a lot of puppies. Except for cats. Cats come afterwards. That's in the second phase of my life.

My mother took in these stray puppies. She gave them baths and took care of them. Soon, there were more puppies, a whole gang of puppies. I had a lot of contact with animals. Another influence upon my childhood was an experience that was very reminiscent of slavery, but with other connotations. My mother took in a lot of lost orphans. Lost in the sense that they had lost their virginity, and were girls whose families had driven them out of their homes. My mother took care of these girls, who were usually black or mulattoes. They were my caretakers. They gave me baths, they curled my hair so that I could be an angel in a procession as my mother wished, they told stories, and they fed me, because my mother had a lot of commitments. She was a pianist, and she couldn't take care of her four children. I was the youngest. So my nannies took care of me a lot, and they were usually illiterate. Very much like *"Casa grande e senzala."*

My father was an unstable man. He traveled a lot from one town to another. He was a very attractive man, and very intelligent, but very temperamental. He liked to drink, he liked to play and he liked to smoke cigars. He gave me cigar rings that I put on my fingers, and I would hold my hand like a parrot's claw to keep them from falling off, because they were too big for my fingers.

My family moved a lot with our Bechstein piano. My mother's family had been wealthy, and my father's family, too, but afterwards, I began to become aware that we were actually poor. Meanwhile there was a certain living standard: a nice house, a backyard, a big garden, enough fruit, enough puppies and enough nannies who told stories and curled my hair that was straight as an Indian's. In a certain way, my childhood was half disheveled, half unkempt and rustic like that. It was the nannies who paid attention to me, and there was nature. After my brothers went to boarding schools I was the youngest, and then I went on trips with my parents in an ox cart.

My father was of Portuguese and Italian descent. On my mother's side, I think that I may have native or Indian blood. My uncle was a revolutionary in Brazil. He opposed the monarch, and he loved the Republic. Mama told me that he died on Mount Vesuvius, that he fell into Vesuvius. I asked my mother, "Where's Vesuvius?" and she said, "In Italy." I was impressed. "What an important uncle! How could he have fallen?" My father said, "He didn't fall. He was murdered." Mama said, "No, he fell. It was an accident." There were two theories about my uncle's death. One is that he was murdered by the guide, who pushed him into the volcano, and the other is that he fell in by accident, because he went too far into the crater. This made me very proud, and, one day, when an arithmetic teacher scolded me and said that I wasn't very bright, I said to her, "I may not be too bright, but my uncle fell into a volcano." Then I went home weeping and saying that the teacher gave me a zero because my uncle had fallen into the volcano. My mother went to the school and said, "It's true. The girl wasn't lying. Her uncle fell into a volcano." That was a glorious moment in my childhood.

Let's jump into your adulthood now. What does it mean for you to be a woman in Brazil?

At the beginning of my career, it was very difficult. I remember that it made a strong impression on me when I had written a book in law school, and one of the critics said, "How incredible! This girl writes like a man!" And I felt that I had disillusioned him, that he would prefer for me to have written about flowers, butterflies and birds, and poems about God. I started talking about things that shocked him. A prejudice.

When I was very young, I knew our great modernist Mario de Andrade. He asked, "Lygia, what would you rather be: beautiful or intelligent?" I said, "I want to be intelligent," and he said, "How dumb you are." Then I said, "Why am I a dummy?" He answered, "Oh, beauty is so important." And I asked him "Why did Mr. Mario say this? It's very important to be intelligent." He said, "No. It's because I'm an ugly old guy. You don't know how much I've dreamed about beauty all my life." I thought that my beauty was attractive, that my beauty would attract men so that they wouldn't take me seriously. I would have to be ugly in order to be accepted. A prejudice.

The situation of women is changing and, consequently, the situation of a woman writer in Brazil should be changing as well, right?

I'd like to quote a great Italian legal thinker who died recently, Norberto Bobbio. He said that the greatest revolution in the 20th century was the women's revolution. When the second world war took place, men went to fight, and women began to take their places, in factories, in hospitals, in universities and in offices. Suddenly, they were found to be extraordinarily skillful at handling machinery, ideas, etc. That was a revelation from the second world war. The women's revolution was the most important cause in the 20th century.

Liberation. That was an exaggeration obviously.

Trotsky said, "Those who go to the battlefront pay the price." Many women didn't understand this revolution. They became victims. They were promiscuous. Sex. Indiscriminate sex. Free women. Free women in a desperate way. It wasn't for love. Complete promiscuity. Diseases. Syphilis. And later, AIDS. This promiscuity was confused with the true liberty that Norberto Bobbio saw in our revolution. When I wrote *As meninas* [*The Girl in the Photograph*], my inspiration was a young woman who had lived in our home. A beautiful girl of 17 or 18. I asked her, "Why are you happy?" She said, "I'm happy because I'm emancipated. I live in a 'republic,' and I can sleep with whomever I want." This was an exaggerated interpretation of sexual freedom. Drugs were part of it, too. She was already starting with cocaine, and she was already starting with crack. Alcohol to excess.

These women didn't understand liberation as a way of gaining access to universities, offices or factories. They had been raised strictly, in the Portuguese way, the Lusitanian way. I have a story "Espartilho" ["The Corset"] that describes this issue. Going back to my novel, *As meninas,* the young woman that I knew was the source of my character Ana Clara, who dies from drugs. Beautiful and completely crazy. The idiocies of burning brassieres, it's all stupidity. Gradually, women are going to lose this urge to attract attention, to tear away veils, to nourish male fantasies. Those who fell were necessarily from the first line, those who marched ahead. Now I think that women will calmly find their place in the sunlight.

What role does family play in your life? Does it inspire you or does it have a negative effect on your work?

I married my professor, Goffredo da Silva Telles. There were only five girls, and more than 200 men where I went to school. One of them came to me and asked "What is it that you've come here to do? Did you come here to marry somebody?" I said, "That, too." I did get married, but I also managed to obtain a diploma and to have a job in the event that marriage wasn't reliable, as, indeed, it wasn't, so that I would have a possibility of being employed. I was a public official.

My family has played a very important role in my life, and I deeply regretted that my first marriage came to an end. I regretted being divorced and being alone with my son. Afterwards I went to work. Afterwards, I married Paulo Emilio Salles Gomes, an extremely intelligent man, just as my first husband was. Both of them were very encouraging about my work. They liked the fact that I was writing, and they encouraged me a lot. Paulo Emilio, the founder of the Cinemateca Brasileira, was an excellent writer, an essayist, a cinema expert and a very close friend of Glauber Rocha. He died in 1977, and I've remained alone. Again. *Voilá.*

Did your work as a public servant have any impact on your themes and style?

I only had this job in order to have some money at the end of the month. Just in order to get by. I knew that I didn't have a calling for it. My true calling was writing. I was an attorney for the State of São Paulo's Retirement Institute. I provided legal opinions about pension applications from extremely impoverished people; poor civil servants who were applying for pensions and assistance for their spouses' funerals. I came into contact with very poor people, extremely humble people. Therefore, I found it easy to get under the skins of my characters who came from the lowest levels of our society. It was also my own experience.

When my father lost everything and Mama separated from him, I stayed with her, and we lived in modest rooming houses. I was ashamed of living in a rooming house. I was very young, I went to parties, I was pretty, very well-dressed and so on, and

I wouldn't say where I lived. I lied, so people wouldn't bring me home after parties. Many times, I went home alone on the trolley so that nobody would see me entering the rooming house. I was dying of shame about being poor. Therefore, my youth which was very difficult, was a good lesson, because later, I came into contact with the poorest groups. In my work as an attorney I knew the most impoverished civil servants: elevator operators, janitors, etc., and I was able to come up with ways of helping. Very often, I wouldn't find a certain document there, and I would conceal the situation, so that the person would end up receiving a pension. I helped them by playing dumb. One day, my boss called me, "Doctor, where's the marriage certificate for this lady who is applying for a pension?" I said, "It's there, sir." I knew that it wasn't there. Luckily, my boss went on leave the next day, and I had given her a pension. This was a poor woman who hadn't married and who had 10 children with her companion and decided to seek a pension when he died. I said, "But don't you have a marriage certificate, ma'am?" She said, "I don't have any kind of certificate. But I did have five children with this worthless man. They all on look like him. I've brought these children to prove it." I had to struggle with things like that, and this was a very important struggle.

One day, I received a phone call that made me very happy. It was a phone call from a man whose name was Edson. He said, "I want to create a show with your story, "A Medalha" ["The Medalion"]." This is a story about a girl who lives with her grandmother. The grandmother is enormously prejudiced against blacks. She hated her granddaughter and tried to upset her. The grandmother said, "You're spending time with men just before your wedding. Your fiancé is an unfortunate guy. I feel sorry for your fiancé." "But he's not innocent," the girl said. "Why isn't he innocent?" the grandmother asked. "Because he's black." So I was very happy when Edson, who is black, contacted me. He told me, "This is the best work that I've read in relation to racial prejudice." If someone says that there's no racial prejudice in Brazil, the person must be thinking about Pele. For Pele, there's no prejudice.

How important for you is mysticism and spirituality in general?

My mystical side began when I was an angel in the procession. I inherited this mystical side from my mother, who brought me up in that environment with nannies, nature, and animals. I always believed in God. Today, I firmly believe in the immortality of the soul. I would like to quote the great philosopher Empedocles who liked to say, "I've already been a girl, and I've already been a young man. I've already been a bush, and I've already been a bird. And I've also been a fish in the depths of the sea." I believe in that kind of transmigration. Not in resurrection, because it would require a similar body. I believe in transmigration according to which my soul would migrate into a cat's body. A cat. A bird. A bush. Therefore, the respect that I have for nature is because it seems to be given life by the breath of something subtle. This is a sensibility that seems universal to me.

Speaking of universality, when you write do you direct your words to a particular reader or a "universal reader"?

"I don't want to be understood," I once told a reader from Asia who complained that he didn't understand my stories. Nobody understands anybody. People are difficult. Life is difficult. I only want my reader to be my partner and accomplice in the act of creation which means anxiety and suffering. It's a search and a celebration.

Before concluding this conversation I'd like to ask you what you think of globalization.

I think that it's dangerous. According to our president, Fernando Henrique Cardoso, it's necessary, but I think that, in Brazil, we aren't as ready for globalization as they want us to be. Our country still isn't developed. We're part of the Third World. Our character, our makeup, our deepest roots are very threatened. I hope that the Amazon region will never be transformed into a tropical Disneyland in this process of globalization. I have strong fears. I think that we aren't ready for globalization. This desire to display development and modernity is an erroneous approach, with the wrong means being used. I'm very afraid that we may lose our character, that our people will lose their traditions, their customs and our nature. Suddenly, we're being obliged to adopt foreign ways. That would be the death of this country. The universalism that we talk about only exists on the spiritual level, as I see it. It's important not to let the channels flow together. It's necessary to have protection, and preservation of the things that aren't ready to be globalized. I have this savage side, a very strong bond with nature, and, at the same time, I have very strong bonds with the people.

In conclusion, I'd like to quote a very good composer who died of AIDS, Renato Russo. "The people of Brazil aren't happy. They're joyful." There are three species in Brazil that are undergoing extinction: trees, Indians, and writers. Why trees? Because they're destroying our forests, and they're selling everything. In an official way, or an unofficial way, they're destroying our trees. Why Indians? Indians are being destroyed because they're part of that environment. And why writers? Because the number of illiterates in Brazil is so high. What hope can there be for a Brazilian writer sitting here with you to be read in Brazil if the level of illiteracy is so high and if the people who do read are going to be reading foreign writers, preferably from the First World? It's a new colonization. Brazil was never as colonized as it is now. Brazilians turn outward with great enthusiasm, like sunflowers. The danger of globalization is that it will disguise and distort this country that, in spite of all of its problems and backwardness, all of its ills and defects, still has its original face.

The Day to Say "No!"

Today is the day, I decided when I woke up. The day to say "No!" Suddenly I thought of Saint Augustine, the *vera artificiosa apis Dei* — God's bee. This admired and loved bee, strong enough to know the yes and the no of its fundamental nature, who gave in, only to resist a moment later, ah! And how he resisted, until he had made a place for himself in the city of dreams. "No!" he told the invader of those times, who probably resembled the invader of today, this invader-collector who takes up space that is not his.

I mentioned the City of God. Here we are in a city full of invaders, from extraterrestrials (who tend to be the most discreet) to the more ambiguous type, the invaders of free will. These ones are hidden. Obviously, they take advantage of the most common of feelings, guilt. In the immense picture of *mea-culpa*, the easiest stance is humility, which is to say, fragility. Is the invader moved by this? No, on the contrary, he is encouraged to keep trying until he bends the sickly will, which gives in, believing that later it will be able to break free. Can it break free? No, because the yes keeps multiplying like the links of a chain in which it becomes passively entangled. And yet, because it continues to hope, it believes that struggle is possible. But hope is blind, and in its foolish blindness, it soon turns into a hope for hopelessness.

Jesus asked us to love our neighbor, I know. But He is aware of what has become of the neighbor in this century. I'm not talking about a real neighbor (the people). I'm talking about the official neighbor, the politician-invader who doesn't really care to hear refusal. He looks bored, has a beer or snorts some coke, and forgets. Nevertheless, he keeps making demands. And, accustomed to asking questions in a voice that suggests that he doesn't like pessimistic answers, the collector is the opposite of the negativist. "How is it going?" he asks, and the invaded is supposed to answer, "Fine!" with the athletic look of someone who seems to be making his way up when he is actually face down on the floor. It is the yes of opportunism. Of blind obedience.

Blind hope. The blind are forced into an obedience that generates insecurity. Fear. The fear of feeling afraid, and the weakened will dreaming of the invasion. Escape. There is nowhere to escape when Misery and Violence (twin sisters) are everywhere galloping on the white horses of the Apocalypse. Is it that man became more cruel in this year of the dragon (Chinese horoscope), or was he always like this?

The day to say "No!" I pray to God to strengthen my faith, I pray so intensely, is it depression? And this pain so hard to localize, is it another flu? Out of decency I don't throw myself on the floor, and I don't pull my hair, already thinning on my sore head. Where is the good invader (the extraterrestrial) who knows how to unscrew a throbbing head and put it on a hat stand? I dissolve some aspirin. One part of me lays down in the dark and the other part (I'm divided) points me toward the street. Because there is a collector in the ether (the phone) collecting and challenging. Why that voice? I swallow saliva and answer quickly that I'm fine. I'm great! I can even tell it to the four winds. Which are the four winds? I forgot. I only know of one wind, which varies in intensity like the Four Cheeses Pizza, which is the main attraction at the restaurant. You order and it comes steaming hot, with four cheeses! Actually, there is only one cheese that changes flavors according to the capricious sauces. The solution is to pretend (to lie) that you believe, and from one lie to another, to keep retreating until you achieve the triumph of an optimism that can only be found in that movie. Remember? The lead got shot in the chest by a machine gun, and though his shirt was still covered with blood (tomato juice or chocolate syrup?), he is still about to crawl to the policeman, who asks the classic question, "How's it going?" And the lead answers, "Fine." Instead of screaming, "Shit! I'm dying!" But at this point the violins begin to play (it's a Hollywood movie) and the lead becomes sentimental because he's thinking about his sweetheart. More violins. *Horas non numero nisi serenas*! — he can quote with the same emphasis as the clock in the Parisian park, I only count hours of happiness!

"Counting dollars!" whispers a euphoric materialist. That's it, emphasis. "Things. Things are so sad when you consider them without emphasis," wrote the poet Carlos Drummond de Andrade. Things seem sad, as does the human race, I would add. Without hurting the atheists' feelings, I would also like to say that emphasis is the soul's home.

My youth was so impregnated by the sound of the colonizer that it is a miracle that I am still disobedient after all of these years, always trying—poor me!—to forge a will of iron.

It's a cloudless morning. The cab driver turns on the radio and asks me if I want to listen to the politician talk. "No," is my answer. I say that I don't like the speech so he suggests some country music, having already found a station with guitar music. I discover that it is out of tune, but I keep quiet: if I don't respond politely to his cordiality he might get annoyed and in his annoyance hit the vehicle in front of us, a bus that is already invading our space. "Be careful!" I whisper, and I shrink down so that I won't be thrown out of the car. If there is a collision, I would surly break my leg, at the very least. I try to relax while these ideas play in my mind. I imagine a woman entering an emergency room with a broken leg on a weekday.

Or perhaps on the weekend, it doesn't matter, there are always too many people there. "Enough!" — yells the doctor whom I quietly address. Insecurity softens the voice so. It is only a fracture, he says. "Look at that!" he explodes, and runs off to take charge of a motorcycle helmet full of brains. The policeman who brought in the helmet is stuttering that the kid had his head smashed against a pole and all that was left from the collision was the pulp, he explains, handing over the helmet. "I picked up whatever I could," he explained, pointing down the hall: "the body is over there…" Or rather, was over there, as the stretcher is being quickly removed. The policeman and the doctor have to run after the stretcher. In vain, because they were stopped by another winded doctor asking about the body of another victim. Another?! The second doctor points to a stretcher where, wrapped in newspaper, an amputated arm drips blood. The doctors and the stuttering policeman are completely astonished. Soon a cleanshaven man dressed in elegant sport cloths appears. He introduces himself as a witness: "It was not an accident but a mugging," he says, zipping his blue jacket. "I was jogging on the street when I saw a finger sticking out of a muddy pothole in the street. It had just rained, doctor. And the drain was clogged — they are always clogged, you know. The arm that those thugs chopped off fell right into the hole. Imagine what a fright it gave me!" The second doctor (the first one had already left with the policeman) leaned over the arm covered with blood and mud in order to get a better look. A few remains of a T-shirt still hung there. It is hot. The witness unzips his jacket and continues. "The victim drove up in a new Golf, stopped at the stop sign, and saw the thug with the broken gun. So the victim rolls down his window and opens his arms. That's what is recommended, that victim should never make a quick move, but rather, act friendly. Unfortunately, the guy didn't understand and went for his knife. His gun was broken, as I already explained. And all these people passed right by pretending they were not there, seeing and ignoring the guy

34

finish his job!" concluded the witness, as he pointed to the stretcher. He took out a pack of cigarettes and then stopped mid gesture when he read the No Smoking sign. The doctor leaned over the stretcher. "What about the body? Where is the body?" The witness stood up upright. "I don't know, doctor. The body must have arrived first and be over there somewhere," he said, gesturing absent-mindedly to the hall filled with stretchers and improvised beds. "I only found the arm, which had been forgotten at the crime scene. As for the rest, I don't know where it ended up. I don't know." The doctor took a pair of calipers from the pocket of his apron and cut into the hardened blood. "A perfect job," he said.

I press my legs into the seat and give a look of distress to the driver, who is talking on his cell phone, while driving with only his left hand. The threatening bus has disappeared into the traffic. I manage to calm my breathing. The guitars continue to twang on the radio but now the cab driver has both hands on the wheel, having put his cell phone aside. I open the window a bit and a street vendor reaches in with a small box. "Strawberries, Ma'am?" I say "No," and repeat my No to the vendor who is now offering me a duster, and to another who offers chewing gum, brooms... Misery at work, I think to myself, and say a softer "No" to a boy who offers me a little basket of violets. Now a small group of beggars approaches. I close the window quickly, and in the mirror, see the flushed face of the driver, who gives me an nasty look. "Hot, isn't it?"

On the sunny avenue, Misery (the galloping one) seemed a bit calmer. But present, still. I opened the left-side window at the intersection when the light turns red. Turn green already! I kept wishing. But this was a distracted traffic signal, so distracted that the boy selling lottery tickets had time to limp over.

Balancing himself on the crutches stuck under his skinny arms, he move quickly, agilely making his way through the line of cars. He must have seen the open window from far away and now he was approaching triumphantly. All right, he made it, I thought, as his thin hand pushed through the open window, selling not lottery tickets, but stationery.

"Perfumed cards!" he announced in a piercing voice, as he opened a colorful array of envelopes. "Send a sweet- smelling card, look at this one, it smells like roses! This one smells like jasmine, it's a beauty!"

I slipped over to the other side of the car, while he kept shaking his paper rainbow. I could smell the sweet perfume as I looked anxiously at the light, which was still red, so red! Is it ever going to change? And the puny, bucktoothed boy kept talking and talking. "A blue card is for a good friend, but this pink card, you see? It is for love letters. This white one is for failed loved, but the purple one is for people you miss, it's got to be purple for people you miss, take them all and I'll give you a deal."

I stared at his crutches, one on each side. These supported the bony torso that protruded from a T-shirt with a political logo on the front. Suddenly I remembered my mother, in her garden, her hands dirty with soil, trying to use two stakes to support a plant that was wilting to the ground.

"I have nobody to write to." The boy laughed and shook the bundle

"Not a single boyfriend, huh?"

The driver apparently thought this was funny as his shoulders shook with complicit laughter. "That perfume is good!" he softly approved. I looked at the traffic light again. Is it ever going to change? And suddenly intimacy pervaded the space, as both the country music playing guitars and the enthusiastic boy, shaking his stationery, reached their climaxes.

"Listen, he might be far away, but he will be back in a hurry if he gets a green letter of forgiveness. I swear!"

"The light! The light is green," I announced to the driver, who had become absent-minded as he turned toward the vender like a sunflower.

He began to drive, I said a definite "No," and the lines of

cars began to furiously move forward. The winged hand flew away like a bird through the crack of the window. I could still see the skinny silhouette slipping away, limping between his crutches and then disappearing behind a jeep.

"Next time," I said, closing the window.

"It was nice perfume," muttered the driver. Was he censoring me or was I censoring myself? I took care of all of my usual errands. First a stop at the bank. Where had the old atmosphere of amenity and trust gone? So many men with guns. Angry faces — had the bank become an army barracks? I listen, unmoved, to the manager's propositions of great investments, which I politely refuse. "No, no"... I leave and go to the crowded post office. The line is quite long, so I have time to hear several requests. A woman with a child wants money to buy her medicine, a toothless man asks for money to get a ticket back to the Northeast, a boy wearing a cowboy hat wants me to participate in a fantastic raffle. I might even win an imported car! "No, No," I keep repeating. I am so tired now that I vaguely acknowledge a beggar who approaches me on the street and stares at me as if asking, "Now what the hell do you have in your chest? A rock?"

"Let's go," I said to the driver, who was waiting for me in the cab. He turned off the radio and was now reading some booklet. Aloof.

"Where to?" I was mute, and felt my face fall, like the faces of biblical character meeting their damnation. I lowered my head and thought again about Saint Augustine, "God's bee producing honey which distills the compassion and the truth." After all, the day of saying "No," was split in half because the other side of the coin was "Yes." The will could serve either side, but the important thing was to pick the right side, and for this one had to be rational. Or should the inspiration come from my heart? Well, I need the freedom to choose, freedom not to feel like I was feeling at that moment, like a sponge soaked with bitterness. An emphasis on inspiration! I lifted my head, shocked by the revelation of the boy on crutches. It was him I was thinking about (and not thinking about) all the time.

"Let's take the same route on the way back," I told the driver. "I want to buy stationery from that boy. I'll buy them all!" I announced, and heard my voice with great joy.

He turned the radio on again and took off.

"The perfume was good." There we were again, at the intersection, on the avenue with the same traffic light, gloriously red once again. I opened the window quickly. What luck ! I kept looking anxiously for the boy. "This is the place where he was, right? The driver stepped out of the car to help me in my search, looked both ways, gesticulating. He asked around, "Have you seen that kid with crutches?"

I opened the window and asked the guy who was selling newspaper. "Where is the stationery vendor, do you know? Oh… that one! Where is his bony hand shaking the rainbow garden, where?" I saw a man selling figs and a girl selling candy. I looked through the other window and bumped into a guy selling flower-filled vases.

"A boy on crutches selling stationery!" I asked people who absent-mindedly tried to help, "Letters?"

The cabbie began to drive, as the light had turned green.

"Where did that boy go?"

I could still see the guy selling newspapers, another one selling watches, and a girl passing out real estate announcements, but I never found the boy with the sweet-smelling stationery again.

— translated by Elzbieta Szoka
with Shanna Lorenz

Helena Parente Cunha

Helena Parente Cunha

Helena Parente Cunha was born and raised in Salvador in the state of Bahia. She studied Neo-Latin literatures in Italy and literary theory in Rio de Janeiro. She made her literary debut fairly late dedicating herself before that to academic research, criticism and pedagogy. She held a chair in Literary Theory at the Federal University of Rio de Janeiro (UFRI), where she also served for a while as departmental chair and graduate advisor. She "launched" various generations of academics, writers and filmmakers; João Ubaldo Ribeiro and Glauber Rocha, among others. Her work has been translated into English, Italian, French and Dutch. She lives and works in Rio.

Her major works include: Poetry: *Maramar* (1980); *Corpo no cerco* (1989, 2nd Edition).

Prose: *Cem mentiras de verdade* (1990, 2nd Edition); *Os provisórios* (1990, 2nd Edition); *As doze cores do vermelho* (1998, 2nd Edition); *Vento ventania vendaval* (1998); *Mulher no espelho* [Women Between Mirrors] (2001, 7th Edition).

Essays: *Os melhores contos de João do Rio* (1990); *As mulheres inventadas. Leitura psicanalítica de textos na voz masculina* (1994).

Helena Parente Cunha

How did you become a writer?

Maybe I could say that it's been a calling, because, since childhood I always liked writing, and my creations were highly praised. I always wrote poetry. I liked to write rhyming poems, like the one that I wrote when I was 7 years old, a poem dedicated to springtime: "Today's the day of flowers,/a day for children/receiving praise/filled with hopes." ["*Hoje è dia das flores/ dia das crianças/ que recebem louvores/ cheias de esperanças*"] I still have a copy that I kept in my early handwriting. There were four stanzas with very poor rhyming verses, "butterfly" ["*borboleta*"] rhymed with "violet" ["*violeta*"], "rose" ["*rosa*"] rhymed with "beautiful" ["*formosa*"]. I also liked reading a lot. I read children's stories, and I wrote speeches. My father kept in close contact with political activities, because he was a friend of the governor of Bahia, and that's why I wrote little speeches that always began with "Distinguished Ladies and Gentlemen…" but they were never delivered and listened to, except by my father and my mother. I also liked to write letters, and I have kept up an abundant correspondence with relatives who lived outside Bahia my whole life.

I like to point out that the first money that I earned in my life was when I was a teenager, in a poetry contest, "Where Is the Poet?" that was sponsored by a radio station. I won the prize, and the poem was read in the auditorium by an actor who became very famous, performing in the theatre, in films, and on television — Paulo Gracindo. At that time, he was an actor in radio dramas.

Helena Parente Cunha

How was your childhood and how has it influenced your work?

My childhood was in the Rio Vermelho neighborhood of Salvador, in Bahia. When I was a child, it was said that this was a very remote neighborhood. It was a beach neighborhood that became important later. Not only because Jorge Amado lived there, but because of the festival on the second day of February, which is dedicated to Iemanja, the "Mother of Water's Festival." At that time, this was a half-prohibited festival, because traditional families didn't look favorably upon the Afro-Brazilian religion *Candomblé*. In some way, it attracted me, because, from my "fantasy window," I could see the boats and the processions passing by. My childhood world passed in front of my window. There were fishermen, there were people waiting for trams and there were people selling things. When it was time for the "Mother of Water's Festival," women dressed in marvelous dresses would pass by on their way to the ceremonies on the beach. All of this stimulated my imagination.

I also liked my backyard, where I played and had my swing, my dollhouse, and all my plants and birds. I loved to watch rows of ants crawling. Sometimes, at night, the ants ate the ferns, and, in the morning, the yard would be full of leaves, which made my mother upset. It was fascinating, however. The Rio Vermelho neighborhood in Bahia formed my mythical geography.

Another part of my childhood was the unbelievably special nursemaid that I had. She was a granddaughter or great-granddaughter of slaves. She was the source of a character in my novel, *Mulher no espelho* [*Women Between Mirrors*]. Rio Vermelho appears in my work very often. Actually, what I remember about Rio Vermelho isn't really a memory. It's more of a fantasy — my own mythic space. My sensibility developed there.

One of my stories in the book *Vento, Ventania, Vendaval* [*Wind and Gale*], introduces two girls who are talking at their windows, which is related to my conversations with a girl who lived across from my house. Our world was there, and that's where we discussed everything about our little lives. Adolescence was more complicated, because my father was very strict, very severe, and I didn't have the kind of adolescence that other girls my age did. I lived in a very isolated way, because my father wouldn't let me walk on the beach, or go to parties. I played with younger girls, and that's why I remained very childish and had problems in my relationships with girls at schools. I think that the rebellion against any kind of authoritarianism that is present in my works arose from that phase. In addition, none of the father characters that appear in my books, especially in *Mulher no espelho,* is an exact image of my father, who has an authoritarian side, but also an extremely loving side.

Are travels important for you?

I like to travel, but it doesn't mean as much for me as it does for some of my friends. "Inner journeys" are much more meaningful for me, to be sure. I did go on significant "external journeys," however. For example, I received my first important literary prize during my stay in Italy. In Perugia, I took part in a contest for stories about Umbria. Newspapers here in Brazil wrote about my award, and reported that I had competed with students from more than 20 countries. With the money that I received, I bought my Olivetti typewriter. I still have it today, although I no longer use it. I stayed in Italy for nearly a year, and then I spent some time in France. That was the first time that I had traveled alone. Many people asked, "If your father's so strict, why would he let you travel to foreign countries?" He gave a lot of incentives for my studies. In this respect, he's completely different from the father that appears in my literature.

I was in Italy on various occasions and in Germany, where

43

my sister, Moema, lives, as well as in the United States in order to take part in conferences, or to give lectures, or to talk about my work on various occasions, or simply traveling. That's without including the fact that, at least twice a year, I go back to Bahia. My sister Zilma has a wonderful house on the beach at Guarajuba. In that dream landscape, I go on long "inner journeys."

Do politics play an important role in your life?

No, I don't have any affiliations, but I feel a deep sympathy for people who fight against oppression. Authoritarianism is naturally unjust. Any kind of social injustice disgusts me. I don't support seeing children sleeping in the street, or people sleeping in the street and going hungry. This is a very profound source of indignation for me, not only Brazil, but in other countries. I've always been in favor of those who struggle for a fairer social situation and less inequality in family incomes, and I try to vote for those who have objectives of that kind. Party politics aren't reflected in my work, but social problems are.

My literature can be regarded as political literature, because it condemns or exposes the conditions of victims of injustice, the poor and beggars. I have many characters who are beggars in my ministories in *Cem mentiras de verdade* [*100 True Lies*], and in another collection of stories, *Os provisorios* [*The Provisional*]. In the book of stories *A casa e as casas* [*House and Houses*], the theme of the final portion pertains to worldwide problems. Especially in relation to women, I'm constantly becoming more involved in issues of inequality and discrimination, or, ultimately, any kind of injustice. These problems appear frequently in my narrative works, and they reflect enormous indignation.

What does it mean to be a woman in Brazil?

I can't say that I've encountered discrimination for being a woman as a university professor and a writer. When I lived in Rio de Janeiro during the 1960s, I went to various publishing companies trying to publish my first book, which didn't appear until 1978. I wasn't rejected for being a woman, but because I was completely unknown.

What left me disgusted was the treatment given to women until the 1960s. Beginning with the 1960s, women's situation changed in Brazil, but, ultimately, there was a vast revolution in people's customs throughout the world: use of contraceptives, the hippie movement, miniskirts, men wearing long hair and ear-rings, pop culture… It was a big shift, a radical change in people's ways, with advances for sectors of society that previously had been ignored by the white, male, heterosexual, bourgeois or middle class establishment, which had been influenced by the European model and later by the North American model. Then the black movement in the United States spread to other countries, and, today in Brazil, there's a very strong movement among people of African descent. Other minority groups are also constantly becoming more significant.

I consider it absurd for women to regard themselves as being inferior to men. I still see women who think that way; even young women. For women to marry and to begin using their husbands' surnames was normal until a certain time. When I was married, I added my late husband's surname, but, if I had married during the 1970s, I wouldn't have done it. Women who still change their family names today abandon part of their identities. They stop being themselves, and become Mrs. So and So. I find this extremely odd. I believe that it's odd to send an invitation to a couple and write "Mr. and Mrs. So and So" on the envelope, as if the woman didn't have a name, instead of "Mr. A and Mrs. B." Certain customs are so deeply rooted that people don't recognize absurdities that had a reason to exist in earlier times, when women didn't have a voice.

Today, however, there are religious weddings for non-practicing Catholics, for example. A spectacle, a scenario, with people going in front of the altar and making a promise of mutual fidelity, but, very often, the marriage ends shortly thereafter, and then they reunite with other partners. What really makes me uncomfortable is seeing people being married in church, dressed as brides and grooms, after they've been living together. Sometimes they even have children, but they suddenly decide to have a church wedding. I don't know why. Possibly, or definately, because the ceremony is very beautiful. The young woman is led by her father or brother to the altar where the groom awaits her. The woman is being given to her future husband, as if she had no capability of managing her own life when, in reality, in most cases, these are women who do know how to manage their own lives.

What could be the inner meaning of this ceremony that is capable of awakening so many people's imaginations? What's going on with the Collective Unconscious? Naturally, everyone wants to be happy through love. The desire for completeness, perfection and happiness that is present in all of us, although it's never fully achieved, awakens the fantasy inspired by a desire that love, through marriage, would create a dream of the "They lived happily ever after" type. It appears that the wedding ceremony may represent fulfillment of the desire to be happy and, even more, to be happy with a loved one. As if the mechanism of the ceremony could give that kind of support or could be a condition for fulfilling the eternal dream. Very often, I look at all of this with a critical eye, and, sometimes, I look at it with a bit of compassion.

What is the situation of a woman writer in Brazil?

Beginning in the 1980s, some extremely important work has been completed here in Brazil in regard to female writers from the 19th century, and, although I didn't belong to research groups in that field, I'm very interested in popularizing their discoveries. I think that it's profoundly unjust that the names of hundreds of female writers who are being rediscovered now have not appeared in histories of literature. They were not taken seriously simply because they were women, to such an extent that the label "poetess" possesses an unfavorable connotation for many female writers today who prefer to be called "poets." "Poetess" referred to women who wrote in sugary language that was considered a typical form of expression for women at that time. Actually, during the 19th century, there were many female writers who rejected that stereotype, but they remained unknown, with only extremely rare exceptions. I find it outrageous that, before the 1960s, the creations of female writers in Brazil, except for Raquel de Queiroz or Cecilia Meireles, were not properly appreciated alongside men's literature.

As I said before, after the 1960s, hardly anyone encountered discrimination because of being a woman. But people did encounter discrimination because of not being white. That's another subject, however. In Brazil, there are movements that socialy alert women have joined as a reaction against this state of affairs.

Does family occupy an important place in your life?

I came from a very well-organized family with a father, a mother and five children. I have two sisters and two brothers. I'm the oldest. My family had a very strong structure within the traditional pattern for Bahia. My father was the "master of truth." He gave orders and made decisions, and my mother thought that this was best. After I married, I left Bahia, and I went to live in Rio de Janeiro. My husband and I were together for 30 years, until his death, and we had one son. My late husband fully supported my intellectual efforts, and he always encouraged me. He died when I was in the United States, participating in a conference in Los Angeles. I received the news of his death by telephone. I returned to Brazil the next day. My family generally gave me a lot of support. My only son has his own apartment, but he lives in the same building that I live in. Sometimes, we go for a number of days without seeing each other and without speaking, but, in a general, I'm very happy with him and with his girlfriend. With my siblings, I've also had a very good relationship. My father was very proud of me.

My first book of poems, published in 1978, although I had prepared it 15 years earlier, was dedicated to my father, who had just died. My narrative works began to be published at the end of the 1970s, at the time of profound changes in our society, when women could speak freely and could criticize the patriarchal system. My texts were considered violent. When I wrote my first short stories, I was surprised by the aggressiveness with which I was treating certain matters. Before, I had never believed that I would write narratives. People who knew me were also surprised. My mother didn't like my narratives very much. She called them erotic and was very upset by them. When I published my novel, *Mulher no espelho,* in 1983, many people found it too daring and aggressive, and my mother asked me, "What would your father say if he read this book?" Do you know what my answer was? "I probably wouldn't have written this book." In fact, I don't think that I had enough courage, because, in this novel, I criticize the entire structure that I grew up in. I dedicated my book of short stories *Os provisorios* to my mother and to an uncle and an aunt who were strongly present in my childhood and who told me the first stories that I can remember. Some people in the family, some of my uncles and aunts, were offended. "People will find out that your uncles and aunts told you these indecent stories." I find it odd that, even though I loved my father so much, there are various passages in my stories and novels where I attack the authoritarianism of the patriarchal system in which I was brought up.

Are mysticism and spirituality in general important for you?

Oh, yes. Mysticism is an integral part of my life. I believe that, without mysticism, I wouldn't withstand the distaste that I feel on account of our human condition, on account of the sensation of being imprisoned, on account of people's not being able to achieve their dreams, even independently of the social context. A concern with the mystery of "What is it that we're doing here? What is the purpose of our journey?" has tormented me for a long time. I can't say that I have any answers today. I've always had a very intense desire for God, a very strong longing for the infinite, as if I were always rejecting the limits of the human condition. Sometimes, I've lived with an impression of being imprisoned within my body. After a lot of searching, I entered a spiritual path that gave me answers for many of my questions. I can't say that it's an organized religion, but it's my belief system. It has been strongly influenced by Eastern thought along with Christianity from the earliest times.

Principally it is the quest for an inner God that inspires me the most. I believe that all of us have this Divine Flame. People who have more layers covering the Flame find greater difficulty in communicating with their Divine side, but, as people go looking for answers and finding them and strengthening their faith they remove these layers and approach the Divine. Whereas my poetry was initially full of metaphysical pain in the presence of the mystery that permeates our condition, my concerns and doubts have ended now. Rebellion from a social standpoint, however, has not changed. Although I don't find answers for certain metaphysical questions today, now I can accept being unable to comprehend something that is beyond our three-dimensional reasoning.

Whom do you write for? Is there an imaginary reader, or an intentional one?

Obviously, I like my readers. It's a matter of communication. When I write, however, I'm not thinking about a particular audience or reader. Sometimes, my literature is considered difficult. Perhaps a person who is less intellectually prepared may find it difficult to follow. I write because I have to write what I write. I can't open a door to my way of inventing reality. I write what I feel most deeply within myself. If my language sometimes avoids grammar or avoids what is officially correct and if I commit various kinds of linguistic or structural transgressions when I create a narrative, it's from a desire to be able to say more of what I want to say.

Currently I'm writing for a specific group of readers for the first time. I received an invitation from the writer Antonio Olinto, at the Brazilian Academy of Literature, to participate in the *Anjos de branco* [*White Angels*] collection that has been introduced by the Federal Nursing Council. For me, it's a challenge to write a narrative with a predetermined theme and for a particular audience on a priority basis. This novel will be released in 2002, and it may find a broader circle of readers, far beyond those who work in the health-care area.

What do you think of globalization?

It's affecting the entire planet at every level, and I think that it could turn out to be very good, but, at this point, it isn't. Today, I have a more optimistic vision of things; therefore, I imagine and I hope that all of the events that have caused so much suffering, so much fear, so many threats and so much unemployment for so many people will serve as experiences that lead to a state of affairs where every nationality and every region can maintain its individuality while also being able to experience global integration, which isn't occurring yet. Maybe we're on the way toward it. Maybe…

Single Mother

My daughter is a single mother, it's true, so what? my daughter is the daughter of a single mother, true, that she is, so did they have to throw dirt on her relationship? Another thing, what kind of man is that, 30 some years old and just because his daddy thinks that a single girl who has a daughter taking the college entrance exam isn't a flower of womanhood, well now, he kept on filling his son's ears, careful, boy, how many lovers has your girlfriend had so far? son, you can't believe her. My daughter dumped the guy just in time, but she is suffering, she likes that daddy's boy, you see, the world keeps coming back to the same thing and lots of people are still tied to the past, when I got pregnant, ah, you depraved girl, I'll only not kill you to keep from being arrested, you've stained my name, spit on my honor, get out of my house right now, disappear from my town.

That woman, swept by a strong wind, the will in her whiplike look forbidding the forbidden, reversed all the signs and signals.

Of course I was a hippie, I made lots of leather bracelets, sold necklaces and earrings in the Praça da Sé, I survived. University? I wanted to be an architect, I went through hard times, but I managed, this scar here on my face, can you see it? The mark from my father's belt buckle, I never needed him or any man to pay my bills, eh, I couldn't live just on peace and love, with so many wars to face.

Impatient to show off the mark of victory, the scar from the belt buckle was a war trophy. From the highest heights, my gaze would strike and explode metal and burst bottles. A warrior, in permanent state of defiance, living each episode as a new test, for the new triumphs to come.

I took a lot of drugs, true, so what? Arrested, I was arrested, my name booked by the police, Mr. Prosecuter, I have a clean background, there must be a mistake, I never sold drugs, I'll never forget that night, but those things are in the past, I've already used up my quota of madness, my first jobs? Maid, waitress at a lunch counter, yes, my dear, how was I going to support my daughter? I miss the ruddy ferocity of those wars.

Residues and excesses, she raised the standard, brandished the shields and the fireworks. Without any brilliant tactics, no medals, I listened to the throbbing of turbines of metal and bottles, in the midst of the whirlwind.

Hunger, yes, I was hungry, but I never stole, never killed, never coveted my neighbor's man, never, and who doesn't like to have a good time? Dance? Sometimes really drunk, true, so what? Please, Mr. Union Boss, pardon the noise, I'll turn down the sound, it was madness, my dear, I was never late to work or missed deadlines, never late with my architecture projects that won a lot of prizes, my construction projects, from hotels and mansions at the beach resort of Ararapugi to the little chalets with gardens in the far suburbs, yes, my daughter is my assistant, and because she wants to be, I don't interfere with her decisions, I don't interfere with my daughter's daughter's decisions, she's going to take the entrance exam in architecture because she wants to, my daughter is a single mother by choice, the child's father wanted to get married, my daughter didn't want to, said no, get married for what, man? What nonsense, we're fine as it is, each one in his own house, but I'm a representative in the legislature, you have to understand, we need to legalize our relationship, you know, the voters, the party, so he ended up marrying another woman, he didn't know how to live without certificates stamped by notaries, want to know something? I don't care what others think or don't think, I am my own person and I don't owe anything to anybody.

Always stronger in her attitudes, she showed off the mark of the buckle, wound and certificate of manumission, eye to eye, from the fortress of her castle, taking the measure of everyone, it was hard for anyone to bear the whiplike eye for long. Culminations and profundities in the ardent winds of hurricanes.

Boyfriends, yes, I had many, many lovers, so what? Sweetheart, it's not because I love you that I'm going to stop working with my partner, why make that ugly face? If men think that they own you, it was never that way with me, listen here, darling, I don't have to ask your permission to serve a client in another city, right, I only stayed with the men I truly liked, how many were they? Ah, how many, become a slave, never, no man can control me, no matter how much I like him, I'll tell you, my dear, once and for all, I don't make up excuses not to meet you every night, I don't cancel my professional engagements, you have to believe me, ah, how many lovers have I had, I don't like to lie, see here, I paid dearly for my liberty, so love me or leave me, that issue is sealed up forever, here, look.

The buckle of the distant belt sparked from the heights of her great attitude, her face entrenched in the warning and the castle, defense against assaults, attack when the trumpets announce an enemy approaching.

The black sheep of my family? All right, you can call me that, my sister pretends not to notice the same relationship of her husband and his children with another woman, you have to decide without fear of fractures and fissures.

Her whiplike eye was dilating into the explosion of metal, always on guard, ready to shoot off arrows, no, I didn't question her high tides and storms on the high seas, but I know that she was in love, and then?

At night, when I return home, he is waiting for me, the table set, flowers and lighted candles, he never asked me for a laundry list of what I do during the day, he hands me a clean and sweet-smelling towel to use after my bath.

The whiplike eye calmed from the great height of storms into small lulls, breezes of satin and jasmine petals, her voice emerging from a glass of champagne, that's it, yes, the whole day full of battles, but night was cushioned. His shoulder's infinite space and the comfort of his warm lap, nest for her fabrics and silks, skin against skin, hair touching hair, smoothing murmurs, culminations, the look of fine violins, mute, autumnal.

The warrior rests in the arms of her lover, after the angry day of battles and trophies.

— translated by K. David and
Elizabeth A. Jackson

Two Girls at the Window
To the memory of Maria de Hugo

When something has happened to you in the fullness of its nature, even if it breaks, passes or comes to an end, you never lose it. It stays with you. It lives inside you. I'm referring to the window in my house in Rio Vermelho, where I used to converse with my undying friend, who was leaning on her window just across from mine. Two windows and two young girls. In the middle, the street. In between, the world.

All that fullness that we had, broke, passed by, came to an end. One of the girls died. But nothing of the fullness was lost. The two girls inhabit secret layers of my body, hidden among cells and pulsations and timelessness that absorb the clarity of voices and the form of gestures and the enchantment of reverberations.

Two windows and two girls. They used to see and hear the streetcar that came from Amaralina. They used to see and hear the world open in mysteries and shapes that came up between the windows and their curious gazes. I would lean over and call. She also called me and leaned out. Mirrors where the girls saw themselves, face to face, one self in the other.

What luck, Dona Lucy isn't coming to give class today, so I can paste in the photographs of Shirley Temple that Aunt Beth gave me.

If you have a duplicate of Shirley dressed like a little soldier, trade with me, my album is already almost full. Look there at Mr. Anacleto the milkman talking with the girl from the pharmacy.

Dona Bernardina is returning from Mass with a golden rosary in her hand. She goes to Mass every day, wrapped in a black shawl, and Marta's mother goes with her.

Dona Bernardina said that no one should play with the rosary because it will turn into a snake and bite you, but I think she's lying. I adore chocolate caramel, if I could I'd eat the whole box.

Dona Lucy said that sucking candy causes cavities in your teeth. When I grow up, I'm going to the United States to meet Shirley Temple, but before that I'm getting a permanent to make my hair look just like hers.

Dona Zuzu is coming for my 10 o'clock class and if I don't have my assignment ready, I'll be punished. I wanted to know why Marta killed herself.

I didn't see Marta's funeral procession because my mother wouldn't let me. When I'm bigger, I'm going to the Normal School, I want to be a teacher.

I hid in my room and watched Marta's funeral procession go by, I don't know why she killed herself. When I'm bigger, I want to go to high school, then I'm going to be a doctor.

Marta was very pretty, we'll never see Marta ever again.

Today Valdete is coming to play with me, I wanted my hair in little curls like hers, the same as Shirley, but my mother says that it's a lot of work, why don't you like Valdete?

What a shame, my hair is very straight and I can't have curls, but I'm getting a dress just like Shirley's.

Mr. Filinto from the store gave me three chocolate caramels, I adore caramel. Have you ever seen you brother taking a bath naked?

I saw Aunt Beth changing clothes. Dona Lucy gave me a perfect score with honors because I knew the multiplication table by heart. Be careful so your teeth don't get cavities.

The Shirley Temple doll is in Sloper's store window, it's the most beautiful doll in the world, I'm going to ask my father to give me one.

I wanted to know why Marta killed herself, she was such a good person, but lately she passed by and didn't even speak to me.

I ask everyone why Marta killed herself. Next year I'm going to dress up like a Hawaiian and watch the clubs parade at Campo Grande.

I wanted to get that beautiful dress just like Shirley's to go strolling on Mariquita Square on Sunday afternoons.

Today is the feast day of the Goddess of the Sea and you can only go to the beach if you take a present to put in the boats, you understand? The boats are all decorated with flowers.

Dona Bernardina said that whoever believes in the Goddess of the Sea is going to hell. I'm going to dress like an angel and go out in Senhora Santana's procession

Mr. Anacleto the milkman is talking again with that girl who works at the pharmacy. They are going out together.

Mr. Anacleto is married and he can't have a girlfriend. Dona Bernardina gave me a little saint and told my mother that it was time for my First Communion.

Look at Carlinhos on his scooter, he is so cute, when I grow up I'm going out with Carlinhos. Every time that Mr. Filinto passes by here, he gives me chocolate caramels, I adore caramel.

Be careful so your teeth don't get cavities. Marta's mother goes to Mass every day, all dressed in black, her head lowered, poor thing, she's crying.

Marta didn't play with dolls any more because she had grown up. Valdete has a Shirley Temple doll, but my dad says that it's very expensive and I already have lots of toys, why don't you like Valdete?

Yesterday Aunt Beth brought a doll with a bunch of dresses just like Shirley's. Aunt Beth is going to have one made for my birthday.

I wanted to dress up like a Hawaiian with lots of necklaces and flowers, but my dad won't let me because my grandmother died.

In Senhora Santana's procession, I'm going to be an angel with a silver star on my forehead, too bad my hair is straight and I can't have curls.

Valdete said that Marta killed herself because her mother

didn't want her to date. When I grow up I'm going out with Carlinhos.

Dona Bernardina says that dating is a sin, that's why Marta's mother didn't want her to date.

I didn't go see Shirley's film because my homework has ugly handwriting. I think the women going to the Goddess of the Sea festival with embroidered skirts and colorful necklaces are pretty.

My dad said that the only people who go to the festival of the Goddess of the Sea are those condomblé *people and that we shouldn't get mixed up with them because they don't believe in God.*

Well I'm not afraid and on February 2nd next year I'm going to take a flower to put in the boat with presents.

I was already in my angel costume, with a silver star on my forehead, but Dona Bernardina said that I could only go out in the procession after I had my First Communion.

My mother doesn't want me to take chocolate caramels from Mr. Filinto at the store. I'm going to study medicine, like Valdete's sister, she entertains boyfriends every night at the gate, her dad lets her. Why don't you like Valdete?

Dona Bernardina says that women shouldn't study medicine and that Valdete's sister is shameful, when I grow up, I'm not going to make out at the gate because it's a sin.

When I grow up, I'm going to make out with Carlinhos at the gate, he's so cute, isn't he? He's going to take the entrance exam for Bahia High, did you know? Next year I want to be a Hawaiian with necklaces and a wreath of flowers on my head.

Next year I'm going in Senhora Santana's procession dressed like an angel, with wings on my back and a silver star on my forehead. I'll only give you the photo of Shirley dressed like a soldier if you give me her tap-dancing on the stairs.

Valdete said that Marta killed herself because she was going out with a married man separated from his wife and her mother didn't want her to.

Mr. Anacleto the milkman is married and going out with the salesgirl at the pharmacy and she didn't kill herself.

On my birthday my mother is going to decorate a table with little dolls with yarn hair and curls just like Shirley's.

Aunt Beth said that the girl in the pharmacy's father went running after Mr. Anacleto with a pistol in his hand.

Valdete said that Marta killed herself with ant poison that her mother put in the garden so the ants wouldn't eat the plants, why don't you like Valdete?

I can't have curls in my hair because it's very straight. What did your dad say to Mr. Filinto at the store who used to give you chocolate caramels?

I told my godfather that on my birthday I want a Shirley Temple doll, but daddy thinks it's very expensive.

Aunt Beth already ordered the dress just like Shirley's for my birthday. Marta's mother hasn't been to Mass for three days.

Mr. Anacleto isn't putting water in the milk any more, but no one speaks to him, not even to say hello. The girl at the pharmacy moved to Jequié.

Marta's poor mother, she's very sick, did you know? Dona Bernardina said that we should forget about Marta.

Mr. Filinto from the store passed by here, but he didn't give me caramels or look at me, he just went by looking straight ahead, why don't you like Valdete?

Do you mean to say that your dad isn't going to take the family to Uncle Duda's farm and you can dress up like a Hawaiian for Carnival, with necklaces and a crown of flowers on your head.

Do you mean that you're going to take First Communion and can be an angel in Senhora Santana's procession, with wings on your back and a silver star on your forehead.

I went to the dentist because of my tooth with a cavity that was hurting a lot and Aunt Beth gave me ice cream and bought me shoes just like Shirley's for my birthday.

Every time that Carlinhos comes by, he winks at me, he's so cute, isn't he?

Marta's mother is going to die.

Marta's mother died.

Dona Bernardina said that I shouldn't speak to Valdete, because at her house no one goes to Mass.

Valdete said that her sister said that Dona Bernardina turned devout because she was secretly dating and her boyfriend left town, afraid that her father would kill him if he didn't marry her.

I don't like Valdete because when she comes by here, she swings her head with all those curls just to spite me because of my straight hair.

I'll trade my photo of Shirley tap-dancing on the stairs for yours with her dressed like a soldier.

Do you think my birthday dress is pretty? It's just like Shirley's.

Just look what Uncle Duda gave me for a birthday present, a Shirley Temple doll, the most beautiful doll in all the world.

— translated by K. David and
Elizabeth A. Jackson

Astrid Cabral

Astrid Cabral

Astrid Cabral was born in Manaus in the state of Amazon. At 16-years old she published her first articles and ediortials in the local press. During the 1950s she was a member of an inovative literary movement in the region known as *Clube da Madrugada*. she moved to Rio de Janeiro to study Neo-Latin literatures at the Federal University of Rio de Janeiro (known then as the University of Brazil). She also holds a degree in English language from the Insitute Brazil-United States. In 1962 she joined the faculty of the University of Brasilia, but she resigned for political reasons shortly after the military coup of 1964. In 1988, after the amnesty, she resumed her academic career. she has held various posts in public affairs and spent several years in Chicago working for the Consulate of Brazil.

Her most important works include: *Alameda* (1963); *Ponto de cruz* (1979); *Torna-viagem poesia* (1981); *Lição de Alice: poemas, 1980-1983* (1986); *Res desgarrada: poemas, 1986-1990* (1994); *De deu em deu: poemas reunidos, 1979-1994* (1998); *Intramuros* (1998).

Astrid Cabral

What induced you to become a writer?

I think that it was the life force. I've always been a person guided by emotions. I felt very ill at ease when I had to speak in public. Any strongly emotional situation drained my spirit. When I was young and even when I wanted to end relationships, I relied upon letters. I delivered my letters in person, instead of speaking. A way of avoiding weeping and stuttering. Writing was my way of channeling this excessive sensitivity and remaining at ease by saying things in front of a piece of paper instead of in front of people. I have a poem, "O vinho de emoção," where I've explained all this.

What was your childhood like?

I was born and brought up in Manaus. When I was very young, my family moved to Recife, and then I went back to Manaus when I was 4 years old, when my father died. I was brought up in my grandparents' house. When I was 18, I went to study in Rio. After finishing my education, I married a man here in Rio and I ended up staying, but my childhood in Manaus was something extremely important for me. The thing that affected me most deeply was losing my father. I kept looking for my father in the shadows, imagining that he was still alive and that, one day, he would return, after being resurrected like Christ. My earliest memories are of the city Recife, the sea and our house in Madalena, but my entire upbringing was in the Amazon region.

I grew up in Manaus when it was influenced by the decline of the rubber industry. On one hand, there was sophistication from the era of wealth, or a cosmopolitan heritage, and, on the other hand, there was a lot of nature. My house was located between two bridges. Just across from it, there was a palace, which was the government building that has become the cultural center today. It was built by a German, and, to the right and the left, there was a collection of hovels and shacks floating on the river. I can even say that, if Gilberto Freire had been an Amazonian, he would have written *Palaces and Hovels*, in addition to writing *Casa grande e senzala* or *Sobrados e mocambos*, because the contrast between the two Brazils was already there, just as it can be found everywhere today: Rio de Janeiro with its luxury condominiums and slums, Manaus with its turn of the century palaces, and the hovels sprouting along the banks, like riverside slums. As for nature in the Amazon region, it's very overpowering. People there were accustomed to having pets in their houses. It could be a favorite monkey, a talking parrot, or a turtle, aside from puppies and cats. In the basements of houses, there were boa constrictors and other snakes that eat mosquitoes. The greatest fear of my childhood was that there could be an alligator sleeping under my bed. There is no doubt that this was another world.

> *You've traveled a lot. Did your trips have an*
> *important role in your work?*

Oh, travel, no doubt about that! During the period when I was living in Manaus, I made two trips to Fortaleza and Belem. My father's family was from Fortaleza, and I spent holidays there twice. After I came to Rio and after I was married, I traveled a lot with my husband who also likes to travel a lot. I entered a competition for the *Itamarati*, Brazil's foreign service. I worked in various places, and all of these trips are strongly present in my work be it the Orient, be it the Amazon, be it the United

States. My other books are more linked to time than to space, but they are more abstract and subjective, more universal.

What was the impact of politics upon your life?

The period with the greatest impact was that of the military coup and the dictatorship that came after it. I was never able to become involved in political agitation, precisely because I was bringing up my children at that time. When the dictatorship began in 1964, my belly was as big as it could be. I remember things such as a summer camp where I enrolled two of my sons. I was shocked to realize that this "summer camp" was a ruse for intensive military indoctrination, for praising the dictatorship, etc. I removed my sons from it immediately.

I always tried to have a position in relation to the simplest day-to-day things. I can remember that, during the time of the dictatorship, there was rationing during a shortage of milk, and, one day, a woman came and said, "Listen, save three liters for the captain's wife." I jumped out from the end of the line and said, "The lady won't do that. The dictatorship can't reach as far as the milk line." The woman went away very quietly. During that time, I took a position about little situations in life, but I couldn't abandon my family and go into the streets.

I signed various manifestos, and I was a victim of the dictatorship at the University of Brasilia, where I was working with hopes of an academic career. I entered the contest for the *Itamarati*, because I had lost my position at the university, for supporting my collegue. He had been fired unfairly because of being suspected of communism. That's why I didn't know until the last minute whether or not I would be accepted to work with the foreign service. But I was accepted. During my youth here in Rio, I had some sympathy with communism, but I never joined any party. I always wanted to keep absolute freedom before the facts, above anything else. I like to be free and to take my own stand in any situation, independently of abstract commitments, and independently of everything. I'm rebellious. I never belonged to any party, and I think that it's good that I didn't make a commitment because after all the communist dream, the dream that inspired even the creation of Brasilia, degenerated into totalitarianism and created so much horror. I continue to believe that capitalism is wrong, but I don't know how people can overcome social injustice without totalitarianism, without endangering freedom.

What does being a woman in Brazil mean to you?

I think that each generation and each place will give a different answer to that question. Brazil is a world, it's a continent, and we have not only a vast geographic space but a huge temporal space. There are people in the inland areas of Brazil who still live in previous centuries, in backwardness, even though this has changed somewhat with television. From any standpoint, I think that, from my generation to my daughters' generation, there was a real earthquake, a revolution. During my era, it was very common for people to be virgins when they married, and for young men to ask the bride's parents for her hand. There was a whole set of rituals and formal requirements that are completely gone.

I was enormously lucky with my marriage, because I married a man who was free from machismo. He always gave me the freedom to do what I truly believed in, and he always supported my literary aspirations. He's a poet, too, and he really helped me with raising our children. He took part in our household chores. Personally, I don't have any complaints, because I had this extraordinary good luck. From what I see around me, that's not very common. There are a lot of burdens, and more burdens fall on women. Women have gained many things, but they've also lost many things. They have to lead agitated lives with a lot of stress, working at home and away from home.

It's also necessary to see the difference between middle-class women and women from the lower classes. I will always say that there are more differences between one social class and another than between one country and another. So, a woman from the lower classes, a middle-class woman, and a woman from the upper class will have greater differences than the two of us talking here.

Are conditions for women writers different from conditions for male writers in Brazil?

There's a lot of curiosity about women. For a long time, women didn't have a literary voice, and now they're beginning to speak in literature. Before, they only spoke to their counterparts. I even think that some people became known by giving this kind of testimony about women. It's something new.

In Brazil, writers generally face a very difficult situation, except for a half dozen who have managed to be commercially successful. For most writers, it's terrible, because there's no readership. With this absence of a readership, it's as if you were speaking in a desert. Someone who writes does it because of the joy of creative efforts and enthusiasm. It's necessary to express what's inside you, because, if you don't express it, you suffer. Society doesn't create favorable conditions for it, however. There is difficulty publishing books, and there are especially difficulties with distribution of books. Because I don't have any sense of marketing, the happiness that my books give me is more important than sales. It's like an initiation, as if I were part of a community, or something that's even clandestine or partially on the fringes.

Have your other occupations influenced what you write?

Undoubtedly. When I was a teacher, I studied a lot. A lot of theory. Therefore, I was intimidated by all of this good literature that had already been written and, because I truly liked teaching, that activity absorbed my enthusiasm for literature. When I stopped teaching and began working as a civil servant, which I didn't like, but which I did anyway because I'm a responsible person, the total lack of enthusiasm for my new job meant that I could return to literature, not for studying it any longer, but for my own creation. Then it was good, and, looking back now from a distance, after a long time, it was good to have my academic career end so that I could read what I wanted to, and have the freedom to spend my time with myself, with my creative activity.

Is your family important to you?

It's very important. I put my family first. Five children who didn't ask to come into this world are a responsibility. My husband and I are very much in love. We're *tucunare* parents, like that type of fish that stays and protects its young in the river. This current of love between us is a rare thing. There's so much frustration dominating the world around us.

What's the role of mysticism in your life?

I've had moments of deep mysticism and moments of deep doubts. I'm a person who can be inspired by passions, but I'm also a creature of investigation and rational thinking. I fluctuate a lot. For me, the issue of belief is very irregular, because I believe and I disbelieve. Perhaps because I was raised in a house where my grandfather was very skeptical and my grandmother was religious. I can say that I was ecumenical before ecumenism developed. When I was a girl, I went to Catholic masses on Sundays, and, on Saturdays, I attended Baptist rituals. My grandmother was appalled: "You're Catholic. You can't do this!" but my grandfather said, "Oh, no, let her go. She knows what she's doing." So I grew up in this atmosphere of freedom and diversity. In Brazil, we aren't orthodox in matters of religion. People need to be very free in this area, because I don't think that anyone can possess absolute certainty.

What do you think about globalization?

At the same time that I applaud it, I'm dying with fear. Imagine everything becoming uniform! I believe that human beings can't become uniform, that the beauty of humanity is variety and that there must be respect for this variety. I'm dying of fear about economic globalization, because I think that an economically interconnected world is worse off. A world of self-sufficient communities would be a lot better. On the other hand, I also think that people can't live in isolation, but that they should have the right to be independent. I'm strongly in favor of globalization in cultural terms, but not in economic terms.

The Orchid at the Exposition

She was surprised to be taken down one morning, carefully, from the trunk of the mango tree where she lived very comfortably. She was angry to be disturbed, then was it right to dislodge her from her home, without the least deference? But soon the idea of adventure consoled her. Nostalgia for travel lit up her sedentary head. Little by little she found herself a captive. She released the roots that at first resisted and confided herself with no further delay to the hands of an unknown.

She felt herself beautiful, velvety, and an uncontrollable exhibitionism compelled her to a prime location where her lavender-purple and her butterfly shape could be praised with songs more varied than the refrain of that flycatcher that she knew. In the mango tree where she lived, only two sang: him and a loud cicada that cried in her ears even when the heat was soft and friendly.

What would the world be like far from there, that was what she at times asked herself in her muteness. Was the sky as distant and the earth as near? Or was there a tree so tall it could invert distances? She hoped to live in such a tree. It should be wonderful to live with the clouds, made from milky camellias and fluffy cottons! To see rain born in her little patch of air. And to be in the neighborhood of stars, what would it be like? But she sighed: Ah, certainly I won't ever reach that giant tree.

I'm not strong enough to grow with it. I know my congenital weakness, my indisposition for grandeur. If only there were someone who could place me in its highest branches... But not even men on the scaffolding of the highest skyscrapers have arms long enough to reach it.

She stopped to imagine the tree. It must be so exuberant that year by year its canopy covers the whole earth and wherever the sun goes, its rays always reach the ground filtered and softened by its leaves. Immense leaves like wide-brimmed hats that men use for protection.

But now where was she going? And if she should ask those orchids open for more than a week? Well, she concluded with a pout, a flower's life is too short to have experiences.

Then she found herself in a closed space, with the same low white sky, just parallel lines and very decorated suns, neatly arranged like pomegranate seeds. She enjoyed the space for some time, until the window near her was opened and she was able to contemplate the sky outside — the patch of blue daubed with white, framed in the square of the window like a flag commemorating spring. That was when she found herself in a storehouse and soon became better informed when groups arrived with loud voices speaking of clubs, halls, dance floors. How would men dance in such a place? She couldn't conceive of dancing and movements unless the wind, like music, created the rhythm: from sky to earth, from sunset to sunrise. When her own image was subject to violent gymnastics, she was not pleased by the easy manipulation of some companions who shamelessly exhibited an anxiety not flattering to their species. She detested the susceptibility and somnolence of the most sensitive ones: "What coquetry, my God!" They didn't know how to straighten up even the slightest. Alas in this respect she had no illusions. She already knew that very few shared her point of view and, among them, of course, the *cactáceas* that, besides their immobility that made them rigid and ferocious, their thorns showing to anyone who dared transplant them.

Such intransigence was much more dignified than the benevolence with which she had surrendered. She was repentant. She longed for the freshness, the horizon, the mango tree, and what was she doing there after all? She posed for impertinent photographers, who frightened her with their lightning, exposed to the caprices of countless visitors. One of them slyly used the wicker basket where she was installed as an ashtray. Either because, unforgivable forgetfulness, there wasn't one in the room, or the windows were all monopolized by strangers, the person pretended to examine her subtle details and while he handled one of her petals (making a farce of the guard's vigilance, who wasn't guarding anything and was just one more decorative vase, wrapped in a shiny uniform, planted solemnly at the door) he tossed the still hot tip of his cigarette inside her basket and left at once, relieved. She was wounded and wanted to cry out for help, since it would do no good to make animal sounds, baby cries. She must denounce him clearly using human language: —Stop this lack of respect, this meddling. But would it be worthwhile to speak out when words had lost their power? In silence she considered and lived her panic. Certain that the heat would increase beyond what she could feel, all her reserve of water exhausted. Before the end that seemed so simple, all destinies would come to the same result, there would be an unbearable point, a moment when all feelings are stretched to a limit that condenses all life itself. That's what she feared.

Meanwhile the heat ceased, throwing off a ring of tenuous smoke. Outside the door, only the smell lasted a few more moments. She liked strong persistent smells, but not that one, others: the stems of tuberoses that the boy brought each week to the small alter at home. From the garden, nested in the mango tree she had also breathed the aroma of peeled tangerines down below, between laughter and eating. She was far from all of this, devoured by melancholy. Had she known she would have stayed there. Oh, she would have put up a firm and tenacious resistance.

When the exhibition had opened it was fun, such lovely visitors with their praises: "How lovely! I didn't know this one." "—Look, it's like the postcard that Belgian sent me." "—Notice its princess airs, Julieta." Then others came saying: "What a disgrace! Just imagine! To bring people out of their houses to see this." "That one shouldn't be in the show, it's too ugly." She was saddened by the lack of respect and then suddenly remembered that no one or almost no one suspected that she could understand what they were saying because of her natural wisdom. With this came the heavy joy of vengeance. She fooled them. As quiet as can be, she enjoyed the frankness, the imprudence of all who spoke without restraint. Her happiness didn't last. Its violence didn't take root. And sadness suddenly came over her: if she lived in order to be beautiful, and she wasn't, why continue? So many are the flowers that abort and rot as seeds in the ground or water!

When she reflected pessimistically, finding herself as useless as the drops she drank, the mango tree's hospitality took her in its arms, a certain little girl on tiptoes touched her with her finger. "—Buy this one for me, Mother. It's the most beautiful of all." Her mother left pulling the girl by the hand, which didn't matter much because moves are tiring and journeys only when they could swear: —the giant tree exists. They would have to give her a map because trails, she already knew, cover all corners of the ground (she had overheard some underbrush say so). There would be the problem of transportation. What was the route like? She couldn't count on the slow and lazy ivies. Who knows maybe the back of a bird?

The young girl's voice brought back her well-being. She was happy again. Beautiful, beautiful! But what if others found her ugly? Doubt took away her happiness, made her sad, took away her sadness and made her happy. Voices of praise and reproach mixed together. Someone was lying. Who? If only she had a mirror always ready, like her friends in the lake (that's why they were so vain) she could vouch for one of the versions.

She could agree with her self-criticism: —I'm beautiful, I'm ugly. That wasn't enough to make her right. She could think herself beautiful being ugly (the most likely result, since all the flowers with which she was acquainted held this illusion). She could be beautiful thinking herself ugly, a mistake for which there is no excuse. Oh, what a dreadful situation. She would like most to unmask the liars. And what if the liars were the ones saying she was beautiful? Oh big heart, have mercy. And those who said she was ugly? Envious, talking uselessly in spite of being convinced.

Oh, oh, she was tired for no reason… Certainly the truth didn't exist and, if it did, it could only be seen from the top of that tree, higher than the highest mountain.

— translated by K. David and
Elizabeth A. Jackson

The Male Soapberry Tree
Sapindus esculentus

Years and years went by and the soapberry didn't bloom. It's enormous branches covered with leaves shot up into the air over the fence. It seemed to wave with its large clusters, bowing as if to practice the moves of its future offerings of fruit. But it didn't go beyond the promise, its agitation useless. Maybe next year. Next year, who knows? It grew old that way, without anyone noticing. Bald with only a few leaves, and a more shriveled trunk, already speckled with moss and mold. Its branches had a vague tired air, flaccid, less erect, drooping towards the ground, although there were those who attributed it to the strong winds that blew through the empty garden where it was planted. There is no immunity from the weather, however, even if the tree's decline was slow, almost imperceptible in its deceptive mildness.

More than one generation of boys passed by with their street cries in the heat of the afternoon: So.. so.. soapa-papapbeeery! So..so..soapapapapbeeery! Overfilled trays spilled the round fruit that rolled down the sidewalks, changed into shooting marbles. Shoulders sank under the weight of the straw baskets that returned in the evenings light from the streets and stops on the corners.

That soapberry was on strike. It ridiculed the fertilizer,

contradicted the ground, a prodigal with other roots. The garden was filled with people and the canopies wove together filtering the days. The guavas swelled and yellowed to the delight of the parrots and birds. If they smashed to the ground, they opened their rosy hearts to the wanderings of the fruit flies. Tall mango trees dropped mature fruits with a crash, their skins tearing on impact. Clouds of mosquitos banqueted, attracted by the fermentation, the reigning heat and humidity. The exhuberant growths of bitter Cayenne limes spread through the stalks, within reach of hands. Rising above the roofs, the thin stalks of the star apple showed constellations of mature fruit. And the soapberries on the adjoining properties?

The sterility of our soapberry seemed to be a provocation, a donkey's stubbornness.

The charcoal man came by saying that he would try something, since he had already cured the fussiness of so many, and he began to enumerate them: two avocado trees and a papaya when he lived on the farm, not counting the decorative plants that he had made to bloom. Taking the ashes from the stove, he murmured while he dressed the trunk of the soapberry in a grotesque boot.

—It's a sure cure, a sure cure.

But it didn't make any miracles. Then it was the mulatto Pedro's turn to come by with a circumspect suggestion.

—Why, everyone, it just needs whipping on Fridays.

He started to come religiously to execute the ritual. He stripped the bark, shook the branches. Overcome with frenzy. He hit it with his belt until his face burst almost pouring out blood mixed with sweat. Then like a man possessed, he started in again with the placidity of the high canopy. Seeing that its trunk was too vertical, most of the branches very high, he didn't dare try to scale them. He remained below with his stick and patience, shaking the branches indefinitely until exhaustion overcame him. But weariness could not sadden him. He went away happy, relieved.

Then the passing of time confirmed what everyone had suspected, aggravating the general disdain. The frustrated hope preferred anger to pity. No one could conceive of wasting that space in such a full garden. Why not plant another soapberry? That one doomed the species bringing to mind a possible extinction.

Condemning it was the uncontrolled appetite with its incurable revenge. The fruit denied seemed to have been taken out of the mouths of everyone there. Thus their unanimous sentence of the death penalty.

Some children came playing games around the soapberry. With their soft hands, they could not protect it for very long. They dispersed on orders of the adults, frightened by the dry moan of the wood and the thump of the body, deaf and meek like a gesture of resignation.

Afterwards, the sun opened wide into the emptiness. An ardent suffocating sun to wither the little plants between the stones and to cause shadows in men's hearts in the shade they had destroyed.

— translated by K. David and
Elizabeth A. Jackson

Marly de Oliveira

Marly de Oliveira

Marly de Oliveira was born in Cachoeiro de Itapemirim in the state of Espirito Santo and grew up in Campos in the state of Rio de Janeiro. She moved to Rio de Janeiro with her family to attend the Catholic University (PUC) where she studied Neo-Latin literature. During her college years she published her first volume of poetry *Cerco da primavera* (1957). She studied Italian language and literature in Rome where she befriended Giuseppe Ungaretti. While in Rome she wrote *Explicação do Narciso* (1960). After returning to Brazil she taught at PUC in the department of Hispanic literatures and in the department of Italian literature at the *Faculdade das Doroteias* in Friburgo in the state of Rio de Janeiro. Married to a diplomat she traveled to Argentina and Switzerland and she spent some time in Brasilia after it was founded. Her second husband was João Cabral de Melo Neto, Brazil's foremost poet, who died in 1999.From her first marriage she has two daughters: Monica, who organizes cultural events and Patricia, who is a painter.

Some of her major works include: *A suave pantera* (1962); *A vida natural* (1968); *Contato* (1975); *Invocação do Orpheu* (1979); *O banquete* (1988); *Obra poetica reunida, 1958 - 1988* (1989); *O mar de permeio: poemas, 1991 - 1994* (1997).

Marly de Oliveira

What led you to become a writer?

I believe that people are born with a predestined vocation, a kind of internal calling, because from my earliest days I felt that I wanted to have a life through words. Therefore, my initial path began with a course in Neo-Latin literature at PUC [the Catholic University in Rio de Janeiro], where first under the influence of Spanish poetry with a predominance of images (García Lorca, Guillén) and some of reflection (Salinas), I wrote *Cerco da Primavera* [*Spring's Boundary*] when I was 17 years old. In the following year, I won first prize in the INL [the national book award]. I then began *Explicação de Narciso* [*Explanation of Narcissus*], and left for Rome, where I did postgraduate studies and met Ungaretti. Even though I was under the guardianship the nuns of the Order of Saint Theresa, they never stopped me from seeing him or going to some classes with Vittorio De Sica. But the biggest surprise is when he read some poems of mine written in Italian on RAI (the Italian radio and television network). It was a combination of joy and commitment. The aesthetic concern was yielding to expression of feeling and not saying.

What was your childhood like and in what way did it influence your work?

My childhood was not very happy, even though I lived in a very large house in Campos (State of Rio de Janeiro), after having been born in Cachoeiro de Itapemirim (State of Espírito

Santo). There were wide-open spaces and gardens, but it was not a time of freedom: it was a time of severely disciplined education and represssion. Today, I am able to appreciate this, reflecting upon where all this limitless freedom can take you.

Do you enjoy travel? Does travel inspire you?

I am idealistic about travel, feeling that it helps one to learn more about things and understand them better. I value the importance of knowing oneself, even without leaving your own room. Returning from Rome, I was at three universities: PUC in Rio, Petrópolis and Friburgo. Shortly after, I married a diplomat who is now the Ambassador to Morocco. It was a time of some great experiences: a long relationship with Jorge Luis Borges in Buenos Aires, for whom I translated *La Nueva Antologia Personal* [*The New Personal Anthology*] (with Maria Julieta Drummond), and about whom I had written several articles. Borges was already blind, but had a fantastic memory.

We then went on to Geneva, my husband's second post, where I was able to read Jung and complete the book *Contato* [*Contact*] begun in Buenos Aires. We went several times to Italy, traveled to Greece and Germany, where José Guilherme Merquior, my great friend (we began literary life together) asked me to translate his book about Drummond, and I spent a little time with Piaget, another of my objects of admiration. I never felt the burden of a social life, since I was always in contact with special people. The only thing was that I didn't know how privileged I was. When we returned to Brazil, we built an enormous house on a piece of beautiful land close to the south lake.

We had two children, but to be in Brasília was in a way still being in a foreign land, because my family was in Campos and my mother was not always able to come to be with my girls so that I would be free to accompany my husband on his little work-related international travel. Circumstances of a special nature occasioned an amicable separation. Some years later, my eldest daughter wanted to go to college. I rented a house in Brasília and a large apartment on Avenida Atlântica. At this time I published *Contato in Brasília*, and later *A Vida Natural e O Sangue na Veia* [*Natural Life and Blood in the Veins*]. I also wrote *Invocação de Orpheu* [*Invocation of Orpheus*] (which won the prize of the Federal District Cultural Foundation) and *Aliança* [*Alliance*]. Then *Retrato* [*Portrait*], *Vertigem* [*Vertigo*] and *Viagem a Portugal* [*Voyage to Portugal*] (1986 prize of the Brazilian Writers Union) were published here.

One month after this move, João Cabral de Melo Neto, ambassador and poet (unanimously considered the greatest after Drummond) unexpectedly asked me to marry him. He was living at that time in Portugal, had been widowed and was depressed. I accepted out of admiration, love, compassion. For 13 years I looked after him, prefacing and organizing all of his works. He died two years ago and yet there was still fight in me, notwithstanding the fact that I had a dislocated vertebra that was always acting up. Fearing surgery, I did not accept the invitation to be a resident at Stanford or at European universities. During this period I published *O Banquete* [*The Feast*] (PEN Club award), *Obra Poética Reunida* [*Combined Poetry Works*], *O Deserto Jardim* [*The Foresaken Garden*], *O Mar de Permeio* [*The Sea Between*] (Jabuti prize), and a year ago *Uma vez, Sempre* [*Once More, Always*], with the second edition of *A Força de Paixão e a Incerteza das Coisas* [*The Power of Love and the Uncertainty of Things*].

Do politics play any role in your life?

Clearly they do in my thinking and in my personal behavior. However, since I was married to two diplomats, I could not be involved. For example, when Saramago received the Nobel Prize, I was called to receive him at the CCBB [Cultural Center of the Bank of Brazil], but I could not accompany him in more public activities. Brazil is and is becoming a more and more difficult place, as you must know. What each person who is not connected to a political party can do is very little, but still that "very little" is absolutely necessary.

What does it mean for you to be a woman in Brazil?

To be a woman in Brazil today is not much different from being a woman in other countries. In addition to looking after the education of the children, dealing with problems at home, she must help her husband in maintaining what all of this represents, unless she is part of the group that controls the major portion of the country's income.

Is the status of the female writer in Brazil the same as the status of the male writer?

To be a woman writer is different from being a male writer, because it is always assumed that men are more cultured, have more time to read, are not involved with the home and children. In a phrase, they always have more time to interchange with other writers. Nevertheless, Clarice [Lispector], who was also married to a diplomat, showed that she was actually a genius after she separated from him.

What role does mysticism play in your life?

The word "mysticism" is very solemn; it makes one think of Saint John, Theresa of Avila and that real union with God. However, I am merely a human being who tries, who seeks, who prays, but I am discovering unbelievable things with quantum physics. And I am concerned about cloning. But I am always trying to push away the doubts and cultivate faith. I do not believe that one can be happy without helping others. This is also a question of temperament.

Is family important to you?

Very, very important, and family not only includes blood relations but also true friends.

For whom do you write?

Will a poem have only one direction? From age 17 to age 59, in 18 books (excluding small critiques in magazines), I have dealt with varied subjects along with a vision of the world that is expanded by contact with other people. I will continue along this path by reading, by expanding my fields of interest to include theology, quantum physics, the mind, and, finally, a desire to understand the world.

What are your feelings about globalization?

For us I believe that globalization is a utopia, an extravagance, given the sharp social and economic differences of the developing nations.

A Suave Pantera

The Smooth Panther

(selections)

1

Como qualquer animal,
olha as grades flutantes.
Eis que as grades são fixas:
ela, sim, é andante.
Sob a pele, contida
    —em silêncio e lisura —
a força do seu mal,
e a doçura, a doçura,
que escorre pelas pernas
e as pernas habitua
a esse modo de andar,
de ser sua, ser sua,
no perfeito equilíbrio
de sua vida aberta:
una e atenta a si mesma,
suavíssima pantera.

Marly de Oliveira

1

Like any animal
she looks at the floating bars
All the grates are firm:
She, above all, is mobile.
Under her skin, restrained
    —in silence and smoothness—
is the strength of her evil,
and the sweetness, sweetness
that runs through her legs
and accustoms her legs
to that way of walking,
of being herself, all herself
in the perfect equilibrium
of her open life:
one and attentive to herself
the smoothest panther.

2

É suave, suave, a pantera,
mas se a quiserem tocar
sem a devida cautela,
logo a verão transformada
na fera que há dentro dela.
O dente de mais marfim
na negrura toda alerta,
e ser de princípio a fim
a pantera sem reservas,
o fervor, a força lúdica
da unha longa e descoberta,
o êxtase de sua fúria
sob o melindre que a fera,
em repouso, se a não tocam,
como que tem na singela
forma que não se alvoroça
por si só, antes parece,
na mansa, mansa e lustrosa
pelúcia com que se adorna,
uma viva, intensa jóia.

2

The panther is smooth, smooth
but if you want to touch her
without taking necessary precautions,
you will see her soon transformed
into the savage she holds inside her.
Her tooth of purest ivory
all alert within her blackness
and being from beginning to end
a panther without reservations,
the fervor, the constructive force
of her long and visible claws,
the ecstasy of her fury
under the finesse that the beast
shows in repose, not touched,
as if she possesses in the singular
form that never betrays exertion
for herself alone, but always resembles
the smooth, smooth and lustrous
pelt in which she is adorned,
a living, intense jewel.

4

Mas é no amor que essa fúria
alcança de si o máximo.
À parte qualquer luxúria,
à parte a flata de tato,
se se alça e ganha a medida
de seu corpo todo casto,
há que ver-lhe a esbelta e lisa
figura de todo lado,
quando toda se descobre
   —como um cristal se estilhaça —
amando a vida, ai, amando
a vida que passa, passa.
Tão projetada num sonho,
nem se diria ama fera,
contida, casta e polida,
com tanto furor interno.

4

But when making love that fury
attains the best of herself.
Apart from any luxury,
apart from her lack of tact,
if she stretches out the full length
of her entirely chaste body,
you can observe her thin and smooth
figure from all sides,
when she can be discovered complete
　　—like a crystal that shatters—
loving life, yes, loving
life that passes, passes.
Thus projected in a dream,
no one would call her a beast,
self-contained, chaste and polished,
with so much internal furor.

6

O olhar tão aceso
revela, revela.
Que força de abismo
na virgem pantera.
Que força de amor
na sua recusa;
o ventre cerrado
    —quem julga? quem julga?
e a sua ventura
violenta, sedenta,
ensaiados membros
em surda paciência.
É vaga e concreta,
como que inspirada:
flutua em si mesma,
parada, parada.

6

Her look so alive
reveals, reveals.
What abysmal force
in the virgin panther.
What force of love
in her refusal;
Her sealed womb
    —who can say? who can say?
and her venturing,
violent, eager,
her limbs well practiced
in deaf patience.
She is vague and concrete,
as if inspired:
she floats within herself,
motionless, motionless.

7

Parada, parada,
quase se humaniza,
todo um viço de asas
na cara tranqüila,
flexuosa aspirando
    —quem mata, quem mata?
como uma pessoa
de forma coleada.
No entanto a narina,
no entanto a pupila
    —relevos de sombra —
ah, se a denunciam
mais que uma pessoa,
poderosa e bela:
macia, macia,
esplêndida fera.

7

Motionless, motionless
almost become a person,
all a vitality of wings
in her tranquil face
flexing, breathing
   —whom to kill? whom to kill?
like a person
in crawling form.
Meanwhile her nostrils
meanwhile her pupils
   —reliefs of shadows—
ah, they do denounce her
more than a person,
powerful and beautiful:
smooth, smooth,
splendid beast.

8

Esplêndida fera:
onírica e lúbrica
como pode às vezes
ser uma pantera.
Negra ela rebrilha,
presente a si mesma,
como se invadida
de uma luz avessa,
como adiamantada
de uma luz escura,
afoita e inefável
quem a subjuga?
afoita e inefável
qual nenhuma besta,
cingida ao que em si
é a sua natureza.

8

Splendid beast,
oneiric and sensual
as from time to time
a panther can be.
Black with shiny flashes
present within herself,
as if invaded
by a lost light
as if made a diamond
by some dark light
bold and ineffable
who can subjugate her?
bold and ineffable
as no other beast,
constricted within herself
by her own nature.

10

A forma espessa da pantera,
um tal negrume e tal pelúcia,
às vezes quase que a confundem
com todas as demais panteras,
mas só naquilo que por fora
tem uma existência concreta,
naquilo só que se objetiva
formosamente sobre a relva:
olhos detidos de tão verdes,
corpo luzindo sobre as pernas,
um certo modo de mover-se
sobre si mesma, terna e quieta.
Porque ela é igual só a ela mesma,
se com ardor alguém a observa,
mas por dentro, tão escondida
como no fundo da ostra pérola.

10

The thick shape of the panther
all blackness and plush
can almost at times be confused
with all the other panthers,
but only in what is exterior
and has a concrete existence,
only in what can be seen
beauteously on the grass:
restrained eyes of such green,
shining body over legs,
a certain way of moving about
over oneself, soft and quiet.
Because she has no equal beyond herself,
if someone observes her with ardor,
but inside, so hidden
as the pearl in the depths of the oyster.

13

A fome de um bicho
—e mais se é pantera—
não tem o limite
que em gente tivera.
Não é como a fome
violenta, direta,
subjetiva, do homem,
a fome da fera.
A fome de um bicho
é cruel e eterna,
e toda inconsciente,
com uma força interna.
É fome indistinta
espalhada nela,
com íntima fúria
que ela não governa.

13

An animal's hunger
—moreover if it's a panther—
has no limits
that people would have.
It's not like violent,
direct hunger,
subjective, a man's,
the hunger of a beast.
An animal's hunger
is cruel and eternal,
and completely unconscious,
like an internal force.
It's an indistinct hunger
spread throughout her,
with an intimate fury
that she cannot control.

14

A liberdade da pantera
está justamente nisto:
que nem ela se governa,
e o que sucede é imprevisto.
Essa a vantagem da fera:
uma força que ela abriga,
inconsciente, dentro dela
— sob a aparência tranqüila —
e de repente se revela,
mas numa espécie de fúria,
que atinge inclusive a ela,
mas numa espécie de luta,
que é o modo que tem a cólera
de mostrar-se uma fera,
e que é a sua única forma
de ser pura, além de bela.

14

The freedom of a panther
consists precisely of this:
that not even she can control herself,
and whatever happens is unforeseen.
This the advantage of a beast:
a force that she shelters,
unknowing, inside herself
    —under that tranquil appearance—
suddenly can be revealed,
but in a kind of fury,
that even controls her,
but in a kind of struggle,
that is the way that anger has
to show that she is a beast,
and that is her only way
to be pure, beyond beautiful.

16

Além de precisa é ubíqua,
outra vantagem mais forte.
Por toda parte é sensível
sua graça, como um broche,
ou como coisa pousada
e em si mesma repentina:
os olhos onde violetas
cobram cores agressivas,
a cauda suspensa e lisa
como nuvem sossegada,
não solta, não qualquer nuvem,
nuvem presa como uma asa,
o corpo todo concreto,
todo animal, perecível,
e mais uma ansia por dentro,
de ser livre, livre, livre.

Marly de Oliveira

16

Beyond precise and ubiquitous
another advantage is stronger.
Every place is sensible to
her grace, like a brooch,
or some other object at rest
within itself, even brusquely:
eyes where violets
veil aggressive colors,
a suspended and smooth tail
like a floating cloud,
not loose, like any cloud,
a cloud captive like a wing,
its body all concrete,
all animal, perishable,
and what's more yearning inside,
to be free, free, free.

— translated by K. David and
Elizabeth A. Jackson

Jandira Martini

Jandira Martini

Jandira Martini was born in Santos in the state of São Paulo where she studied Literature and participated in University Theater. After moving to São Paulo she studied acting in the department of drama at the University of São Paulo (EAD/USP). She made her professional acting debut in 1970. She appeared on stage in various Brazilian and international plays: *Medea* by Euripides; *A longa noite de cristal* by Oduvaldo Vianna Filho; *Candide* by Voltaire; *Richard III* by Shakespeare; *Bodas de papel* by Maria Adelaide de Amaral; *Jogo de cintura* by Jandira Martini and Marcos Caruso; *Porca miseria* by Jandira Martini and Marcos Caruso to mention only the few. She also directed various theater productions in São Paulo. Jandira Martini is also a known TV actress. Her most recent role was Zoraide in the very popular soap opera *O Clone*. She has written various plays, some of them with her ex-husband Marcos Caruso: *Sua excelência, o candidato* (1982) [Moliere award winner]; *Jogo de cintura* (1988); *Porca miseria* (1991) [three prestigious awards: Mambembe, Shell, and APCA]; *Os reis do improviso* (1996); *Brava gente* (miniseries written for TV) (1993). *A vida é uma opera (1990)* [APCA award of the association of art and theater critics from São Paulo]; *Imagens descongeladas no verão* (1999, unpublished).

Jandira Martini

How did you become an actress and, later, a writer?

I think that I became an actress because reality doesn't appeal to me very much. With everything that I see, in terms of how the world is organized, how things happen, the social hierarchy and human relations, everything seems far inferior to what it could be. So, the thing that made me get involved with theater is being able to live other realities while trying to change this one. Theater offers various opportunities to live various lives, various characters and various circumstances, while trying at the same time to communicate new ways of relating and new forms of social organization to people. With all this, the theater serves as a judge, or as a teacher. I think that, with these two possibilities being combined and as a result of this discontent, I started doing theater when I was still a student at the university in the literature department. There was a theater group in the department, and, at that time, there were many student theaters in Brazil.

I'm from Santos, which is a city that always had a lot of experimental theater and a lot of amateur theater, and that's how I began doing theater. Then I became enthusiastic and studied at the School of Dramatic Art that already existed here in São Paulo. At that point, I became a professional actress and I gave up my academic program in literature. I had wanted to be a teacher, and I even entered a graduate program, but it wasn't possible to do both things, and I chose the theater.

I think that the time in the country and in the world led me into the theater. I had started with the theater in my department in Santos in 1964, at the point when everything was very turbulent. Not only in Brazil, but throughout the world. People picked up this entire phase in 1968. So it wasn't just a matter of a vocation, "Oh, I always wanted to be on the stage…" I think that reality made me choose.

Did your childhood influence what you are doing today?

The city where I grew up was a big influence. There was a very extensive amateur theater movement in Santos. Professional theater was only for traveling companies. In my family, no one did theater, but everyone was very eager to see plays. My father, who was the son of Italian immigrants, liked opera a great deal, and we went to a lot of the operas that were performed in Santos. I think that all of this is present in what I write in a certain way. There are also memories of actors whom I saw when I was a child. Characteristically Brazilian actors.

We were influenced by Italian theater, Italian directors who came here during the 1940s created a more European and more intellectual type of theater when the *Teatro Brasileiro de Comedia* was established. The School of Dramatic Art where I studied was strongly oriented toward that type of theater, which is very different form the popular actors whom I saw when I was young. Those were actors who had been trained on stage, and they didn't have any other kind of training. It was the type of theater that certain people have sometimes referred to as "second-rate," but it's actually a highly authentic kind of theater that is much closer to Brazilian personalities. The comedy is typically our own. Our great actors are comic actors, and our first author was the comic dramatist Martins Pena. Therefore, it doesn't help to try to deny it. Nor does it help to deny what comes from outside sources. I think that everything is added together. There was some resistance to this kind of popular theater, however. In my case, the fact that I had seen it and the fact that I didn't have this prejudice influenced the type of theater that I'm doing.

Jandira Martini

What does it mean to you to be a woman in Brazil?

I don't see a difference. I think that it's being a Brazilian. For me, it's social class. And the type of education that I've had. With the luck that I've had, because I can consider myself a privileged person in a poor country and an illiterate country, where I managed to arrive at a university and at the School of Dramatic Arts, which is a luxury. Therefore, I don't feel this gender difference, even in the profession that I chose. Actors and actresses don't compete. So, I don't perceive differences between men and women. I feel that the difficulty is the same.

It's not difficult to be a woman in Brazil. It's very difficult to be a Brazilian. It's very difficult to be a Brazilian actor, and it's difficult to be a Brazilian author. This is very difficult. I don't think that being a woman holds me back. Depending upon a person's social class, it may be that popular culture has more to do with inequality for women, but, in terms of occupations, I don't see this. Poverty is so extensive that people are in it together. This division between men and women doesn't exist. The whole world is trying to survive. It's obvious that, depending upon people's culture and education, family relations may be more difficult for women than for men, but, in social terms, I don't see it. Perhaps it was different many years ago, but today, we've already gone through the changes that were inspired by the feminist movement.

Is there professional equality for actors and actresses in Brazil? Are the expectations the same?

In Brazil, there's a phenomenon that's a worldwide trend: worshipping youth, worshiping the beautiful, worshiping the body. In Brazil, this is extremely pronounced, because everything here is the body, everything is the butt because of the tropics, the heat and the beach. Therefore, the factor of physical beauty exists. After a certain age, an actress or an actor loses physical appeal, and the public usually loses interest. There are always a lot of young, good-looking actors emerging. I don't think that it's different for men or for women, however. I think that actors end up having fewer roles, because nothing is written for older people. More is written for young actors because people in Brazil are strongly influenced by television. The *Globo* Network is a large Brazilian company and, perhaps, that's why there's this predominance of young people. On television, physical beauty has a much bigger role, and I think that our theater has also been somewhat contaminated by it.

Does family stimultate you or is it a limitation?

The fact of having a family is a restriction that varies depending upon the education that people have had, and that's logical. Today, I think that I'm a lot freer than I was 20 years ago because my children are adults. Today, I have much greater autonomy, and I'm prepared to do many more things, including traveling if it's necessary, and those are things that I didn't do. Perhaps that's one of my characteristics. It's also an option. I don't think that it's been a bad influence, however, or that there has been resistance.

When I began doing theater, it was very difficult to do theater in Brazil. It was television that gave actors status. Actors even became wealthy then, and people didn't hold it against them. In those times, when I started, it was an occupation considered somewhat marginal, and actresses were thought to be semiprostitutes. In those times, my parents didn't think that it was acceptable to do theater. They found it acceptable to attend, but not to act. Now it's not that way. There was a general change of outlook. In my home, there was never any resistance; it was very much the opposite. Even at the point when it was unacceptable to do theater, they were displeased, but they let me.

What were the practical means that helped you overcome obstacles and reach a point in your career where you are respected and have options?

It was very difficult. The practical measures in Brazil are like this: you have to do everything. Preferably, you have to write, to direct, to produce and to perform so that you will manage to survive, because we don't have producers, and we don't have people who invest in the theater. The people who have always produced have been actors. It was always that way: the actor was the leader of his troupe. So when I started doing theater we did group theater. We were a group of actors who produced their plays very poorly, because that was the only way that you could get some money from the ticket sales. That's how it was, and it's still somewhat like that. If you open the newspaper, you're going to see that there are about 60 plays being performed in São Paulo. At least 40 of them are groups of young people who are supporting themselves like we used to.

Our group, which was a comedy group, was known as the Royal Beixigas Company. People chose that name, because, at that time, there was a budget appropriation from the state government for bringing the Royal Ballet to São Paulo. The government had an absurd idea of financing for keeping the Royal Ballet in São Paulo, and it wouldn't put up a cent for the young theater companies that were starting out. We kept working for four years. We dissolved the group on account of financial problems, because we couldn't find another way of supporting it. We were relatively successful, with good audiences. One of our shows went to a festival in Nancy, France, and it stayed on the stage a long time. It came back, but, even so, it wasn't enough to keep us going. Then each of us went on to perform with other companies in order to earn money, and the group began to dissolve. That's what happens with most groups.

Many people went into television, too. I think that it's a pity because I believe that the best productions in the theater are group productions. Currently, I'm doing a series on *Globo*, which is *O Clone*. During the coming year, I want to do a show that I already wanted to do this year, although I couldn't obtain backing for it. This is a text that I asked Leilah Assumpção, Renata Pallottini, Consuelo de Castro and Maria de Adelaide Amaral to write. I also wrote a portion. Each of us wrote her part. The theme is women on the telephone. Each author wrote a different section without knowing what the others were writing. It was very interesting, but I didn't manage to put it on this year. When I finish my novel, maybe I'll do it. It's a very fine monologue, and the title is *Por telefone* (*On the Phone*).

What's the role of mysticism in your life?

None. I'm not mystical in any way. I'm an absolutely nonbelieving person. I don't believe in anything, and I don't get involved in these things. I'm a materialist. I think that many things in nature haven't been discovered yet. That doesn't have anything to do with religion, however.

What type of audience do you want to reach?

I've always been concerned with attracting large audience numbers. I have no interest in doing limited things. I have no interest in doing things for an elite. My aim is to reach the middle-class public and the masses. I don't have any intellectual concerns. For me, the ideal in performing is the Greek theater, with large areas for large numbers of people. I can do theater for 30 people in my living room. I think that the professional theater should be impressive event. In order to have a show, it's necessary to have a large audience.

When I write, I always think about actors. I always think about characters. Always in relation to the actor. I think that actors are the interesting part of theater. As for the author, however good the author may be, he or she is less important in comparison with the actor at the time of performing. The fact that I've principally done comedies is because comedies attract bigger audiences. Although I had dramatic training at the School [of Dramatic Art], I haven't had many chances to perform in tragedies.

Do you ever do politically engaged theater?

I know that when I was at the university, people performed a few plays that were censored. It wasn't exactly political theater, but these were plays that spoke against the regime. Afterwards, when I started my professional career, censorship was so strict that everything was done with metaphors. Nothing was done directly, and words like "strike," "workers," etc., couldn't appear in any script. So, I never actually did free theater, because this kind of freedom would be the basis for political freedom that didn't exist at that time. Afterwards, when there was liberalization, there was such severe economic oppression that theaters didn't have any freedom either.

You only have freedom if you have the means of doing what you want to. Therefore, I never managed to do political theater because I never had the opportunity. People just ended up in prison. I don't accept theories that say that oppression can be stimulating for artists. Those are rare cases. Those are unique examples that would occur with censorship or without it. Those are geniuses. Hence, I don't think that it was productive for people to be obliged to speak in metaphors. It would be more productive for people to be able to speak freely. Or even to protest because that would lead to something. Contrary to a situation where you have to regress, turn back and use metaphors, and, then at the time of liberalization, you no longer know what to say because you've already lost your way. I don't believe in this. I don't think that it's creative. I don't think that any kind of repression is creative.

What do you think of globalization?

Oh, that's difficult. I think that, for the time being, it's very early for us to know whether this is a good direction for the world. I also think that anything that brings unity, anything that clarifies and anything that brings knowledge is good. The fact that today we can know about everything that goes on everywhere is much better than the ignorance that we lived in. Where is this process going to lead? I think that it will lead to greater understanding among people. That's my hope. It's merely an intuition that isn't based upon any deeper analysis.

Life is an Opera is a grotesque, symbolic play that takes place in a library which has just been shut-down. Two of the three characters, Virgilia and Tonica, are librarians, and the third character, Lair, is a schoolteacher doing research on Machado de Assis, Brazil's outstanding novelist from the 19th century. In the play, a statue of Machado de Assis has been removed from the town square and placed in the closed down library. During the first act and the first half of the second act, the characters reveal their frustrated selves to each other through dialogues and monologues that are for the most part comic, bordering on the sarcastic. Virgilia, the head librarian, turns out to be a failed opera singer, who gave up her dream of becoming a diva because of her intolerant boyfriend who, during the military dictatorship in Brazil during the 1960s and 1970s, believed exclusively in political activism to fight against the regime. He dumped Virgilia soon after she gave up singing. Lair is a shy schoolteacher who always wanted to be a novelist. She is now writing a dissertation on Machado de Assis in order to move up the teaching hierarchy and improve her salary. Tonica, the most cynical of the three characters, is a librarian by choice but she did dream of becoming a missionary in Africa after a painful affair. As the three characters cope with the closing of the library and various challenges ahead, details of bureaucratic corruption are revealed as is the contraband whiskey and a stash of cocaine that was kept in the men's bathroom.

Life Is an Opera

Act II

*Music: **Recondita Armonia**. Tonica is standing next to the recliner posing in a 19th-century costume. Lair, also dressed in period costume, is observing her. The statue of Machado de Assis has been placed in front of the door, blocking it. On the table are two bottles of scotch, one of them empty, and plastic cups. The trunk that in Act I was purportedly in the men's bathroom now stands open to the recliner, some of the clothing spilling out. When the curtain opens, the atmosphere is timeless, as if this act were actually taking place in the 19th century.*

The telephone rings. They look at each other. Then they stare at the phone. After a pause, Lair breaks the silence.

LAIR: You better answer it!

TONICA: I don't want to talk to him…

LAIR: Maybe it's not him…

TONICA: Of course it is. Who else would be calling here at this hour?

LAIR: Want me to answer? (*She goes toward the phone.*)

TONICA: (*Holding her back.*) No. You better not. He doesn't even know who you are. Let me. (*She speaks into the phone.*) Hello. No, it's Tonica. Virgília?…

LAIR: Don't tell him she went out for pizza…

TONICA: She… she can't come to the phone right now. What deadline? Oh, sure. Armando, I'm… I'm… I'm not sure how to express it… shocked… dumbfounded… I don't know… What about? I found what you hid in the bottom of the trunk… What to do mean you don't know what I'm talking about, Armando? You don't know anything about the trunk? Don't be so childish! You must have suffered a psychotic break to get mixed up in something like this… (*She listens for a moment and is totally flustered.*) You wouldn't do that, would you, Armando? You can't… Armando, Armando… (*He has hung up on her. She puts the telephone down. She pauses.*) My god, he can't! He can't be such an asshole!

LAIR: What is it! What is it he said?

TONICA: That we're the ones who had a psychotic break. That we're seeing things, that he doesn't know anything about any trunk, that we're hysterical… and that there's something else he can do…

LAIR: Is he going to call the police?!

TONICA: That's the least of it!

LAIR: What do you mean?

TONICA: … he's going to call the police and then call Dr. Fontoura. He's going to say he only decided to take action because he suspects we refuse to leave because we're hiding something…

LAIR: Hiding something? But he's the one who's hiding stuff!

TONICA: Just when you think life has played every dirty trick on you…

LAIR: Right now this Dr. Fontoura's the least of our worries. But bringing the police into this, frankly…

TONICA: Dr. Fontoura's not the least of our worries, no ma'am. He's thick as thieves with the government in Brasília. Dr. Fontoura's friends with "the man," and the bastard Armando's going to use Mr. All-Powerful as a witness on his behalf. To avoid the risk of being turned in he's turned us in. That's it, Lair…

LAIR: (*Getting her things ready.*) Let's get out of here, Tonica. This is a bad situation. I can't, you understand? I can't take the chance… A scandal like that! You know, I was just stupid. I was an idiot to get mixed up with you two…

TONICA: (*Ironic.*) Oh thanks, Lair. That's all I needed to hear right now…

LAIR: But it's my job that's at stake!

TONICA: Oh! And what a great job it is!

LAIR: Yes! My great shitty job! But I can't afford it, I can't be stuck in here... I'm not going to throw away 20 some years of having to put up with...

TONICA: And what about our job? Did you ever consider that?

LAIR: There's still time, Tonica! You're going to leave this place and turn the keys over to Armando.

TONICA: What about Virgília?

LAIR: You can explain everything to her later...

TONICA: Explain what?! That we chickened out and ran out of here to save our necks? Not our necks. Mine. You just wanted to check out a book. You're not responsible for anything that goes on here... I'm not leaving until Virgília gets back.

LAIR: And... what if she doesn't come back?

TONICA: Are you crazy? Why wouldn't she come back?!

LAIR: Maybe she changed her mind, and...

TONICA: I will not allow this! I will not allow it! You hear me, you louse? Who are you to think I'd ever distrust Virgília? You come in here acting like a poor little waif, a frustrated novelist, an exploited teacher, a betrayed wife. Then you get the wheels turning, set up your circus tent, start hooting and hollering, get sauced, confess you're not really interested in writing your lousy dissertation and you even have the nerve to... Oh no, my dear, you are going to write your dissertation! And try to put a little love into it and get the highest grades and receive honors. Because the grade is yours but the honors are ours! Write!

LAIR: (*Frightened.*) What??

TONICA: What I'm going to dictate!!

LAIR: About Virgília... I spoke without thinking...

TONICA: (*Shouting.*) Write! (*She dictates in a cold, military manner.*) Which leads him to conclude in regard to destiny, colon, quotation marks. Destiny is not only a playwright, comma, but is its only stage manager, comma, that is, comma, it designates the entrances of the characters on stage, comma, it gives them the cards and other props and, comma, according to the corresponding cues in the dialogue, comma, it produces a thunderclap, comma, the sound of an automobile, comma, a gunshot.

Sound of pounding on the door. The two women are frightened.

LAIR: My god? Could it be...

TONICA: It's Virgília. It could only be her. (*She goes anxiously to the door.*) Virgília, is it you?

VIRGÍLIA: (*From outside.*) Of course! Who else would it be? Open up quick.

Tonica opens the door. Virgília rushes in.

VIRGÍLIA: Damn Chinaman! How can he make a pizza so hot?! Ow, it's burning me! Take it, Tonica, take it! (*Tonica takes the pizza but doesn't move. To Lair.*) So, you feeling better?

LAIR: … feeling better… (*She drinks.*)

VIRGÍLIA: Are you drinking again? Come on, have something to eat. I brought a pizza with chicken and sweet corn. I don't know if either of you like it that way but there were so many choices that I was overwhelmed…

TONICA: Nobody's interested in pizza, Virgília…

VIRGÍLIA: What do you mean?? I ran like a bat out of hell and I even had to stand there carrying on a conversation with the Chinese guy while the pizza was in the oven… Conversation in a manner of speaking. Listening! Because I didn't understand a word he said…

TONICA: (*Very serious.*) We discovered something… terrible, Virgília…

VIRGÍLIA: (*Thinking it's a joke.*) That Armando has an acute case of split personality! A kind of **Dr. Jekyll and Mr. Hyde!** You know, that's what I was thinking on the way back…

LAIR: It's something like that. Except it's much more serious than you imagine…

VIRGÍLIA: Out with it! What's he up to this time?

Lair and Tonica look at the trunk and then at each other.

VIRGÍLIA: What's going on? Why are you looking that way? Are you going to tell me or not?

TONICA: (*Uncomfortable.*) Take a look in the trunk…

VIRGÍLIA: In the trunk? But I've already seen the trunk. (*She guesses.*) More contraband, is that it?

TONICA: (*Losing control.*) Look, Virgília!!

Virgília runs over to the trunk. She looks inside and without saying a word she collapses and sits on the floor.

LAIR: We have to get out of here! We were just waiting for you to get back…

TONICA: Don't you see, Virgília. He called the police.

VIRGÍLIA: What do you mean he called the police?!

TONICA: He said he was going to…

LAIR: Let's not wait to find out if it's true, for god's sake! Let's get out of here!

VIRGÍLIA: Let her speak, Lair!

TONICA: I know Armando. The way he talked to me on the phone…

VIRGÍLIA: (*She doesn't understand.*) But why would he do that?

TONICA: Because he's scared shitless he won't get his transfer to the Ministry of Agriculture. He'll do anything to make sure he doesn't lose that position…

VIRGÍLIA: That's not it. There's something wrong with this story…

LAIR: But there's no way to find out what. Please, let's just go!

VIRGÍLIA: Take it easy, Lair. (*To Tonica.*) Did you say anything about the trunk?

TONICA: Of course I did…

VIRGÍLIA: What did he say?

TONICA: He said we're crazy, we're seeing things, and he doesn't know anything about…

VIRGÍLIA: Maybe he really doesn't…

TONICA: Stop acting like an idiot and protecting that fool, Virgília!

VIRGÍLIA: You're the one who's an idiot if you believe that story! Whoever heard of someone who's guilty calling the police? Think he'd turn himself in? Is that it?! The police show up and find all this stuff…

TONICA: And they'll think it's ours!

VIRGÍLIA: What makes you think that?!

TONICA: It's obvious! We're the ones locked ourselves in here. He planned everything very carefully to incriminate us, Virgília.

VIRGÍLIA: But I can explain…

TONICA: To the police?! "You see, officer, we're working on a dissertation: life is an opera!" It won't work, Virgília. It won't! We're going to leave here and go directly to Dr. Fontoura's house. You can explain everything that's gone on here to him. Give him all the details… (*She gets ready to leave.*)

VIRGÍLIA: To Dr. Fontoura?! Really, Tonica! Now you want to get Dr. Fontoura mixed up in this?!

TONICA: The one who got Dr. Fontoura mixed up in this, as you say, was our dear Armando. He snitched on us to Mr. All-Powerful, if you'd like to know… Come on, let's go before the police get here!

LAIR: Come on, Virgília! Please… If the police show up here and they don't find anyone who're they going to suspect? Armando… Besides, you can always claim you never said you refused to leave… it's your word against his…

VIRGÍLIA: You don't know anything about me. I'm not going to say any such thing.

LAIR: Why not?!

VIRGÍLIA: Because it's a lie!

TONICA: Wake up, Virgília! This is no time for the truth!

VIRGÍLIA: A can't accuse somebody without any proof, somebody who's always behaved…

TONICA: He didn't have any problem accusing us without proof, did he?

VIRGÍLIA: I'm not responsible for what other people do. Anyway, what makes you so certain it belongs to him?

TONICA: Fine, Virgília, fine! We don't have any proof. But if it's not his... whose is it?

LAIR: (*Losing control completely.*) Alright! If you want to sit there arguing about who it belongs to or doesn't belong to like a couple of retards, go ahead! I'm getting out of here!

TONICA: (*Confronting her.*) Just a minute, girl, retards...

VIRGÍLIA: (*Holding her back.*) Take it easy, Tonica. She's drunk...

LAIR: I'm drunk and you're blind! Are you just going to sit there? What about you, Virgília? Are you really going ahead with this? Are you going to challenge these people? Well, be prepared! You don't fool around with these people! Get ready for your big scene! (*Picking up the knife that is still on the table.*) Want some advice? (*She offers it.*) Take this knife and hide it behind your back!! (*She laughs.*)

Virgília doesn't move. She looks at her intensely.

TONICA: (*Standing between the other two women.*) Please, Virgília... Let's get out of here!

LAIR: Alright! Do what you want! (*She drops the knife on the floor and goes toward the door. She laughs but her laughter dissolves into tears.*) "It is the law of *humanitas*! To the vanquished, hate or compassion, to the victor… "

A police siren approaches. Lair stops.

VIRGÍLIA: We better stay. It could be dangerous to leave now.

Lair is terrified and retreats to the recliner. She sits down and lets her head hang down. Tonica and Virgília wait, rigidly still. The siren grows louder. Automobiles screeching to a stop. The police car spotlight moves around the set.

OFFSTAGE VOICE: (*Megaphone.*) This is the police!

TONICA: (*Very serious.*) My god, how obvious can you get!

VIRGÍLIA: Be quiet, Tonica!

OFFSTAGE VOICE: Miss Virgília! Miss Virgília! Can you hear me? This is officer Motta! Leave peacefully and nothing will happen to you!

TONICA: We better leave now… Before this cop gets mad! These guys are nuts…

VIRGÍLIA: Maybe I'll go out. But I'm going to tell them.

TONICA: You're not saying anything now. We didn't see anything! We don't know anything!… Come on, Lair! (*Lair looks at her without expression.*) You don't have to be afraid. Everything's going to work out!

OFFSTAGE VOICE: Miss Virgília! Don't force us to take drastic action! You'd better come out now! I give you my word nothing will happen to you…

A gunshot breaks one of the panes of glass in the door and part of the statue's head explodes. Lair screams. Virgília pulls Tonica back from where she was standing in front of the statue. The three women are terrified. A cacophony of voices outside.

LAIR: (*Going over to Tonica by the statue.*) It could have hit you! My god!… If it weren't for the statue…

VIRGÍLIA: Get away from there, Lair! Move away from the door!

OFFSTAGE VOICE: Calm down! Calm down! (*The voices outside grow dimmer.*) Everything is ok, Miss Virgília! Calm down! Don't be afraid! It was an accident! They didn't mean to shoot! (*His voice lower.*) Who was the sonofabitch took a shot!

The cacophony of voices resumes. The three women, standing stock still, look toward the door. Pause. The voices subside again.

VIRGÍLIA: Now what?… I wonder what they're going to do.

LAIR: We better get out of here now! (*She tries to leave.*)

TONICA: Get back here, Lair! What guarantee do you have they won't shoot again?

OFFSTAGE VOICE: Miss Virgília! Dr. Fontoura has just arrived. He's standing here next to me. He insists everything can be resolved in a civilized manner. He's going to speak with you…

VIRGÍLIA: Dr. Fontoura's here?!

TONICA: Strange! Very strange!

FONTOURA: (*Offstage. Megaphone.*) Virgília! Can you hear me?

VIRGÍLIA: What's he doing here?!

TONICA: There must be some explanation!

LAIR: Answer him, Virgília. He's our only chance.

VIRGÍLIA: (*She shouts.*) I can hear you, Dr. Fontoura! Tell me what you want!

TONICA: My god, why?! Why did he take the trouble to come here?!

FONTOURA: Oh, my dear! I know you only did what you did because you're under a great deal of stress. You need a vacation! And I'm working things out so that when you get back the two of you will have a position in Mines and Energy!

VIRGÍLIA: What are we going to do in Mines and Energy?!

TONICA: Sonofabitch!

VIRGÍLIA: Why is he a sonofabitch?

TONICA: He's trying to buy us off!

VIRGÍLIA: What do you mean?!

TONICA: Of course, Virgília. This is his doing. All this crap.

VIRGÍLIA: Him?? It can't be…

TONICA: Why do you think he came all the way over here to offer us a transfer to Mines and Energy?

FONTOURA: Virgília! We're going to forget this unpleasant incident. Pretend it never happened. We're going to erase tonight from our memory… You understand me, don't you, dear?

VIRGÍLIA: (*In a low voice.*) Yes, I do, you scoundrel!

TONICA: (*Trying to stall for time.*) Answer the man, Virgília!

VIRGÍLIA: (*Loud, ironic.*) Yes, Dr. Fontoura, I understand.

FONTOURA: So, my dear?! Come out now! Don't be afraid! I'll work things out with the police officer and then we can all celebrate your new position!

TONICA: (*To Lair.*) You hear! He's trying to buy us off! And you're our witness!

LAIR: A witness?! Me?!…

VIRGÍLIA: Celebrate? He can wait 'til kingdom comes! I'm going to let the cat out of the bag!

TONICA: Not yet. This is no time for foolish heroism, Virgília.

VIRGÍLIA: I have to speak, Tonica, I have to. People need to know what kind of country they're living in!

LAIR: (*She laughs.*) They already know. They've had a stomach full…

VIRGÍLIA: The more they know the better! Who knows, maybe they'll do something about…

TONICA: Virgília, please, listen to me: there's no way out! You have to keep quiet and accept the transfer. If you say anything now we're going to jail because obviously if you mention this shit he's going to say it's ours… Proof, my god, we need proof…

VIRGÍLIA: (*She suddenly goes over to the trunk and begins removing the cocaine.*) That's not a problem! We've lost our library, haven't we? So he can lose his contraband!

LAIR: What are you going to do?

VIRGÍLIA: Return all of it to the men's bathroom. That's where it came from and that's where it should end up. I'm going to flush it down the toilet! Help me with this, Tonica!

TONICA: (*Blocking her way and removing the packets from her hands.*) You're not throwing anything away! You want to flush our job down the toilet? All you're going to do right now is shut your mouth and go along with Mines and Energy! (*And she resumes putting things away in the trunk, including the costumes. Lair helps her.*)

VIRGÍLIA: What do I care about Mines and Energy?

TONICA: What are you planning on doing with your life?

VIRGÍLIA: The truth, Tonica! I want everyone to know...

TONICA: Don't be a romantic! We don't have any proof...

VIRGÍLIA: But they have our word...

TONICA: Who cares about our word, Virgília? Two librarians against the world. Unemployed. Forced to retire. Living off the crumbs of social security. Shut-ins. Alone and useless. Is that what you're after, Virgília? Growing old, shut up in your house, like a useless piece of junk?

VIRGÍLIA: (*Touched.*) ... But I can't, my god... I can't! I'm tired of putting up with crap!

TONICA: So you put up with a little more... What difference does it make? Mines and Energy? Social welfare? Agriculture? We have to go along to get along, Virgília...

VIRGÍLIA: Go along? How long?!

TONICA: ... Until we learn how to face our fears...

VIRGÍLIA: (*Smiling.*) Wouldn't it be better if we overcame them?

TONICA: Sometimes fear can be useful, dear boss. Who knows... in the future... But until then... We're just going to have to put up with a lot of crap.

And… someday… who knows?…

VIRGÍLIA: (*Bitter.*) And we'll choke on it!

TONICA: (*Picking up the knife that was on the floor.*) Or hide the knife behind your back! (*When she's about to place the knife on the table she sees the camera. She picks it up without saying a word.*)

FONTOURA: Virgília!! What's your decision?! We're still waiting, my dear!

LAIR: (*She looks anxiously at Virgília.*)

TONICA: (*Still holding the camera.*) Answer the man, Virgília!

LAIR: Think, Virgília. Think about what's best for your life. For you.

Lair and Tonica stand there looking at Virgília, waiting for her to respond.

VIRGÍLIA: (*She looks at them briefly and then decides to bite her tongue.*) We're coming right out, Dr. Fontoura! Just a minute! (*To the two other women who are hugging each other emotionally.*) When I wake up tomorrow I'm going to be so ashamed of what went on today…

TONICA: Then… turn the other way…

VIRGÍLIA: Why?!

TONICA: So you don't see what I'm going to do…

VIRGÍLIA: After all this!… Nothing you could would be worse than what I've just done…

TONICA: (*She picks the book up from the table and moves toward Lair.*) For now… it's all we can do… all we have left… I'm not sure you deserve this… but anyway… (*She slips the book into her purse.*) Do us proud, girl!

LAIR: (*After a brief pause.*) Are we going?!

VIRGÍLIA: (*She smiles.*) Are we going?! You come with me, Lair. And don't open your mouth. Let me explain everything. And don't embarrass us. Please put down that cup!

LAIR: (*She looks at the cup she's still holding and then looks at the books.*)

TONICA: Now what? What is it?

LAIR: "Someday, when all the books become useless and are burned, there will be someone to teach this truth to men. Everything is music. In the beginning it was do, and the do begat re… This cup! This cup is a brief refrain. Can't you hear it? Nor can you hear the wood, nor the stone, but everything belongs in the same opera"… (*She crushes the plastic cup and throws it up in the air.*) I know that I'm not a brilliant person, but I promise… I'm going to do you proud!

VIRGÍLIA: Then let's not waste any more time! Don't forget you've only got two weeks! (*She puts her arm around her for support. The two women begin their exit.*) Come along, Tonica!

Tonica waits for them to exit and runs over to the table.
She grabs the camera and begins taking pictures: the broken
pane of glass, the head of the statue, the inside of the
trunk… she then hides the camera in her purse and looks
sadly around. She glances briefly at the books. She passes
her hand over them as if she were caressing them. She
turns to go and notices the piece of the statue on the floor.
She picks it up and carefully replaces it.

TONICA: (*She covers the statue as if she were covering a child.*)
Good night, master! And if you can — dream with
the angels!

She lifts up her head and takes a deep breath. As she
*disappears through the door, the music begins: **Va pensiero**.*
The lights dim and only the police spotlight remains,
sweeping across the set. There is also a spot focused on the
statue. The music gets louder and mixes with the opening
*chords of the overture of **O Guarani**, as the spotlight fades*
to blackout.

— tranlsated by David S. George

Leilah Assumpção

Leilah Assumpção

Leilah Assumpção was born in Botucatú in the state of São Paulo. Her great-grandmother founded the first school there. Born into a family of teachers, she enrolled in the department of Education at the University of Campinas in 1960. In 1962 she moved to São Paulo and studied literary criticism, acting and fashion design. She appeared as an actress in *Vereda de salvação* by Jorge Andrade in 1964 and in Bertold Brecht's *Three Penny Opera* in 1965. She also worked for a while as a fashion model for Valentino and Pièrre Cardin. She lives in São Paulo with her husband Walter and daughter Camila. Her most important plays are: *Fala baixo senão eu grito* (1969); *Amanhã, Amélia de manhã* (1973); *Vejo um vulto na janela, me acudam que eu sou donzela* (1979); *Sede pura e alfinetadas* (1980); *Boca molhada de paixão calada* (1980); *O segredo da alma de ouro* (1980); *Lua nua* (1987); *Quatro mulheres* (1988); *Quem matou a baronesa* (1991); *Era uma vez... Luciana* (1993); *Adorável desgraçada* (1994); *Intimidade Indecente* (2001). She also authored and co-authored various TV shows and is a recipient of various awards granted by Brazilian theater critics.

Leilah Assumpção

How did you become a writer?

I'm from a family of professors and writers. I grew up in that context. I think that my first impulse was to communicate with my mother. I became a writer to please my mother. I wrote, and she was delighted when I wrote. That was my first impulse: to communicate with her. She died when she was 42 and I was 13. And I continued.

Before becoming a professional writer, I studied education, I worked with a fashion designer, I was a fashion model and, for a year, I was an actress, performing in the *Opera dos tres vintens* [*A Three Penney Opera*] and in *Vereda de salvação* [*the Road to Salvation*] by Jorge Andrade. After all of these experiences, I began as an author in 1969. All of my experiences before 1969 contributed to my training as a writer, but real life experiences were what helped the most. Life inspires me more than studying.

Tell me about your childhood...

I had an unhappy childhood. An alcoholic father, even though he was brilliant and was a professor, a pianist, and a writer who had a column in a newspaper in the São Paulo hinterland. He made me suffer a lot. My mother died very young from cancer. We moved from city to city. As soon as I had roots in one city, I always had to move to another. I was always surrounded by books, by my family's erudition. My great-grandmother founded the first school in Botucatu. My mother taught rhyme and meter. When I was 5 years old, I'd already written my first poem.

You did travel a lot. How did all of this traveling influence you?

I like to travel a lot. Now I only like to travel to foreign countries and to Rio de Janeiro. Within Brazil, I only go to Rio. I traveled a lot, and I'm continuing to travel a lot. All of these trips have inspired me, but inner journeys inspire me, too.

Do politics play an important role in your life?

I always sympathized with the left. I was never an activist. I was a feminist. My work is feminist to a large extent. In that time, however, it wasn't politically correct to be a feminist. So, I didn't become involved in that kind of feminism. I didn't even know what it was. Now, when I think about my work, I can see how much I was a femenist and how much I still feel that way.

What does it mean to be a woman in Brazil?

Being a woman in Brazil during the past 50 years has meant a lot of movement and change. I think that women's consciousness is among the things that have changed the most and developed the most in Brazil. The difference between my sister, who is almost 10 years older than me, and myself is enormous. It's as if she were my mother, or my grandmother, with the values that she has. I think that being a woman in Brazil is a blessing, because people had something to fight for, because they had an ideology and because they won something. There are still things that need to be won: equality in wages, for example, but the gains have already been enormous.

What about the situation of a woman writer in Brazil?

I think that there isn't much difference between female and male writers today. When I started in 1969, there was a preconception. Most of the public and most critics expected rose-tinted playwriting from women. And when a woman wrote well, people said, "Wow! It's almost like a man's writing!" I had to combat this, but, today, that's not the way it is. I think that women have their place, and they aren't discriminated against for being women. Even to the contrary, I think that playwriting by women is more readily accepted in Brazil now precisely because we have more to say than men do. Now, difficulties in handling this space will always be there.

The success that my last play, *Intimidade indecente* [*Indecent Intimacy*], had here in São Paulo is a miracle. Producing a play in Brazil is the most difficult thing. Succeeding is a miracle. We don't have agents or anything here. When we write a play, the first thing that we have to do is to find an "accomplice." Someone who is as enthusiastic about the text as you are. It can be an actor, an actress, a producer. Normally, it's an actress, because I create a lot of female roles, but, very often, it can also be an actor who does his own production. Having a well-known actor or actress interested in your script is like winning the lottery. On account of my family's financial situation, I had the opportunity to produce various plays of mine. Even though I had the money to produce, however, I had to be lucky enough to find a great actress who would be interested. It's not enough to have the money and to ask them. If they don't like the role, they won't do it. With *Intimidade indecente*, everything went well. I had enough money to produce it, Irene Ravache was enthusiastic about it, and she also wanted to produce it. Everything went well that time, but what happened in that case is a rarity.

What is the role of family in your life? Does it inspire you or block you?

I always had double feelings in relation to the family. Attraction and repulsion. Love and hate. Yet, I was always looking for a family, because of having lost my mother very early. I always had a lot of fears, too, because, for me, family meant fights, alcoholism, etc. Then I was married, and for 20 years, I succeeded in having a stable family. I managed to live in a comfort zone, and it was also a period when I wrote less. I enjoyed happiness. Now it has ended, or, to express it better: the relationship became open. It became open. My husband keeps his belongings here, but he lives in a hotel, even though we aren't officially separated. There wasn't any kind of breakup. There are only three of us, and each of us goes his own way, because my daughter is 20 years old, and she is following a brilliant career. I feel the lack of a family. Now I'm going to look for a family in a religion. I also feel a great lack of religion. I never had one. I was always an atheist. Now I feel the lack of a deeper kind of family, a spiritual family.

Is mysticism a brand-new experience for you? You had no previous interest in spirituality?

No, I was never interested in it, it's recent. I was always an atheist. I'm Catholic, but I never practiced. On the other hand, I always recognized something rather unique in creation. I always recognized it because, many times, when I was writing, I had an impression that it wasn't me, that I was just serving as a medium.

Now I'm looking for a religion and for God. Not long ago, I also found out that my difficulty in finding this God is that I'd been looking for a male God. Everyone says that He is male. It can be seen that I had blocked it out, too. Because God is neither male or female. It's abstract, an entity or an essence… Let's think about it. When I was young, I went to *Candomblé* rituals, Spiritism centers, and I switched around, etc., but that's because I had a panic syndrome and I was looking for a cure, even though there was no cure at that time. That was during the 1970's and 1980's. Before then, I had suffered from a panic syndrome, and, with *Candomblé* and Spiritism, I was looking for a form of Reichian therapy with movement of the body, and I managed to create circular energy. Afterwards, it was with antidepressants. Actually, at that time I was looking for a cure instead of a religious experience. Now I'm looking for the latter.

Whom do you write for? Who is your audience?

Each play is for a person. At times, it's even unconscious. After time passes, I'll say, "Listen, what I said is for so and so." This abstract thing of saying, "I'm writing for mankind," doesn't exist. The need to say things exists, and when I go to paper and can't express myself, I die, I truly die. It's a matter of life and death: I need to speak. Sometimes, it's just for me. Before, there were other women. They were always my age. Men like my most recent plays, too, since *A lua nua* [*Naked Moon*]. And now there's *Intimidade indecente,* where men have been deeply affected, and they are even showing their emotions. I'm trying to find out why. I think that it's because I talk about male fragility and impotence. Men are much more inhibited than women, and they discover that they aren't the only ones who feel the fragility that's in my play. I think that's why men like it so much. In the instance of my earlier plays, most of the audience was from my generation. Now *Intimidade indecente* has an audience from my generation upward. The elderly adore it. Just think about it…

Leilah Assumpção

What do you think about globalization?

I think that it's something irreversible. Now globalizing from just one location, selling a product for the whole world, setting up McDonald's throughout the world — I don't think that's fair. In my generation, it was known as imperialism. On the other hand, there are things about it that can't be controlled anymore.

Leilah Assumpção

The Passion of Miss Congeniality, a one act monologue, was first performed in 1994, starring Claudia Mello and directed by Fauzi Arap. It tells the story of a friendship, better a love-hate relationship, between Guta, the only character physically present onstage, and Maribel, who is invisible but present in Guta's flashbacks to their childhood and adolescence in a small town in the state of São Paulo and later during their trying times in São Paulo itself. Guta, is between 40 and 50-years old, introverted, shy, depressed, yet friendly and generous. Maribel is the same age as Guta, but in all ways the opposite. Other characters brought in by Guta are: Silverinha, a handsome and distant young man who both young girls had a crush on, but only Maribel was able to satisfy her desire; Iraní and Teresa, both childhood friends from the same town as Guta and both working the same lousy job in São Paulo. Before the final scene, which is published here, Guta recalls different episodes from her past in which Maribel would always take over, intentionaly or not, all that Guta held dear.

The Passion of Miss Congeniality

The neighbor's TV gets louder. The music now becomes dramatic, like the soap opera

GUTA: Do you mind turning that TV down now? I don't want to hear it anymore. I've had it with soap operas. "Who killed Lavonhani?" I could care less! Finally it's my story that's taken over and now I'm the soap opera. I'm the story, I'm the heroine, MARIBEL AND I! SHHH! Show some respect. This is my moment!

The sound of the TV stays the same. She shrugs her shoulders.

>Alright… Actually, that music works… gives me the right atmosphere… Background music for the letter. For Maribel's letter… Is that OK, Maribel? Oh, the sound doesn't bother you. In fact, it's the right touch… Alright, then…

The sound is turned down a bit but remains in the background.

>How did you end up in Italy? On a freighter? Or did you go directly from Morocco and the white-slave trade? The last letter you wrote came from Virginia,

from the ranch that belongs the guy who raises buffaloes. Teddy, right? Right, that was his name. An American with Belgian ancestors. You think I'd forget that? A millionaire... Your chance to escape... from that life. You think I don't know? That was your chance to become a decent woman, with a little dignity, with your husband's name. Everything legal and sanctified by the church. But it didn't work out, that's what you were telling me in your letter. That's what I expected, of course, I knew, I was certain. Poor Maribel... Sure, you didn't marry him, and a few months later you were alone, on your own, thrown out on the street, in a strange country. And then what? What happened? Come on, spill it. You can tell me, I'm Guta, your trusted friend. Your best friend. Your Guta, more faithful than a watchdog, ever since we were kids. And you were right to trust me because you knew I would NEVER tell anyone and I NEVER did tell anyone your second great secret... "How" you managed to get through college. "Where" you got the money. (*Softly.*) But since there's no one listening now, it's my turn to talk. Now it's me talking, Maribel, just to the two of us.

Guta takes a long pause. Suspense. Then she speaks, loud and clear.

You got through college because you worked as a PROSTITUTE AT NIGHT IN A CLUB called *La Giselle*, on Major Sertório Street.

Guta closes her eyes. She breathes deeply.

Oh, Maribel... Even today I still feel that dull throbbing in my scalp when I remember that... A blow to my solar plexus. It was a... disaster, a sacrilege, worse than that, a goddamned earthquake! I was flabbergasted… but you wouldn't turn back, it was the way you wanted it. I tried using logical arguments but then you came back with that Karl Marx business. As far as I'm concerned it was HIM, Karl Marx, who was responsible for everything. It wasn't quite so bad in my case because from what you told me about him I learned that the early bird gets the worm, love your neighbor as yourself, the meek shall inherit the earth, this earth right here. But according to you… the Capitalism business… You twisted everything, Maribel. I remember just like it was yesterday you going on about how your body was your own property and you could do what you wanted with it, with God's blessing! Are you listening?! "With God's blessing!" Just think how far you were willing to go! I know this letter contains the whole sordid tale, I know what this letter's bringing me, it's telling me everything, and that's why I'm afraid to read it. The things that you, my dear friend, have done… And everything you've done is just the opposite of what's right and what's legal. Even… (*Awkwardly.*) whore… "with God's blessing!" (*Softly.*) I even suspected Father Pedótti found out about it but he didn't care. No, that's ridiculous, because he would care! Just like God cares! Oh, what God wouldn't have done with you now, my friend… "He knows if you've been bad or good"… You've always realized that. Well, whatever, here I am and I'm willing to help you. I'm not doing so good, maybe you can tell. I need money, I need…! A TV, a gynecologist, a dentist, my dearly departed mom and dad, time that keeps slipping away… and slipping away… And this humidity in São Paulo, it chills you to the bone. But I'm better off than you and I'm ready to help. I told you to be careful when you met that wealthy rancher from Virginia in

Giselle. Nobody invites a pro, sexually speaking, to live with him on his million-dollar ranch with the promise of marriage. That only happens in the movies, Maribel. I thought you had it all figured out clear as a bell when you told me in your letter that marriage or no marriage all that American really wanted was some Third World cheap labor to take care of his 90-year-old senile mommy. "But even so it was neat and it was worth it because he got me out of Brazil." Or so you said in your letter. How naive can you get… worse that a blind man who refuses to admit he can't see. And then what? You got rid of him and what did you do? Go back to the oldest profession in the world? Did you go to Miami? Did you get mixed up with Cuban pimps, Caribbean drug addicts, Columbian pushers? Maribel, have you become a pawn of the Medellín Cartel? What is it you're telling me in this letter, Maribel? What's happened to you…? What kind of holy purifying fire did the all-powerful hand of the Almighty burn you with, my poor, poor friend Maribel?

The music coming from the neighbor's TV gets a bit louder. Music from the film, "The Ten Commandments." Guta turns toward the letter.

GUTA: Come on now!!! Let's hear it!!!

Total silence. Guta and the letter are face to face. She then goes decisively over to the letter. She again removes the sheet of paper from the envelope.

GUTA: Now I'll find out. (*She reads.*) "Rome… November, 1993. I'm not sure what day." (*She laughs.*) Still the same old Maribel… "My forever dear friend Guta. I can imagine you surprise you hearing from me after all

these years. I hope it make you happy like does me."
"You surprise you hearing...." "Make you happy
like..." Yup, the same old Maribel. Her grammar, my
god! And to think she went to college. What would
her writing be like if she hadn't... (*She continues.*) "After
Teddy, my buffalo rancher from Virginia (remember?),
my life went in a such a crazy direction, everything
went by so fast, I suddenly realized... I had completely
lost contact with you, my dearest and bestest friend."
Sure, so crazy and so fast she didn't have time to tell
me a thing. (*She continues.*) "I picked up English pretty
good." But I was the one who was good at Portuguese.
And SHE was the one who studied journalism. (*She
continues reading.*) "... and I managed to work in the
United States and London with the help of some dear
friends and lovers, wonderful folks who helped me get
past the legal hurdles. Some newspaper and TV work,
a few modeling gigs, you know, photography and
fashion shows. Seems they go for my looks more here
than back there. As to the OTHER profession... look,
I was just an adolescent thumbing her nose at the world.
Oh, the good old days... *Giselle* was a wonderful
experience. Sometimes I miss it."

Guta puts down the letter, tense, nervous.

God, are you listening. Are you there, reading this with
me? I'm finding this letter... weird. Don't forget, God,
that Maribel chewed on the communion wafer! And
in the procession You even let them choose HER to
carry the bier with the statue of the Virgin! And after
that she even carried the flag!

*Guta gets up nervously, goes over to the boxes containing the presents
for Maribel, and opens a box of perfume. She fitfully tries to control
herself.*

151

She NEVER respected the Holy Water, God! Are you listening? She cringed at the idea of putting her hand in the water, "where everybody else sticks their hands!"

She opens the bottle and begins "blessing" the living room, as if it contained holy water.

(*In a singsong voice.*) Let us purify, Loooooorrrrrd... There're two gals for every single guy in the town of Sertãozinho where I'm from... Either Guta or Maribel. The two of them together, it doesn't add up. For every decent job in São Paulo there are two candidates: either Guta or Maribel; two of them, doesn't add up. For every grave in the cemeteries of Brazil, there are two dead people...

She suddenly "comes to."

My goodness...! Everything's all wet...! What have I done...! Her... imported perfume... I spilled all of it. My god... such good perfume, doesn't come cheap... That's why I started smelling this strong odor. (*She puts down the bottle.*) Well, I really did spill it all. TOO BAD! Let's get back to the interesting part: THE LETTER!! (*She pauses for effect.*) Let... us... continue... (*She reads.*) "...Oh, the good old days... But now if I want to I can work legally," parenthesis, "even though I don't need to anymore" (*Anxious, fearful.*) end parenthesis, "because... I got married."

Guta, bewildered, stops and stares at the letter.

"even though I don't need to anymore because I got married..." Because I got married... I got married..." (*She pauses.*) That's what it says: "I GOT MARRIED... here in Rome..."

Guta is stunned. But she continues reading, as if she no longer understood any of what she was reading.

"I also picked up Italian pretty good. It's so romantic…! I write articles now and then. Politics when my life is a whirlwind of parties, fashion when things start to feel kind of heavy. But I don't have much time because our daily life is so intense, in every way imaginable. My husband has a very important position in Italy's economic, social, and political life. He's (*She reads with emphasis.*) Felipo Vergari Chiafarêllo, Lord Duke of Graba, Marquis of Savoquétti, and a bunch of other titles I'm not going to list here. We have two beautiful twin girls, our pride and joy. Besides our Villa Damasco Palace here, of all our properties the one I adore most is the Casita Bianca in Greece. From there we take these awesome cruises — we're terrific skin divers! I just remembered you get seasick and airsick and you're afraid of water. Too bad. I'd just love to invite you here! The bottom of the sea is fantastic! We always have elegant, fun and brilliant guests like Princess Stephanie of Monaco and Alain Delon…

Guta crumples the letter. She hangs her head and cowers, like an animal. She emits a low, deep moan. She is dumbfounded, mute. Silence. Suddenly, from deep within her comes a piercing scream, a veritable howl from a wounded animal; the howl brings her to her feet. When the howling dies down she takes a deep breath and speaks slowly and decisively.

GOD DOES NOT EXIST. (*She pauses.*) No… God does not exist. Got does not exist.

Guta takes a moment to recover from her howling.

I want to die. I'm going to stick my head... in the oven and turn on the gas. I'm going to swallow... 30 pills. I'm going to cut my wrist, I'm going to disappear... disappear... Will "that" slow down "a little" the (*She closes her eyes.*) nonstop exhilaration and joy in her life? Damn her! Or maybe she won't even suffer, feel hurt, keel over, crawl on her hands and knees...

Guta goes over to the fern and yanks it out of the pot by its roots and howls like an animal.

HAHAHAHAHAHAHAHAHAHAHA!!!!! DAMN HER DAMN HER DAMN HER DAMN HER!!!!! A THOUSAND TIMES, GODDAMN HER!!!!!

She slowly recovers. She catches her breath. She sits on the floor, defeated, crushed.

No... If I die... maybe she'll feel a little sorry... Maybe she'll even shed a... tear or two. But then right away... she'll be distracted... by some other concern. She'll call someone, engage in some silly chitchat, and laugh. It won't affect her bit. And by the next day she'll have forgotten all about it. No... If I die I might die in vain. My death could be meaningless.

Soberly, she makes up her mind. She goes over to the telephone, firmly and decisively. She dials.

Hello. Iraní... This is Guta. (*She pauses.*) Hello, Iraní! (*She pauses. She smiles bitterly.*) The answering machine. She'll never pay me what she owes me.

She dials again.

Teresa…? (*Irritated, she speaks quickly.*) Don't give me that "maid" business, Teresa. I recognize your voice. This is Guta. (*She pauses.*) Everything's going… I…

Guta is cut off by Teresa, who begins speaking. Guta reacts with increasing surprise, shock, and she is left even more perplexed than ever. After listening for a while she slowly puts the phone back on the hook, lost in thought.

(*She impersonates Teresa, but in Maribel's voice.*) "Listen, Guta. It's nice you called. I've got some news for you. And it's important I give it to you all at once. You're an adult woman. And you'll understand this like an adult. A civilized adult. The fact is, you're on the list. You're through. I'M SORRY, MY DEAR, BUT THAT'S LIFE." (*She pauses.*) I've been fired. Coldly. That's how they break the news nowadays. I'm out of it. I've been fired. After 15 yours with the company, I'm unemployed. "That's… life." Just like Maribel. "That's life, my dear."

Guta begins acting strangely. She walks like a zombie. But a zombie who is now soft and tender.

But the Lord is my shepherd and I shall not want.

She goes over to the presents for the people at the store.

Sandalwood… sandalwood… "Be as the sandalwood, which perfumes the…" Maribel was right, Teresa's terrific. Maribel taught her well. (*Softly.*) Shhh, girls. Let's turn out the lights…

She picks up a package and opens it. She removes a packet of June Fest sparklers. She turns out the lights.

Nights during the June Fest. Remember, Teresa? Remember, Maribel? We couldn't wait till the fireworks started. That was our favorite part… The sparklers that looked like silver tears. That's why I was going to give you these Christmas sparklers, Teresa, so we could reminisce… Look…

She lights a sparkler. The flame sputters and suddenly forms a silver tear. Then another. And another. Guta, like a child, watches until the last tear goes out.

Since I won't be exchanging any presents this year I can light all of them.

She lights another sparkler.

The wedding showers, the fiancés, the children, such happiness… !!!

She watches the sparkler in silence until it goes out. She lights another one.

Who's going to be my Secret Friend? No, there won't be any more Secret Friends. I mean, there will be, but not for me. (*Heartbroken.*) My god, who would've been my Secret Friend this year? No… I'll never know, never. For the rest of my life I'll never know who would have been my Secret Friend for Christmas 1993.

She watches the sparkler. The tear goes out. Guta turns on the lights. She opens the package with the book. She tries to open it but the pages are stuck. She picks up the scissors next to her and tries to cut open the pages delicately. It doesn't work. This makes her nervous and she rips the book open violently. Startled, she drops the scissors on the floor. She sees the fern that has been yanked from the pot. Fear. Pain. She rushes over to the fern.

> No, it can't be... My dear fern, what happened?...
> What have I done?... Please, show me a sign of life!
> My dear fern that my little boy toy gave me...! I didn't
> mean to, I didn't mean to, it was a moment of... It
> was idiotic, brutal, criminal!

She attempts to revive the fern. She tenderly picks it up and tries to put it back in the pot.

> I lost control but you've got to show me a sign of life.
> Poor baby, you're so fragile, so dependent, so alone, so
> sensitive. But now you've got to be strong. You've got
> to help me. Please don't die. Show some life.
> Nowadays you just can't be so fragile... I didn't mean
> to. Show me a sign... You're not in the middle of some
> busy intersection at streets like Ipiranga and São João.
> Give me a hand and push your roots into the dirt...
> help me...

The fern is more or less planted again but clearly precariously.

> I don't feel so well... oh... somebody help me... I don't
> feel so well...

She goes over to the telephone and dials again.

> Answering machine forever. I'll never see Iraní again...

She dials another number.

> She left the phone off the hook. Teresa. (*She pauses.*) I
> don't feel well... (*In a singsong voice.*) "Let us purify,
> Looooooorrrrrd..."

She goes over to the presents and opens the package with the flashlight.

I'll never know who would've been my Secret Friend for Christmas 1993.

She thinks for a moment. A ray of hope. A faint smile.

Why not…? It's just that… I'll feel braver in the dark.

She turns out the lights again. She turns on the flashlight and shines it on her own face. Extreme fear. Like a detective, she shines the light around the living room looking for the phone. She finds it and dials a number. Tense, nervous. When someone answers at the other end of the line she immediately turns off the flashlight and talks in the dark.

Hello. I'd like to speak with Silveirinha, please. (*Flustered, she pauses.*) Silveirinha…? Is it… really you?

Guta becomes excited, breathless.

What a… coincidence… Just a… moment…

Guta puts her hand over the phone and catches her breath.

Oh, I'm so nervous…

She speaks into the phone again.

Hello. Excuse me. This is Guta. (*She pauses, disappointed.*) Guta who…? Let's see if you can guess. You were a guest in my home, you and a male friend of yours. We had English tea and tiramisu. The two of you fancied my grandmother's antique soup tureen so

I gave it to you. Some times I'd bring you fruit when you lived in that boarding house on Pará Street. (*She pauses and smiles.*) Sertãozinho, of course... I called you because... (*Nervous.*) because... MARIBEL SENT A LETTER! YOU WERE SUCH CLOSE FRIENDS WITH HER... (*The person on the other end of the line interrupts her and she pauses.*) Rome... Calm down... Of course I'll give you the address. Obviously... (*She pauses.*) To your wedding...? You're going to invite her... you... you're getting married, Silveirinha? (*She pauses; she begins speaking softly in a singsong voice again.*) "Let us purify, Loooooorrrrrd... The sinner's sooouuul... (*She pauses, surprised.*) No, nothing... It's a carol from my childhood... It's just that... Look, I'm sorry, Silveirinha, but it's just that...

Though Guta is now in a state of anguish, she is clear-headed and serious. Her tone is pleading.

It's just that I'm not feeling well... I'm calling to tell you I'm not feeling at all well.

Guta listens for a while. She slowly puts down the phone. She turns on the lights.

(*She impersonates Silveirinha, but in Maribel's voice.*) "Now, now, Guta, stop thinking that way... Anyway, who does feel good nowadays...?"

Guta repeats what Silveirinha has said, but doesn't speak in an effeminate voice. Her voice is mechanical and robotlike, with some of Maribel's inflections.

"Of course I'm getting married, birdbrain. Everybody's catching that awful disease... The girl's my boss's daughter; that cross-eyed redhead you saw. You know the best man, Sweetie... my fellow, of course!" "That's life, my dear." Just like Maribel. The Lord is my shepherd and I shall not want. Let me be thy instrument, Lord, let this moment be thine.

Guta goes over to the Christmas tree and takes it down. She picks up the crumpled letter from the floor.

It was terrible to crumple my dear friend's letter. My bosom buddy. Maribel... Maribel... How I miss Maribel. But you can still read it.

Very carefully and lovingly she smooths out the letter.

"It so happens that Father Pedótti in Sertãozinho heard about me from the Vatican. When I've got time on my hands I do some charity work, stuff high-society ladies do. Well, the priest decided to honor me by naming a plaza after me. You know, you remember, the one where we used to play hopscotch...! I have to go back to Sertãozinho and take care of some family business. Want to go with me? Don't worry, you won't have to take a single minute off from your all-important job. I'll be passing through São Paulo on Friday, November 16th. Of course I know you'll go with me. Be ready about 8:30..."

Guta calmly looks at her watch.

Nearly 9:30. Friday. November 16th. Today. (*She pauses.*) No, I'm not surprised. Now I know: it was destined to be. I've sensed it since this morning. No, I've always known. Yes, Maribel, I'll be ready. You must be on your way. You're certain I'm going with you... You've always be certain of me.

She turns the key in the door, leaving it closed but unlocked.

> *(In a singsong voice.)* "Let us purify, Loooooorrrrrd... The sinner's sooouuul..."

She goes over to Maribel's presents and begins opening them. First the incense, which she lights and which perfumes the living room. She continues in a singsong voice.

> The Lord is my shepherd and I shall not want. Let me be thy instrument, let this moment be thine.

She carefully opens the box with the Japanese flowers. She affectionately smoothes them out.

> So lovely...

She gently places them on both sides of the living room "door."

> Thank you, Lord, for making me understand at last. For understanding my mission. God works in mysterious ways. Let me be thy instrument, let this moment be thine...

From the largest box she removes the muslin smock from her first Communion. She continues in a singsong voice.

> Let us purify, Lord... My strange mission.

The smock is much too small for her. Guta is a pathetic figure. She opens the packet of beads, smells them and breathes in deeply. The intercom buzzes and Guta goes to answer it.

GUTA: Hello. Yes, Simão. There's a friend of mine downstairs wants to see me, right? *(She pauses.)* How did I know?

161

I know about these things, Simão. (*She pauses.*) Yes, that's her, Miss Maribel. You can tell her to come on up, Simão. I'm so happy. She's my best friend... (*She pauses.*) Thank you. (*She disconnects the intercom.*) The happiest day in my life. To see Maribel again, my great mission. The Lord is my shepherd and I shall not want. What kind of music should I put on? What will please my dearest friend?

She goes over to the tape player. She puts on Gounod's "Ave Maria." It plays softly. Lovely and tragic. Enchanted, she listens briefly. She then opens the large box and removes the veil and tiara from her first communion. She puts them on. She opens another gift box containing wax candles and places four of them by the door, two on each side. She lights them with the sparkler, one by one. She is deeply resolved. She is still for a moment. Only the "Ave Maria" plays in the background. A climate of deep respect for the ritual. Once the candles are lit, Guta turns out the lights. She stands before this "altar" and solemnly waits. The beautiful "Ave Maria" continues playing in the background. A short time passes. Then the doorbell rings. Guta goes over to the small table next to the sofa and picks up a piece of white cloth. She moves to the door and spreads out the cloth in front of it, between the candles and the flowers. Total silence. The doorbell rings again. Guta goes back to the table and picks up the large pair of scissors. She stands beside the door holding the scissors. She holds them tightly with both hands. In a single powerful and decisive movement she lifts both hands above her head and holds the scissors firmly. She stands still in a waiting position. Suddenly the jingle announcing the news comes from the neighbor's TV set while the announcer speaks.

NEWS ANCHOR: Last night in her apartment Guta Mello Santos murdered her friend Maribel Vergari Chiafarêllo with a large pair of scissors. There were 17 stab wounds. The victim had just returned from Italy, where she was well known as the Duchess of Graba, Marquess of Savoquétti and Countess of Lavonhani. The crime remains a mystery and the murderer is in a state of shock. She says over and over that she has completed her mission and has now become a saint. A new Brazilian saint: Saint Augusta, a saint, a SAINT!!!

Guta, her hands holding the scissors firmly over her head, then speaks in a child's voice. She has totally regressed and her voice is absolutely sincere and happy…!

Come on in, Maribel…! The door's open, come on, come in…!

Blackout.

THE END

— tranlsated by David S. George

Maria Adelaide Amaral

Maria Adelaide Amaral

Maria Adeliade Amaral was born in Porto, Portugal. She moved to Brazil with her family when she was twelve years old. She now lives and works in São Paulo. She is the author of 18 plays and seven novels, as well as the writer and co-writer of various mini-series and soap operas for Brazilian television. Her most acclaimed plays are: *Bodas de papel* (1978); *Chiquinha Gonzaga* (1983); *De braços abertos* (1984); *Querida Mamãe* (1994); *Para tão longo amor* (1994). With the exception of *Evangelho Segundo Jesus Cristo*, an adaptation of José Saramagó's novel, and the "period play" *Chiquinha Gonzaga*, which portrays a famous composer of African descent, her work deals mostly with social and existential dilemmas experienced by Brazilian middle-class, particularly the Brazilian baby-boomers. Among her theatrical translations are plays by Samuel Beckett, Jean Paul Sartre and Edward Albee.

Maria Adelaide Amaral

How did you become a writer?

I was always a person who found it extremely easy to write when I was still in school, and, at a given point, I decided that I was going to be a writer. At that point, I started orienting my life toward being a theater critic. During that period, I was working for the large publishing company Editora Abril in the cultural department. I produced a series of cultural publications, mainly about theater. One day in 1974 we were facing the problem of mass firings at Editora Abril. They were going to fire many people all at once. It started as a rumor, and the rumor went on spreading here and there, with people panicking and beginning to have the most varied attitudes and responses to the possibility of such an event. I was strongly affected by it, and I was actually very disturbed by what I saw. This was an experimental laboratory in human behavior. One night, I came home, and I felt a great need to write about it, so I sat down to write. I didn't know what I was going to write, whether to write a letter, or a chronicle, or a report for a newspaper. The next night, I finished this thing. I didn't know what it was, but I contacted Sabato Magaldi, who was the municipal secretary of culture at that time, and I said, "Listen, Sabato, I've written something and I don't know what it is. Could you take a look at it?" I sent my text to Sabato, and he answered in less than 24 hours, saying, "What you wrote is theater, and it's very good theater." That text was the foundation of my first play, entitled *A resistencia* [*Resistance*]. That was the starting point that motivated me to write *Bodas de papel* [*Paper Wedding*] the following year. In 1976, I entered two plays in the National Theater contest, and *A resistencia* won fourth place.

However, the first of my plays to be performed wasn't *A resistencia* but *Bodas de papel* in 1978. What was shocking for me was that I won awards and praise from critics, and I hadn't expected it to have such a big impact. *Bodas de papel* was a play that was relatively successful with the public, but it was principally a big success among critics, who were unanimous. I suddenly considered myself obliged to become a playwright. I was perfectly comfortable with my situation as a journalist. I had spent a long time working for the publishing company, and I truly liked what I was doing there. Suddenly, I had to face a new occupational possibility and the need to choose. Therefore, I made a choice, and I decided upon writing as a sole activity.

How was your childhood?

I was born about 5 kilometers from Porto in Portugal. My father had a small business. He was very prominent and very active in the community. He was one of the founders of the Volunteer Firemen in Ermezinde, which was the place where our family lived. He had a relatively favorable economic situation for a certain period of time, and then he ended up in a terrible situation, but, because there were appearances to maintain, we were poor people who were ashamed of it. It was all very difficult, and there was a very complicated and conflictive situation in my home. That is why I began reading when I was very young. I went with a book, looking for people who would read to me when I didn't know how to read yet. I was pestering so many people that my father sent me to school ahead of time, so that I would learn how to read by myself without annoying anyone. I quickly learned how to read, and I discovered that reading was something wonderful, because it was a parallel universe where I could live in order to get away from the problems of a life that was very difficult; with a lot of conflicts, a lot of quarrels and deprivation. I was always strongly attracted to cinema and the theater, too. I was strongly attracted to fiction of any kind. That was my way of escaping from what I was experiencing.

I also had the examples of my parents as readers. My father read excellent authors, and my mother read junk from the *Coleccao das mocas* [*Girls' Collection*] with authors who turned the heads of women in the 1920s, 1930s, and 1940s, but at least she read something. I was a voracious reader, and I still am. I read everything that they were reading. When I was reading, I was living in that scenario, and I was living with the same characters, becoming a part of fiction. That's how my childhood was. Many books, many films. Less theater because literary theater wasn't esteemed in Portugal. Commercial theater was the main form of expression in Portugal. I listened to radio plays also.

In 1954, when I was 12 years old, I came to Brazil, because my family's financial situation had become unbearable. My father had already lived in Brazil, twice. The first time was when he was a child. He went to school in Brazil. The other time was when he had been recently married. He came with my mother and spent one or two years here. He had an entire sentimental background with Brazil, and he knew people. Therefore, the family came here and began living in São Paulo. I continued to go to the cinema and to read a lot here. It was in Brazil where I started going to the theater. Not commercial theater, but literary theater. At that time, I started doing children's theater, because I had dreams of becoming an actress, too. I wasn't terrible, but I wasn't exceptional either. Then I dropped this acting career when I was about 18 years old, because I didn't have a calling for it. That's how it was.

Maria Adelaide Amaral

Do you like traveling? How does traveling influence you?

Actually, my main trips have always been inner journeys. Without a doubt. I went to France many times before I got to know France. I went to the United States many times before knowing the United States, and to England. I experienced many centuries of these countries' literary history. When I began traveling to other countries, I was already married. I was already an adult. What did these trips contribute to me? Very little. From the standpoint of literature and the theater, they contributed very little, because my imagination and my prior learning were infinitely more interesting than the short visits that I made. A trip can only be a milestone in your life when you go for a long-enough period of time. After a certain point, I started going to New York every year in order to see plays. My type of theater is entirely unrelated to theater on Broadway. Furthermore, I've already read or seen plays by good American authors. Therefore, I can't say that they have influenced me, even slightly. Prior information is what has influenced me.

Do politics play an important role in your life?

I haven't participated as a citizen. Obviously, I went through a Marxist period, like everyone in my generation. From the age of 16 to the age of 38, I was a Marxist. I was relatively disillusioned with communism, but I never stopped being a leftist. I never allied myself with the right wing. I'm very rebellious, too, and I have an extremely anarchist approach. One of my problems with Marxism was that I allowed myself to criticize when I thought that criticism was necessary. Usually, that's not allowed. You have to bow your head and go in the party's direction. So, I was always an unpopular person. The truth is that I didn't belong to the Communist Party. I never belonged. I sympathized with it, and I considered myself Marxist because of my ideology. Now I reserve the right to criticize anything that I think is horrible. I think this turn to the right in the world is awful.

What does it mean for you to be a woman in Brazil?

During the 1970s when feminist movements were actually beginning in Brazil, I didn't think of myself as a feminist. I think that I was somewhat irritated with their ill humor. They were very angry. Today, I have a clear understanding that I was extremely feminist, that my life has been an example of it, much more so than the banners, throwing away brassieres, etc. I'm a person who took care of herself, by means of her own efforts, and I married, had children and ended a marriage. I live alone, and I'm in charge of my life, and I have a career. I don't know. It's possible that it's a misconception on my part, but I've never felt discriminated against because of being a woman. I've felt discriminated against for being a beginner during the period when I started writing. I've felt discriminated against for being poor, but, throughout my professional life, no one ever discriminated against me for being a woman. Furthermore, poor women have a very difficult situation that's extremely different from the situation of middle-class women, without even mentioning the upper class, but I think that it's different not only in Brazil, but throughout the world.

A woman's situation is always more difficult among the less-privileged classes, even in the United States. Many people have an erroneous vision of this idea of women's independence. Actually, autonomous women with careers and importance are a minority everywhere, even though the number is constantly becoming larger. There are many areas of life throughout the entire world where male violence still prevails, unfortunately, it's still a daily event that's extremely adverse for women. In addition, it's obvious that the number of women within the labor market has increased and, in many cases, it has increased because women have become heads of families. Formerly, men provided, so that, even if a marriage was a disaster men were responsible for providing. Today, there are men who don't feel obligated to provide or to maintain a marriage.

What is the situation of a woman writer in Brazil from your perspective?

Personally speaking, I was very lucky. When I say that no one discriminated against me as a woman in my professional life, it may be that I was distracted. I began in the theater, and I began very favorably. There were delays. It took four years for my first play to be performed, but, once my career began, I didn't slow down. First *A resistencia* was performed, and then *Bodas de papel* was performed in Rio with enormous success. Afterwards there was *Ossos de oficio* [*Occupational Hazard*], followed by *Chiquinha Gonzaga,* which was performed at the SESI Theater for two years. That was followed by *De bracos abertos* [*With Open Arms*], which was performed for four years and won various awards. In 1986, I wrote a novel, *Luisa,* which won the Jabuti prize as the best Brazilian novel. There was an extremely favorable series of circumstances.

In 1990, I was invited to write for television. In the beginning, I helped specific authors with writing television dramas, and that was very convenient for me, because it gave me time to write plays, and to write another novel, *Aos meus amigos* [*To My Friends*] in 1992. When I decided to take a job in television I was extraordinarily lucky. I began with a remake of a novel that was very successful. Afterwards, I wrote six episodes of a serial drama, *Mulher* [*A Woman*], which was a very successful serialization on Brazilian television. Afterwards, I was asked to write a miniseries, *A muralha* [*A Wall*], which was also successful, and it ultimately brought me my first television award. This year, I did a miniseries, *Os Maias* [*The Mayas*], which was a phenomenon with a significant impact and was considered to be one of the best miniseries on Brazilian television in years.

Therefore, I feel very respected by the public, by critics, and by the media, without any preconceptions. If I were to tell you otherwise, I'd be lying. It's obvious that it was different before, and there's no one better to explain it than Lygia Fagundes Telles or Renata Pallottini, because they began publishing during the 1950's. They can tell you what it meant to be a woman and what has changed. Or there's Raquel de Queiroz.

What is the role of family in your life?

At the present time, my family consists of my sons, my daughters-in-law, and my granddaughter, Ana Luisa. I'm extremely close to my sons.

My family inspired me in various works. *Bodas de papel* was inspired by my experience as the wife of an executive of a multinational company. I lived that story. My married life allowed me to write a few plays. My parents' difficult, sad and turbulent life inspired intense magic. My books and my plays are permeated with situations that my family actually provided for me, that family life gave me, or allowed me, or offered to me. In that sense, I'm very grateful to my family, including times when it was difficult. Actually, I'm a result of all this. I'm a product of all of it. A product of the good, the bad, the love and the distaste — I'm a product of all of it, and, obviously, my work is a product of all this, too.

What is your attitude toward mysticism?

I'm Catholic, and, during the period when I was a Marxist, I stayed away from religion. I decided that God didn't exist, but, curiously, I always prayed to a guardian angel, even during those times. It seems that the guardian angel was something separate from this world. I have always been deeply fascinated by the occult. I was always strongly attracted by card readers and astrologers. All of this intrigued me even more in the sense of "pursuing everything and not believing in anything." Principally in the area of astrology, certain things were far too significant for me not to believe. I returned to religion because I had a need. I'm a believer, and my belief was even being expressed during the period when I was a Marxist. In the end, what is ideology other than a form of belief, what are ideological books other than a catechism, and what are ideologues other than prophets, evangelists and apostles? Ultimately, the psychological component is the same. I returned to religion, and I feel very good. I feel very comfortable being a Catholic. I'm a very Brazilian Catholic in the sense of practicing religion my way. I don't follow every dogma or commandment.

Whom do you write for?

For my generation. I'm always talking about my generation. I began writing for people in the over-30 age group, and now I'm writing for those in their 50s. This doesn't mean that older or younger people can't enjoy it, but what I put on the stage tlaks about my experiences, and the principles, values and concerns of my generation.

What do you think of globoalization?

This is a delicate matter, because I think that globalization can't be stopped, just as it wasn't possible to stop the commercial revolution, or mercantilism, or the industrial revolution. The industrial revolution caused so many difficulties that people believed that they could solve them by smashing machines. Unfortunately, the hole is much deeper. What is necessary is for people to go out to struggle in the streets. At this point, I'm completely in agreement with people who are protesting against the insensitivity of the big powers. It appears that they don't see what's happening. Globalization is very advantageous for those who have already obtained big advantages. For underdeveloped countries, and Brazil is an underdeveloped country in certain sectors, it is a tragedy. Therefore, we need to go into the streets and warn people and protest.

Globalization also has its positive aspects. The European Union is so prosperous. I was in Portugal in June 2001, and I was impressed by that country's prosperity. Not long ago, it was very poor. The number of Brazilians working in Portugal as household servants, in civil construction, the number of Ukrainians and other nationalities... Portugal had the Revolution of the Carnations in 1974, but it only entered the 20th century 10 years ago. It did get there, however. And that's fantastic.

Maria Adelaide Amaral

Cherish Thy Mother is a psychologically intense and action-less play. Two women, mother and daughter, confront each other with their old, unresolved conflicts and hidden dramas. Ellen, the daughter, is a middle-aged woman who works as a doctor without much satisfaction. She is also unable to stay in a relationship, according to her, because of her bad luck with people. She is divorced and has a teenage daughter who decided to live with her father because she did not accept Ellen's "promiscuous" lifestyle. Ellen also holds a grudge against her mother for always having favored the other daughter, Beth, who lives in the United States, is happily married and has a brilliant academic career. Ruth, the mother, plays a similar role to that of thearpist, at the same time provoking and consoling her troubled daughter, until she herself reveals a long hidden secret of her own. In spite of the ever-present rancor in Ellen's attitude toward Ruth, there is also a feeling of profound love and dependency, the two last feelings being reciprocated by Ruth.

Cherish Thy Mother

SCENE 6

Glenn Miller's "Pennsylvania 6-500" plays. Lights come up. The set has been transformed into a secondhand store displaying in a more creative manner all the objects that in the first scene Ellen had taken out of the trunk. Ellen is wearing the taffeta dress, evening gloves and shoes with very high heels.

ELLEN: (*Putting on the finishing touches.*) What do you think?

RUTH: Don't you think this looks more like a secondhand store than a living room?

ELLEN: It's very theatrical, isn't it?

RUTH: It is theatrical... I just hope she doesn't think I live this way.

ELLEN: (*Going over to the record player.*) That song is too much of a cliché for my taste. Don't you have anything less obvious? (*She takes off the record.*)

RUTH: I think there should be a Beatles record in there someplace.

ELLEN: I want something from the right period. (*She puts on a record.*)

RUTH: Which period?

ELLEN: Yours, of course. (*She presses the button.*) What did you dance when you were young?

RUTH: Foxtrot, bolero, boogie-woogie, rumba.

ELLEN: (*Taking off the waltz.*) Rumba! Where can I find a rumba record?

RUTH: There aren't any left. Cecília took them all.

ELLEN: Quiet! (*Listening attentively.*) Is someone buzzing the apartment?

RUTH: No.

ELLEN: What's the noise?

RUTH: It must be the neighbor lady's telephone. (*Ellen looks at her watch.*) What time was she supposed to be here?

ELLEN: Around 9. She's not very punctual… (*She takes off her shoes and sits down and rubs her toes.*) I'd like to kill the guy who invented high heels.

RUTH: I find them quite elegant…

ELLEN: Masochistic chic… (*She studies her mother.*) I'm really grateful for…

RUTH: (*Interrupting.*) You don't have to thank me.

Ruth takes a few steps. She's ill at ease but she tries to contain herself.

ELLEN: This isn't easy for you, is it?

RUTH: No…

ELLEN: I just want you to know I think it's really neat what you're doing…

RUTH: (*Attempting to change the subject.*) Your sister wrote. Want to read it?

ELLEN: (*Affirmatively.*) Mm-hm. (*Ruth hands her the letter. Ellen begins reading but suddenly stops.*) Are your test results ready?

RUTH: They'll be ready on Monday.

Ellen returns to her reading.

ELLEN: You must have loved this section: "I miss you horribly, Mommy dearest. Right now I wish you could be here holding me in your lap…" (*She hands back the letter.*)

RUTH: Of course I liked it. What mother wouldn't?

ELLEN: It's so phony. Beth is doing great, she has a fantastic goddam house, goddam husband, goddam university career.

RUTH: She has everything except her fantastic goddam mother.

ELLEN: She seems to have done very well without you.

RUTH: Everyone needs to be held once in a while, don't you think?

ELLEN: Come off it, Lady Ruth. Stirring up your dear little daughter's need for love?

RUTH: I'll stir up yours, too, if you want me to.

ELLEN: My need's of a different color, Mamma.

RUTH: Really? (*Ellen checks her watch.*) I'm going pick out a period piece for you.

Ruth goes over to the record player and puts on Fred Astaire, "Let's Face the Music and Dance."

ELLEN: That's lovely.

RUTH: It is...

ELLEN: (*Straightening up.*) I've seen a bunch of Fred Astaire films on TV... (*She dances.*) He's so light on his feet, so elegant. I was so goddamn jealous of Ginger Rogers! If I hadn't gotten married, I would have been a great ballerina. (*She stops.*)

RUTH: Why didn't you keep dancing? Am I inhibiting you?

ELLEN: I'm not light on my feet anymore... It's awful when you can't do what used to be so easy... It's unbearable...

RUTH: Why do you always have to be so hard on yourself? You should give yourself a break.

ELLEN: That's what Leda always says.

Ruth looks at her watch.

Pause.

RUTH: What's this Leda like? Physically...

ELLEN: Six years older than... She's not pretty, but she has beautiful skin... She's big...

RUTH: Fat?

ELLEN: No!... A little... She's big all over... She has brown hair, brown eyes, a friendly smile...

Pause.

RUTH: How do you... do it?

ELLEN: (*Embarrassed.*) We stroke each other...

RUTH: Is that all?

ELLEN: Do you really want to know?

RUTH: No...

Ellen looks at her watch.

ELLEN: That story you told about grandma... about her running away the night before her wedding... I thought it was incredible. It has this dignity, it's a noble gesture... (*Pause.*) Why do I always have the feeling nothing like that will ever happen to me? Why didn't I run away from home when I was a teenager? Why do I always give in and chicken out? Why do I fuss and fume and always end up doing what other people want me to do? Why am I always so miserable? Why do I always feel something terrible is going to happen?

Ruth, in the face of her daughter's distress, looks at her compassionately. She would like to intercede in some way. To stop Ellen from being so unhappy.

ELLEN: I don't think she's coming.

RUTH: Something must have happened.

ELLEN: If something had happened she would've phoned... Nothing happened. It's over, that's all. (*She takes off the gloves.*) You're relieved; admit it...

RUTH: I'd be lying if I said I wasn't.

ELLEN: The whole time I knew she wasn't coming, but I still staged this whole thing... Isn't that strange?

RUTH: Want to have dinner?

ELLEN: If you could do something for me, Mamma... If you were a fairy godmother, what gift would you have for me?

RUTH: A good man, a true man...

ELLEN: Can you find that man for me, Mamma? A guy who cares for me, who won't hurt me, who'll treat me the way Papa treated you?

RUTH: In one week you'd be sick of someone your father's type.

ELLEN: You think I like to suffer?

RUTH: I think you make your life very difficult, very complicated, very sad.

ELLEN: But I do manage to have fun once in a while. Every time I get invited to a party, I go...

RUTH: (*Beginning to take down the set, gather up the costumes and props.*) You don't have fun. You just try to dull the pain. You're always looking for an excuse not to stay home. You'll accept any invitation just to avoid the risk of being alone... You don't have fun, Ellen. I don't even think you fall in love... Those people who go out with you... They just fill your time...

ELLEN: I really cared for Leda, Mamma. I was very happy until last week. I had someone to love and we did have a lot of fun. (*Ruth gives Ellen a look of despair.*) Who do you dream about for me, Mamma? Is the guy tall, blond...

RUTH: (*Interrupting.*) A man who respects you and you respect him. A man who understands your problems, who doesn't lie to you, a man you admire, you're proud of, a man your daughter respects.

ELLEN: I don't have enough going for me hang on to a man for more than a couple of weeks, Mamma. I thought Leda was different. I thought this was it, for keeps, but I couldn't hang on to her either. (*Ruth strokes Ellen's hair and embraces her. Ellen yields for a few seconds and then awkwardly moves away, trying to pull away from Ruth.*) It was worth it, Mamma... worth it...

RUTH: Why do you always cringe and push me away when I touch you?

ELLEN: You still wonder why?

RUTH: Don't you regret the fact that things are so difficult between us, that our relationship is so painful?

ELLEN: I do regret it, but it seems a little late for us to be thinking about family counseling... There was a time I considered it. It was in a period when I believed therapy could solve all people's problems. Look at me... I don't know how many therapists I've been through, and what good has it done?

RUTH: Do you want me to cradle you in my arms and console you?

ELLEN: (*Halfway between bitter and compliant.*) Mommie dearest...

Blackout.

Music.

SCENE 7

Lights come up.

ELLEN: Do you mind turning off that song? (*Ruth goes over to the record player and turns it off.*) Thanks.

RUTH: Anything you'd like to hear?

ELLEN: No, nothing.

RUTH: Did you come straight from the hospital?

ELLEN: (*Tired.*) Yes.

RUTH: Have a hard day?

ELLEN: Extremely.

RUTH: Any news from Priscilla?

ELLEN: No. And Mamma: how about knocking off the interrogation?

RUTH: I only wanted to see how you were doing?

ELLEN: You know I'm not doing well. So why do you keep... (*Ruth picks up a box of chocolates and offers one to Ellen.*) No thanks.

RUTH: It was your cousin Edu who brought them over for me. He stopped by late in the afternoon and stayed to chat until just a short while ago... He said to say hello... (*Ellen isn't listening.*) Edu is wonderful company, a wonderful young man... so cheerful! so much like his father… (*She smiles nostalgically.*) He was very fond of my brother… Don't you remember? Remember, dear… how much you used to play with Edu when you were children?… Remember once when you stole grandmother's hearing aid?… (*She laughs.*) And that time you put a firecracker in Cecília's birthday cake? (*She and Ellen smile.*) Edu misses you very much.

ELLEN: Well, he never tries to get in touch with me.

RUTH: What about you? Do you try to get in touch with him?

ELLEN: I called him once, and the secretary said he'd call back. I'm still waiting for that phone call.

RUTH: You could have called again… He's a very busy doctor!… But he was kind enough to spend the afternoon with me; it was so enjoyable. He told stories, he remembered all kinds of things… Oh… and he brought last Sunday's New York Times so I could pick out the plays I want to go in New York.

Ellen watches Ruth set the box of chocolates down.

ELLEN: Why can't I be like you? Pleasant, friendly… A person everyone wants to be with. (*Ruth looks pityingly at Ellen.*) Last night Leda came by… You don't have to give me that panicked look, because we're not getting back… She just stopped by to pick up some of her things. Books, records… She said she didn't show up for dinner that time because she didn't want to hurt you. She knows you didn't approve of our affair, she knows you felt threatened. She thought she was no good for me. She said she was harming my relationship with Priscilla. She thinks the only reason I fell in love with her was to hurt you. And since she wants the best for me and the best for you, Mamma, (*She cries.*) she left me.

Ruth places a supportive hand on Ellen's shoulder.

RUTH: You better sleep here. You're in no shape to drive.

ELLEN: You've never been through this.

RUTH: I wish there were something I could do for you, something I could say to comfort you, but the only thing I can think of is to say that what you're feeling will pass...

ELLEN: Life is so hard... (*Ruth nods her head.*) Everything is so strange, so empty, it's so hard to go back home... I can't stop asking myself: "What now?" (*Pause.*) It's not just the pain. It's as if I were suspended in thin air. It's like a nightmare. It's as if the very ground beneath my feet had disappeared, the walls that protected me... nothing, absolutely nothing can take away this sense of loss. Not Priscilla, nothing. I realize that never in my life have I ever been so alone... Not when I separated from Sérgio, not when... at least I had some hope... Now it's just me and my grief.

Ruth pours a shot of scotch and offers it to Ellen.

RUTH: Take a big swallow. It won't help the way you feel, but at least it'll help you sleep better.

ELLEN: (*After drinking.*) I know sometimes I'm more than you can take... It's not just with you. I'm sorry...

RUTH: I'm used to it.

ELLEN: I'm so insensitive whenever you make an effort to… chamomile tea, the canceled dinner, this scotch…

RUTH: I've also been insensitive to your pain.

ELLEN: It hurts so much, Mamma.

RUTH: I know.

ELLEN: Today I felt like jumping out the window but I live on the second floor and the worst thing that would happen is that I'd break my legs and cause you even more trouble. (*She laughs nervously.*) Sometimes I feel like sticking my head in the toilet and flushing myself down.

RUTH: That girl wasn't the first person who ever hurt you but you've never talked about killing yourself before.

ELLEN: I know you think I deliberately get involved with people who're going to hurt me, but that's not the way it was this time.

RUTH: It wasn't?

ELLEN: What do you know about love affairs, Mamma? You've never been passionately in love with anyone; the only thing you've experienced is a trivial relationship with Papa.

RUTH: (*Suddenly.*) I had a lover.

ELLEN: What?

RUTH: I had a lover! From 1963 to 1975.

Pause. Ellen digests the information; she's dumbfounded.

ELLEN: Did father know about it?

RUTH: No.

ELLEN: Did anybody?

RUTH: Nobody.

ELLEN: Is this true, Mamma, or are you just making up a story to...

RUTH: (*Interrupting.*) It's true.

ELLEN: Then why were you so hard on me, Mamma? Why were you so strict with me, why did you give me such a hard time if we're in the same boat?

RUTH: We're not in the same boat! I said I had a man, not a woman!

ELLEN: You had a lover. Or do you think you're beyond good and evil just because you went to bed with someone of a different sex?

RUTH: No one was the wiser, I never failed to take care of the rest of you or anything else because of that man, I didn't create a scandal, I didn't hurt anyone... I don't know what I could have been thinking just now when I told you the story.

Pause.

ELLEN: From 1963 to...

RUTH: 1975.

ELLEN: Why didn't you split up with father?

RUTH: In our generation people didn't split up. And he was married, too, he was in the public eye, a very important lawyer, it was all very complicated...

ELLEN: Did I ever meet him?

RUTH: No.

ELLEN: Did you feel guilty?

RUTH: Very.

ELLEN: And yet you...

RUTH: It was worth it.

ELLEN: Where was your meeting place?

RUTH: In a downtown apartment.

ELLEN: What a great romance...

RUTH: It was a great romance... A long and passionate romance... (*Pause.*) We met at a party at your Uncle Oliver's house in 1958. Then we ran into each other in social gatherings... One day he called me! After that he started sending flowers... It was a long courtship, but that's how it was in those days... (*Ellen examines*

Ruth with interest.) When we wanted a breath of fresh
air, sunlight, we met at a beach a long ways away...

ELLEN: What time did you meet?

RUTH: In the morning or in the afternoon... Once a week,
sometimes twice... It depended on our availability...

ELLEN: That song...?

RUTH: (*Nods.*) It was our song.

Pause.

ELLEN: What ever happened to the guy?

RUTH: He... died. Ten years ago... We weren't involved with
each other any longer when he died but still it was a
terrible shock... He was so healthy...

ELLEN: What did he die of?

RUTH: Heart attack.

ELLEN: Did you go to the funeral?

RUTH: No.

ELLEN: Why not?

RUTH: I would have cried, I would have given myself away!
But the day of the seventh-day mass I went to another
church and attended mass for him and cried all the
tears I couldn't cry at home because of your father.

ELLEN: I thought you didn't care about father and I'm finally right.

RUTH: I cared so much for your father that he was the one I stayed with.

ELLEN: You stayed with father because you didn't have the nerve to separate.

RUTH: That's not how things were then… It was…

ELLEN: (*Interrupting.*) Come off it, Mamma!

RUTH: And I was afraid.

ELLEN: Afraid of what?

RUTH: Afraid of scandal, afraid of punishment, afraid of losing you. Afraid people would point at me, afraid of being an outcast… But mainly I was afraid that great passion would end up in marriage and one day he'd look at me and say: "My god, I deserted my wife and children for you!…"

ELLEN: Poor Papa. No wonder you didn't feel like making it with the old man for all those years. (*Pause.*) How could you live with a man for 30 years and be in love with someone else and never let on?

RUTH: Your father never would have accepted it if I'd told him. He wouldn't even have believed it… There would have been only one way out for me: forsake him, forsake you children. I never would have had the courage to do…

ELLEN: Didn't you feel like a traitor?

RUTH: I felt very guilty, very guilty...

ELLEN: I obviously don't have to ask you if you enjoyed sleeping with your lover.

RUTH: Of course I did! I loved it! But that's not the only reason I met with him every week. I loved the feeling of being in love, of romance, of the emotions the relationship entailed...

Pause.

ELLEN: Just why did you tell me this story?

RUTH: I wanted you to see that I understand every iota of the pain you're feeling... I wanted you to know that I spent years walking the fine line between joy and terror... I knew the agony and the ecstasy... I was happy and unhappy like anyone who's capable of falling in love and experiencing overwhelming passion... That's what surprised you... my willingness to experience overwhelming passion... I wanted you to get to know me because I don't think you know me at all ... I'm just not some conservative housewife with no imagination... I'm a virtuous, old-fashioned woman. I'm a woman with a reasonable understanding of the human soul. I think.

ELLEN: As long as it's two heterosexual souls... I could've actually stayed married to Sérgio and had an affair and you would've covered for me. Right?

RUTH: Don't be unfair. I opened up my home to your friend. She didn't accept because she chose not to.

ELLEN: You opened your home after praying fervently that she wouldn't show up!

RUTH: Why are you giving me such a hard time now...

ELLEN: How can someone who's experienced passion the way you have be so unwilling to give? Why were you so hard on me, Mamma?

RUTH: (*She gives Ellen a look of despair.*) And on myself, too... I'm going to make your bed.

ELLEN: Don't trouble yourself, I'll make it myself.

Ruth puts away the knitting in a basket on an easy chair covered with multicolored skeins.

ELLEN: Beth knows the story?

RUTH: You're the only one who knows.

ELLEN: You planning on telling her?

RUTH: I don't know.

ELLEN: She's going to be very disappointed in you.

RUTH: More than you are?

ELLEN: I'm not disappointed. I'm sad...

RUTH: Perhaps I'll tell her, perhaps not... it has to be at the right moment. Or maybe it doesn't have to be, I don't know…

ELLEN: She has a very idealized image of you, Mamma.

RUTH: And so do you.

ELLEN: Probably. The truth is, some people have a vocation for happiness. I'm not one of them. Papa had it. Beth has it. Leda has it, too, and she figured out I didn't, she figured it out, Mamma… that's why she left…

RUTH: I'm going to bed… (*Running her hand through her hair.*) I'm very tired.

ELLEN: I didn't even ask about your tests.

RUTH: I took them over to Dr. Drummond this afternoon.

ELLEN: I'll call him tomorrow.

RUTH: Good night.

ELLEN: That story about your affair… I envy you a lot… Something like that could never happen to me… No one I ever met was romantic, no one has enough money to keep an apartment anymore, no one can keep a love affair going for 12 years anymore…

RUTH: It was more than 12 years…

ELLEN: And no one noticed?

RUTH: We hardly spoke to each other in public. We hardly looked at each other. We respected other people too much. But not in our fantasy life. In our fantasy life we let ourselves be disgraceful... (*She smiles nostalgically.*) One day he said: "Shall we have a child?" And I often imagined that child: a handsome boy, and in my imagination your father raised him as if he were his own... Then, when I was a little old lady and my son a grown man, I'd reveal everything. (*She smiles.*) Just like in the old melodramas... like in the movies... I feel like I experience something sort of out of a movie... Every time I met with him it was as if we were in a darkened movie theater and I could see myself on the screen... I was taking part in a fabulous story... (*Pause.*) I loved meeting with him, I waited so anxiously for that moment... But I also enjoyed going home again... I adored the feeling of having you children, your father, our little space, everything in its proper place... (*Pause.*) And when your father asked me what I'd done that afternoon, I answered: "I went to the movies." And in a way it was true. That afternoon, I'd lived a dream and it had lasted as long as a movie...

ELLEN: Papa never suspected you had another man?

RUTH: He found out. Just before he died... One afternoon in the hospital, your father looked at me and he saw the guilt I was carrying inside... I squeezed his hand to ask for his forgiveness and he turned his head away... (*Pause.*) There was no one else in the room... Alone at last, exposed at last... At that moment there was nothing else between us: not you, not your sister, not his career, not our family problems, not the household budget... (*Pause.*) he looked at me... His eyes were wide... and he turned his head away... (*Pause.*) We live our life side by side with another person and we don't even know each other...

Lights fade.

"As Praias Desertas" indicates the end of the scene seven.

SCENE 8

ELLEN: Mamma!

Lights up full.

ELLEN: Did you know Beth's coming tomorrow? (*She hands her the telegram.*)

RUTH: I knew.

ELLEN: So why didn't you tell me? She wants me to go pick her up at the airport! Doesn't she know it's my shift?

RUTH: Cecília can substitute for you.

ELLEN: What's this business about Beth coming here when you're supposed to be going there? She having problems with her husband?

RUTH: No. It was I who asked her to come. (*Ellen looks at Ruth without understanding.*) Dr. Drummond has decided to operate on me down below. Take out some of my insides, as he puts it. It's nothing serious, but...

ELLEN: (*Interrupting.*) So why did you have to ask Beth to stay with you? I'm here, aren't I?

RUTH: I didn't want to inconvenience you. You have enough problems of your own. You're at work all day.

ELLEN: I could take some time off!

RUTH: It wouldn't make any sense for you to waste your vacation time in a hospital. You're going to need it for a trip with Priscilla!

ELLEN: Priscilla doesn't live with me anymore!

RUTH: She'll come back to you. She came over for lunch today...

ELLEN: (*Interrupting.*) I don't want to hear about Priscila, Mamma! I'm so pissed at you!

RUTH: (*Loud.*) I never imagined you'd behave this way toward me!

ELLEN: How did you think I'd react, Mamma? I'm a doctor! I'm here! I'm in a much better position to do something for you than Beth is!

RUTH: No one has to do anything for me. My problem is simple...

ELLEN: (*Interrupting.*) If it were so simple you wouldn't need an operation.

RUTH: It's nothing, Ellen. He's been wanting to take out that growth for years.

ELLEN: Well, I'd like to know why he decided to take it out at this precise moment!

RUTH: Everything's under control, Ellen. He says that I'll be able to travel to the U.S. in a little over a month.

ELLEN: So when are you going to be operated on?

RUTH: Monday.

ELLEN: And you waited until now to tell me?

RUTH: I thought you were going to call Dr. Drummond.

ELLEN: I forgot! I thought everything was fine. You told me
yourself everything was fine!

RUTH: Well, it was. According to the clinical tests. But then
after we did the ultrasound he got worried.

ELLEN: You never told me he was worried. You said he had
you redo the test because he didn't trust the first lab.

RUTH: And that's exactly what he told me.

ELLEN: Have you done a biopsy yet?

RUTH: (*Affirmatively.*) Hmhm...

ELLEN: Where're the test results?

RUTH: He has them.

ELLEN: That day when Cecília went with you...

RUTH: No, it was after that...

ELLEN: Who went with you?

RUTH: Edu and Lívia. Your cousin insisted on going with me...

ELLEN: (*Crying.*) Why didn't you ask me to go with you?

RUTH: (*Crying.*) Because I wanted to spare you!

ELLEN: No, you wanted to punish me! That's always been your way to punish me. Pushing me aside by using some noble excuse! It happened when Papa got sick! You left me out because I was splitting up with my husband!

RUTH: I didn't ask you to say with me in the hospital because I was afraid you'd say you wouldn't be able to!… I was so afraid you'd hurt me again!

ELLEN: Before you figured I wouldn't have time to take care of you, did you consider how humiliating this would be for me?

RUTH: Who knows how you're going to react? The other day you said if I got sick you wouldn't be able to take care of me!

ELLEN: So you went right ahead and called Beth… "You see? All I had to do was call and she came right away…" Is that what you're rubbing my face in, Mamma?

RUTH: No… But to tell you the truth it's a relief to find out that Beth isn't that coat hanger where I hung all my maternal fantasies…

ELLEN: If you weren't sick, I think I'd hit you… (*Ruth gives Ellen a shocked look.*) I'm sorry, but I think you should know how angry I am at you…

RUTH: I'm sorry…

ELLEN: Why are you doing this to me?

RUTH: I'd like you to accept my apology… I'm going to feel terrible if I have to go into the operating room feeling that the gap between us is bigger than ever…

ELLEN: For once you've got to realize this wasn't my fault…

RUTH: (*Picking up her knitting.*) I guess our relationship hasn't worked out very well… I guess all our efforts have been big fat failures…

Pause.

ELLEN: How long will Beth be here?

RUTH: At least two weeks…

Pause.

ELLEN: Was it your idea to have Priscilla over for lunch?

RUTH: (*Affirmatively.*) Hmhm…

ELLEN: How's she doing?

RUTH: She's gained a few pounds.

ELLEN: Sérgio must be stuffing her with hamburgers and french fries.

RUTH: She misses you very much. She can't wait to come back home, but, as I understand it, she's waiting for you to make the first move.

ELLEN: Why do I always have to be the one to make the first move?

RUTH: Is it that much trouble to call your daughter and tell her you miss her?

ELLEN: Did you tell her I'm alone again?

RUTH: She already knew you were alone.

Pause.

ELLEN: You always take me so seriously. You believe everything I say and when I'm so mad I can't see straight I say things I don't really feel… (*Pause.*) Or maybe I do feel them but only at that moment… (*Pause.*) Like that business about hitting you… I felt like it when I said it but now I don't… (*Pause.*) I know it hurt you. I'm sorry…

RUTH: (*Taking a long look at Ellen.*) Sometimes you're so childish… (*She returns to her knitting.*)

ELLEN: Well, you've never treated me like a grownup. (*Ruth looks up to respond: she changes her mind and returns to her knitting.*) Do you think you treat me like a grown-up, Mamma?

RUTH: When you act like a grownup.

ELLEN: No. You treat me like the baby of the house, the youngest daughter, the one who's unprepared, the one who lacks maturity, the one whose opinions don't count, the one who's left out of important decisions!

RUTH: I don't want to argue with you anymore. Enough is enough!

ELLEN: I'm not arguing. I'm just telling things like they are.

RUTH: You're just indulging in your favorite pastime: feeling sorry for yourself.

Pause.

ELLEN: When you were pregnant with me, Mamma… Did it make you happy? Did you want a son? Were you pleased when I was born and you found out it was another female? Weren't you disappointed because I wasn't the boy you wanted so much?

RUTH: What is it you want? What are you getting at? Why do you always make me say the same things over and over? How many times have I told you that you were loved and wanted? What is it you want to hear? That I couldn't stand you? That you were the cause of all the problems? Alright, you were! It's true! You were sick all the time and you never stopped crying and throwing up! You were always a troublemaker at school! You hung out with a bad crowd, and I'm not just talking about that girl. Oh no, I'm talking about Sérgio. You just had to get pregnant with him so you could force us to put up with a marriage that obviously would never work out! But you didn't stop there: you dumped all your marital problems on me, not to mention your professional and personal problems. And to make matters worse you left it up to me to raise your daughter so you could study a subject you had no aptitude for! And during that whole time I never received a single thank you, a word of kindness, you never had the slightest consideration for me, all you did was blame me, blame, blame, blame. So there you have it! It's true. And it's also true there are times I regret it's Beth and not you who lives far away from me! It's also true there are times I hate you. But not matter how crude and warped you may be, you're still my daughter. And I love you.

ELLEN: I love you, too.

RUTH: Then stop tormenting me. Or go away. Disappear.

Silence. Ruth nervously resumes her knitting.

ELLEN: (*Observing her mother.*) You've gotten thinner...

RUTH: Actually, I needed to get thinner...

ELLEN: (*Apprehensive.*) Are you feeling tired?

RUTH: Now and then...

Silence.

ELLEN: Have you been sleeping ok?

RUTH: (*Affirmatively.*) Hmhm...

ELLEN: Do you always take your chamomile?

RUTH: (*Affirmatively.*) Always...

Pause.

ELLEN: Are you frightened about the operation?

RUTH: I'm frightened about what might happen afterwards… radiation therapy, chemotherapy…

ELLEN: Maybe none of that will be necessary…

Pause. Ellen puts on a record.

ELLEN: (*While the music plays.*) I read all the poems in your notebook… I liked the love poems very much… (*"As Praias Desertas" plays.*) Was he handsome?

RUTH: (*She stops knitting.*) He was seductive, very seductive…

ELLEN: (*Smiling.*) A scoundrel?

RUTH: No.

ELLEN: You can be open with me. Women love scoundrels.

RUTH: He was a gentleman. Of a different sort than your father. More gracious… more… (*She returns to her knitting.*)

ELLEN: Interesting? (*Ruth nods her head.*) Are you going to tell Beth about him?

RUTH: No…

Ellen looks gratefully at Ruth.

ELLEN: You haven't told me how your affair ended.

RUTH: The way all affairs come to an end. Life drew us apart.

ELLEN: Didn't you ever have anyone else?

RUTH: There was never any room for anyone else. (*The skein of wool runs out.*)

ELLEN: Weren't you even tempted?

RUTH: I just wasn't available. Even though there were many times I would have liked to… Life had more meaning during the period when I was in love. After that, it's not that life was no good anymore. It just became more confined. It was almost 20 years of romance… (*pause*) When you think about it, I was a very lucky woman.

ELLEN: Yes, I think you were.

RUTH: Sometimes I feel totally empty, and I miss those times so much… I miss what I was capable of feeling… Sometimes I have this tremendous desire to go back and feel it all over again, but my fantasy doesn't jibe with my figure… All the images I conjure up about myself have to do with a lighter, younger person. They don't jibe with a face that's aged, a body I'm ashamed to let other people see undressed… (*Pause.*) When I remember the time when I was truly happy there's always a song in the background, a memory of the route I took when I went to meet with him! The intense feelings! And the painful certainty that I won't ever experience anything like it again… That phase of my life is gone forever, it belongs to the past, it can't be brought back, it's dead and gone…

Ruth smiles sadly.

ELLEN: You're still young. You still have the chance to be passionately in love. Maybe your trip to the U.S. Maybe you'll meet someone on the plane! (*Ruth smiles compassionately at Ellen's attempt to cheer her up.*) Don't give me that look, Lady Ruth. You're still very attractive. (*Making a supreme effort not to cry.*) You were always prettier than the rest of us. The most beautiful woman in the world, as Papa used to say!

Ruth smiles. Ellen impulsively embraces Ruth. Ruth's hands caress Ellen's face and hair. Suddenly, surprised by her own gesture, Ellen pulls away. It is a gesture expressing mostly fear. But Ruth does not feel hurt; rather, she feels pity for her daughter's impossible situation. The two woman look at each other.

RUTH: I'm not going to die... I'm not going to die...

ELLEN: (*Averting her gaze.*) No...

— translated by David S. George

Myriam Campello

Myriam Campello

Myriam Campello was born in Rio de Janeiro where she lives and works. She made her writing debut early. In 1972 she received the prestigious Fernando Chinaglia award for her novel *Sortilegiu* (1981). She spent three years in the United States associated with the MacDowell Colony in New Hampshire. Her work has been translated into Polish, German, Dutch and French. Among her works are: *Ceremônia da noite* (1973); *São Sebastião Blues* (1993); *Sons e outros frutos* (1998) [nominated for the Jaboti award]; *Como esquecer (anotações quase inglesas)* (scheduled for 2002). Her work is also included in various anthologies: *Antologia de consistas novos* (1971); *O conto da mulher brasileira* (1978); *Muito Prazer* (1981); *O prazer e todo meu* (1984); *Os cem melhores contos do século* (2000).

Myriam Campello

What led you to become a writer?

I was a child who read a great deal. When I was 12 years old I read Dostoevsky, even without understanding most of what he wrote. But the human chaos, all of those electrifying dramas and tragedies, attracted me enormously. I discovered that the writer, a person capable of bringing life to these imaginary worlds, was the most glamorous figure in the world. Pure romance. Oh, yes, I wasn't thinking rationally; on the contrary, this was the dreamy intuition of a child. There was this standard question asked of children, "What do you want to be when you grow up?" One child would answer, "dressmaker," and others might respond, "pianist" or "teacher." And that is without counting all those who answered, "housewife" (the options open to women when I was a child were far more restrictive). So when I would say that I wanted to be a writer, all of the other kids were puzzled.

This love of literature continued in me and grew during my adolescence. I went to law school only to satisfy my mother's wishes who felt that journalism had no professional substance. Finally, I did decide to study journalism as a kind of trampoline to a literary career. Big mistake, for journalism has nothing to do with literature (unless we're talking about Hemingway and the kind of writing he did). Today I know that journalism can confuse the fiction writer, since journalism engenders the bad habit of having to write according to a specific pattern.

What was your childhood like and the role of your family in your education? In what way did your childhood influence your work?

I come from a very small family and I am completely turned off by the expression "family values," which I question politically. For me, even your question is surprising. I have an aunt who is very important to me. She was practically a substitute mother. I am an only child and my mother died in an automobile crash when I was a little over 20 years old. My father was a distant figure who lives in São Paulo. Therefore, my memories of him have grown very faint. Thus, my big family connection is to my aunt.

Childhood is always very influential, and there is no event that occurrs during that period which doesn't cast a reflection later in life. What remains very vivid to me is my connection to plants and the world of plant life. I lived in a villa that had a large, lush garden, with trees everywhere. I lived on top of the trees, brought my books there, ate my afternoon snacks there. My grandmother would always try to bring me some homeopathic remedy, but I was always hiding in a mango tree. That world of green left an indelible mark on me. Even today, I have an intimacy with it, a profound love. I would even say that it is the source of my myths.

Another aspect that was important in my training as a writer was that I read everything in sight, from fairy tales to popular stories to the classics. I devoured everything. My passion for reading knew no boundaries; it bore good fruit for me. I enjoyed traditional and pop culture at the same time, and this, I believe, is reflected in my work. I can go from so-called cultured writing to so-called popular writing without any problems; in fact, I take pleasure in both.

Do you enjoy travel? Does travel inspire you?

I enjoy travel very much. I have been to the United States many times, and have taken a few trips to Europe. Indeed, I'd like to travel more. However, Brazil is far away off from many of the places that attract me, and fares are very expensive. But I must also confess that there is some laziness at work here. Nonetheless, I do like to travel frequently, for remember that when one travels a whole psychological and emotional turnaround ensues. There is a enormous break with our daily realities and routines. The foreign land, even more than you can imagine, is always a challenge. You change the environment, the geography, the language, the food, your view of the world. It is like a cultural recycling, however fatiguing, and at times it is even terrifying. But to be your own pilot and navigator in foreign lands enriches you profoundly. I never return from a trip with empty hands.

As part of this recycling, I travel throughout Brazil. Rio de Janeiro, the city where I was born and will always live, is impregnated with memories, with places of memory, with very emotional recollections; the whole nine yards. When I leave there it is a relief. To live in other places, even speaking the same language, is like being reborn.

Do politics play any role in your life?

I feel that politics is very important to everyone, since it defines our steps. This applies to all persons and countries, but above all to those who lived in a period of military dictatorship, such as in the case of Brazil. One cannot pay enough attention to politics. For some time I was very active in feminism, including in the United States. But now I feel that I haven't enough internal space for this. In very simple terms, I haven't time to do everything that I would like to within my personal and professional lives, because in addition to being a writer, I am also a translator. I just haven't time for everything. However, I do feel a sense of guilt because I am not involved more actively in community affairs.

What does it mean for you to be a woman in Brazil?

It's a problem. It is much more problematic to be a woman here than in the United States or in Europe, for obvious reasons. Feminism is poorly assimilated in Brazil, even in our major cities. There is only a slight veneer that covers certain points here and there, however tenuous. The system pretends to accept women, but that acceptance, whenever it does occur, comes in very small doses. It was only recently that women began to hold more important positions in Brazilian politics. Just a short time ago, we finally placed a female justice on the Federal Supreme Court. The prefect of São Paulo is a woman named Marta Suplicy, and Senator Benedita da Silva is the first black woman to have held such a position. These women are merely the exceptions to the rule. Also for the first time in Brazil we have a woman who is a candidate for the presidency of the nation. But again, these are the exceptions. There is no de facto equality. And moreover we still have that rigmarole of a woman earning less than a man for the same work. Women are less recognized than men, and if they want to hold the same positions as men, then they are required to be ten times better than their male counterparts. And all of this is without saying anything about those little acts of discrimination that occur in our daily lives, whether or not disguised, which women suffer.

What is the status of the female writer in Brazil?

The female writer has the same problems as women in other occupations or professions. She is treated with reserve. She has to have nerves of steel and be sufficiently tenacious in her desires, in her vocation, in order to secure a minimum place in the scheme of things. Male writers are viewed a priori with more consideration, more respect. Since the woman is always viewed as a secondary being, her battle is double. With rare exceptions, generally only women who know how to fight and claw are those who can play the system's game.

Do your other activities as journalist and translator influence your work as a writer in any way?

My passage through journalism was minimal, not to say nonexistent. I did literary reviews for almost 10 years for the newspaper O Globo, and had other associations with some newspapers and magazines. But I never worked as a day-to-day reporter. Translation is another story. I am a professional translator, and if there are advantages to working at home, there are also enormous disadvantages. The translator must produce and produce if she or he wants to earn a livelihood as such. Consequently, the time allotted to literature must be signficantly sacrificed. In truth, there is an eternal battle between my literature and translation. In *A Room of One's Own*, Virginia Woolf says that the person who wants to write needs 500 pounds and her own room. She was being realistic. But no matter how you say it, there is still the problem of how does one get those 500 pounds? When you yourself have to produce it, matters get more complicated. A certain type of literature is somewhat more expensive. Fortunately for Virginia Woolf, she was spared this battle, for she received an income, much to our — her readers' — eternal happiness.

What role does mysticism play in your life?

I haven't any religion. From very early on, I mistrusted the rigid and so-called pasteurizing content of all of them, even the most seductive. Religion for me is an invention of men to flee from their worst fears. I was baptized in the Catholic faith,

as are most Brazilians, but beginning at age 14 I saw that the
emperor had no clothes. And I never returned. I had an affair
with Hindu transcendental meditation, but this was merely a
marvelous relaxation technique. Buddhism and Zen Buddhism
are very interesting, but they only interest me intellectually.
Leonard Woolf, a total agnostic, said that when he observed
the puppy of his dog, he believed in God. It was a joke, but the
point was understood. When the surfer rides the crest of a 20-
meter wave, can it be said that in this miracle of equilibrium
with the water, is there not some divine stature in the meeting
between the surfer and nature? Certain beautiful faces, certain
moments also reveal this. Art, and above all, literature. As the
centaur said in the Pasolini film, "Everything is sacred."

For whom do you write?

Most of all, for myself. Afterwards, for people who might
understand my work, that is, who attempt to connect with it.
I don't write for specific persons, but rather for ideal, abstract
readers who will be able to follow the path that my text takes
them on.

What are your feelings about globalization?

At one time I was openly in favor, but now I have serious
doubts. Before, it seemed to me that globalization was a process
of modernizing the world, especially the underdeveloped
countries, and that the process would benefit us. However, now
I see that the process has serious problems. Brazil is being
prevented from exporting because it was introduced to
globalization without being able to compete with highly
industrialized countries that have very powerful export policies;
tremendous protectionism. And if Brazil does not export, it
doesn't finance itself. And if it doesn't make money, the FMI
will call us incompetent. On the one hand, there is enormous

pressure for the so-called peripheral nations to open their markets more and more, but reciprocity from the wealthy nations is not there.

It is a perverse situation, and all it does is to accentuate the world's imbalance. If no mechanisms are created to compensate for the economic inequality between the poor and the rich, the prognosis of globalization is alarming. And I believe that this situation is not desirable for the wealthy nations, who in the future will have to deal with the weight of general impoverishment. With the collapse of the Soviet Union, we saw the end of the mechanism of the political balance that the world had, for better or for worse. It has already been said that power corrupts, and total power totally corrupts. I do not feel that the hegemony of the United States is desirable for itself or others. Hegemony ends up in paralysis of will, desire and vitality. History itself shows this. It is necessary to share more for the benefit of all of us.

The Woman of Gold

She was different from me, simple and shy. She worked in some governmental office which, in my imagination, was always covered with dust, and swamped with documents that nobody would read, as in a short story by Kafka. In the midst of hypnotic disco music I noticed her body towering over the heads of the dancing crowd, a strong, well-built body — perhaps androgynous. I was curious and I got closer, not knowing that her shyness would never admit such boldness. We chatted happily in the middle of the noise. For me it was a game. Then she touched me unintentionally.

A note: Proust waited until his mother died to talk about things. However, my mother is alive and she will have to deal with it. It's all right, Mom. I know about the neighbors, the relatives and the friends, but the truth burns, crazy to break free. Besides, we might as well get used to it. This is the decade when the wolf will eat pretentious people, licking his lips; for me it's as clear as water.

Then she touched me unintentionally. I say unintentionally not because she didn't feel desire (it was burning in her dark, expecting eyes) but because at that moment she was pushed by the dancers, who were suddenly electrified by the hysterical music. Her body touched mine, stuck there and, shazam, lightning cracked the air bringing the Olympian gods to earth. She wanted to go on like this but I moved away, the hot blood beating in my body, bubbling vocanically. I got lost in the crowd, terrified by the violence that I felt. It hadn't been long since I had gotten out of my last marriage, my hair still dripping wet from the big wave that caused the shipwreck which took with it broken habits, faith, the ruins of a cathedral. Had I not been a strong swimmer with three championship medals, I might have been lost in the dark depths. So I decided not to get involved again. I took my lute to a nearby square and burned it in front of the astonished eyes of the mothers and baby sitters staring at the scene. "She must be crazy," they were thinking. But I persisted with the alcohol and matches.

They didn't know that I was burning centuries of medieval inheritance and eternal love, all the stupidity that had been thrust upon me since I had first opened my eyes to the world. Man, it took guts to do it. I didn't play my lute well, but I did play, and it was the only path I knew. And there I was, down on the ground and furious as I undertook this ritual, mothers and baby sitters watching me suspiciously, as I watched the flames consume the wood of the instrument that I had bought years ago in an antique store that was no longer there. From now on, a new life, I thought foolishly. Finally I was putting an end to this erratic career of Isolde, to bathing in obsolete loves that had nothing to do with the harsh reality of our times. The fire on the ground greeted my triumphant individuality. From now on, I'd only look for a new type of relationship, one that would satisfy my needs without causing damage. One thing was certain: I'd never get trapped again.

I got lost in the crowd, terrified by the violence of my feelings. A tidal wave covered my body with fury. I was scared of this loose energy and the fear of the unknown gave me a chill. If I stayed for even one more minute under the paralyzing paw, I would sink into an abyss so deep that I would never return. But I waited ardently for the following Saturday. "What was that?" I kept asking myself in a stupor, unable to think of anything else but the amazing moment when the body of the woman of gold discharged millions of volts into my distracted body. I arrived at the disco confused, trying to hide what I was looking for. Once again we attracted each other like moths to a lamp. The look in our eyes gave us away, and our movements were out of control. We brushed against each other, no longer pushed by the crowds in an accidental way. Once again, I was totally on fire. Who said that desire doesn't hurt? It hurts and it frightens. I was consumed by panic, adult enough to see the danger swelling in my veins: touching her body turned the inside of my body into a marshmallow melting in the summer heat. Oh Lord, what shall I do about this desire? And, Lord, a woman!

Well, I have to confess modestly that in spite of my fear she wasn't the first one. But I had left that behind, along with magic lanterns and steamships, when I discovered that men are much less complicated, and more transparent in their cunning. Even a babe in the crib could see through their tricks. They love and forget with the regularity of a metronome. One needs no foresight to see what's coming. By the time a gal figures it out she has already been transformed from a beloved sweetheart into something traded in for a younger model. A woman, on the other hand... I can say no more. Words fall short. If the Black Forest of the female soul has not once been described with precision, how could I, who has not even been to Germany, hope to do so. But the ball of destiny unrolled its woolly threads without asking for permission. And once again I was completely on fire.

On the fifth Saturday of agony I invited her to my apartment. The smell of jasmine swept through the streets of Ipanema, which seemed mysteriously tropical. "This will be my test," I promised the tops of the trees. A new life, free and easy, like the life of the girls who advertise deodorant on TV. But there we were, in the apartment, with the blue lamp illuminating the sociology book, which I had left open after preparing my class with attentive love. My world. That was the last image I had before the woman lay her body of gold on top of mine on that aromatic night, one that I kept with me like sailors who carry the image of the port, with its masts and the smell of food coming from the land as they set sail. An oceanic fever devoured me there and then, a storm ate me, the entire Hindu mythology visited my lonely places, while Brahma, Vishnu and Shiva ran through the nerves of the exposed root. What was it, oh Lord, this eye of a typhoon pushing me to the distant limits, so distant that I didn't even know they existed, that annihilating wave that sent me into oblivion?   Surprised and bewildered, I said, "yes, I want it." Oh, Molly Bloom, now I can understand you. And it wasn't just the orgasms shuddering though my body like the chimes of a cathedral that led me to this perplexity of pleasure, it was a perfect space which had been traced into my soul, an annulment so big in that plenitude, that I found myself on the verge of a religious ecstasy.

When I temporarily came back to my senses I imagined that there must be somebody in the distinguished audience anxiously asking, what can two women do together? Send replies to the Ministry of Education. Anyone who is correct, or even close, will receive a new car, guaranteed.

A new life, free and easy, like the life of the girls who advertise deodorant on TV. This was my iron will. Iron, of course, to please and deceive myself and the world. I was afraid of the fatal vulnerability that always swallowed me up, like a mosquito trapped in butter. To avoid repeating this mistake I began to build walls, keeping in mind that I didn't want any bonds, no changes, no commitment to tarnish the new chrome of my freedom. "Just good friends," like movie stars. We would get together, we would be together for a while and that was all. This summer, I told myself, I will taste victory.

I thought it was great how she just looked at me in silence. I wasn't interested in her opinion. My phone calls were short, dried up by my controlled voice, which didn't distill any sweetness. To enhance the strange and dangerous perfection of our encounters, I shared my life with other beings, noise and movement. I wanted to surround myself with impregnable shields like those of Caesar's legions. I couldn't afford to give up anything to the enemy. She accepted the martial law that I imposed on the relationship with her delicate silence. She saw that I was at war, intuiting the depth of my wounds by the kicks that I gave out to defend myself. But she didn't care. She absorbed the blows with the proud serenity of a samurai.

I didn't ask her any questions. I barely knew her name and I avoided giving her any information that might hang uncomfortably like a ragged flag at the end of my romantic journey. I was a woman of the times, living the moment, which didn't stop me from thinking that one of these days I'd end up getting shot like Marlon Brando in *The Last Tango*. I was watching myself coldly, observing the sexual restlessness that installed itself in my body like heat. My disheveled senses wouldn't let me be. Neither would my memories, which were slaves to that warm and flexible form, to the smell of ripe tamarinds of that wild body extracting sparks of pure sun from my body. Her fuming lava covered my streets and cul-de-sacs, leaving me no space to breathe, and panic took charge like wild horses, setting off all of my alarms. I felt cornered all week, swallowing the heat of the acerbic sky, motionless, without a shadow of rain to refresh the humus of things.

Perhaps fate knows better than us. That Friday, when the humidity reached 67 percent, the woman of gold forgot about our agreement and in a moment of fierce tenderness she said what was absolutely forbidden: she looked me in the eyes and said that she loved me. It shocked me. The cigarette stopped in midair, the match burning my hand. It was our last night. I didn't want to see her again, and I didn't return her phone calls. Speaking to the empty wall in front of me, I said through my teeth, this summer I will know victory.

— translated by Elzbieta Szoka
with Shanna Lorenz

Sonia Coutinho

Sonia Coutinho

Sonia Coutinho was born in Itabuna in the state of Bahia. She moved to Salvador, Bahia's capital, when she was eight years old. She made her literary debut at the age of 19 and at 20 she launched her career as a journalist. In 1968 she moved to Rio de Janeiro where she lives currently. In 1989 she abandoned journalism and dedicated herself to literary translation. Among the 70 books that she has translated are works by Graham Greene, Doris Lessing, Eudora Welty, Joyce Carol Oates, Christopher Isherwood and E. M. Forster. In 1977 she was a visiting writer at the University of Texas at Austin. She has also participated in the International Writing Program as writer in residence at Iowa City. Her most important works include: Novels: *O jogo de Ifá* (1980; 2002); *Último verão de Copacabana* (1985); *Atire em Sofia* (1989); *O caso Alice* (1991); *Os seios de Pandora* (1998). Stories: *Nascimento de uma mulher* (1971; 1996); *Uma certa felicidade* (1976); *Os venenos de Lucrécia* (1978); *Mil olhos de uma rosa* (2001). Essays: *Rainhas do crime: ótica feminina no romance policial* (1994).

How did you become a writer?

I had this fascination with words and literature from a very early point. When I was a little girl, I loved to read. I was a very introverted girl, and it was difficult to relate to other people. Instead of going out to play, I would stay at home, reading. I think that my literary career began with my introverted temperament and an infinite love for books. Things that were written seemed more real to me than so-called reality. In addition, my father wrote poetry, and there were a lot of books in our house. From children's books, I went on to adult prose in one leap, very early. I would make constant incursions into my father's big bookcase. I read those books, even without understanding everything that was written in them. My writing exercises at school were little stories, that my teachers praised very highly, and that encouraged me. I started writing as a result of all this.

What aspects of your childhood and adolescence have had an impact on your work?

I have been doing psychoanalysis for so long that if I sincerely go into the deep waters of my childhood and adolescence, a very complicated history will emerge. I can try to summarize, or to follow an easier path. My literature has varied a lot, but it's always been said that I focused upon many female characters. One constant for me has been an enjoyment of literature written by other women, and an awareness that this literature involves a specific territory that's ours.

The consciousness of being a woman who is writing came to me very early. Perhaps this was partially on account of the contrast between the education that I received and what my brother received. I was strongly attracted to intellectual life and reading, as was my brother. In my case this attraction didn't please my family, while in his case they were pleased. Therefore, he received preparation for professional and intellectual success, while they only thought about the marriage that I would have. That was what my mother thought, and my father shared this vision of women, even though he was an intellectual. This contrast between my brother and myself seemed unfair, and it affected me. They convinced me not to attend the university, which is not what happened with him. They thought that I would find a job just so that I could buy clothing while I waited for a husband. I was disgusted with all that, and, later, as an adult, I completed a graduate program and, afterwards, I managed to complete a master's degree, just to overcome the trauma.

All the while I worked hard as a journalist and translator. During that time, a diploma wasn't required to be a journalist. Professional standing came with length of employment. I should point out, however, that all of this occurred at the end of the 1950s and during the early 1960s, while my family had a mentality from the hinterland of Bahia. We were from Itabuna, where I was born in 1930. Probably, even during that era, none of this would have happened if we had been in Rio de Janeiro. From all this, I developed a very critical attitude in relation to preconceptions about what a woman can do, and also a very critical attitude in relation to Bahia, which are elements that appear in my literature. From the beginning, I reacted to the Bahian myth that Bahia is a paradise, where all of the women are *Gabriela, Clove and Cinnamon*. Good-hearted and ready to do whatever a man wants. I was always entirely different from this, and I think that it left a mark upon my literature.

Are travels important for you?

They occupy a very important place. Because I came out of this narrow environment, filled with restrictions upon women, which I've just been describing, I had a strong desire to travel, to see what things were like in other places. In fact, I have traveled a lot. I went to Spain when I was 20, for a few years, and I spent nearly a year studying art history. During that period, I traveled in Europe, and I became familiar with North Africa. At another point, I spent months in London, studying English and literature on my own. As a guest, I took part in the International Writing Program in Iowa, in the United States. There were various other trips, but these were the longest ones. I think that these trips broadened my vision and turned me into another person. References to different places appear in my literature.

Do politics play any role in your life? Do you have any political sympathies?

I'm an extremely independent and individualistic person. I never managed to join any parties. Even in terms of feminism, I always said that I didn't have a program, that I wasn't creating literature based upon political commitments. So, I don't have any party affiliations. My personal history already put me in a position, however. I belong to the middle class, and I can't think like a financier. I've been working hard to survive, and, sometimes, I've spent 12 hours working on a newspaper. I would come to the office at noon and leave at midnight. So, it's clear that all this also left a mark. I've been a worker with words. I find that this gives me a specific literary position.

What does it mean to be a woman in Brazil?

I already described part of my experience as a woman. A

very difficult experience. Today, I think that the scene has changed in Brazil. The women's viewpoint has at least been triumphant here. It has even become a type of cliché. Everyone says the same thing, and feminism has become an official form of expression. This doesn't mean that differences and inequalities, or injustices, don't exist, or that they've been entirely eliminated. Nevertheless, the feminist way of talking was generally adopted and it has even become hackneyed. As a writer, I was one of the first to speak about women's condition as something specific. Today, I think that I'm sort of a post-feminist, if you understand. My book *Nascimento de uma mulher* [*Birth of a Woman*] was published in 1971, when many female writers were afraid to identify themselves as feminists.

Is the practical situation the same for male and female writers in Brazil?

No, they're still different. The number of male writers, and the space that they receive in publications is still larger than women's space. Many women, when they manage to appear are taken there by men. They don't forge paths by themselves. There are a lot of women who write, but they are ignored, and they don't manage to be recognized, even though they're good. Just to give an example, I was included in an anthology entitled *Os cem melhores contos brasileiros do seculo* [*The One Hundred Best Brazilian Stories of the Century*]. Within this total, I don't think that there were more than 15 women. The preconception about women writers has undoubtedly diminished a lot, however. Women aren't thought of as people who don't need to have any dimensions other than what they do in their families, as they were in my era in the place where I was living.

What role does family play in your life?

Because I never accepted my family's way of thinking and

because there had been marriages that didn't last, I rejected Brazil's patriarchal tradition of the woman who always lives under her family's authority. I spent a good part of my life living alone and away from my family. Nevertheless, I have a daughter and two grandchildren who live in Salvador, and, today, I deeply miss having them close by. My relationship with my mother, which was awful in those times, is much better today. Difficult family relations marked my life and my literature, too. In personal terms, I regret a lot of this now, and I wish that it had been different.

Are you interested in mysticism?

Yes, I'm a person with a partially mystical temperament, but in an ecumenical way. At the same time that I'm interested in *Candomblé*, I'm also interested in Buddhism. When I was very young, I read about Zen Buddhism, partly because it was fashionable. Afterward, I was strongly interested in *Candomblé*, and I wrote about it in several of my books. In nearly all of them, there are references to Afro-Brazilian religions. Just as I don't have an exclusive political affiliation, however, I've never been interested in a particular religion, and I don't have a particular label.

Whom do you write for?

I think that I'm basically writing for myself, and that's a very dangerous thing. You can end up being your only reader. Clarice Lispector has a saying that appeals to me strongly: "The deeper I plunge into myself, the more I find everyone else." That's how I feel when I plunge into the interior of a character. I wish that all kinds of audiences would read me, but I don't write in order to please a particular audience. Formerly, I would say that I especially hoped that other women would read me, but I concluded that this was a utopia. This audience in solidarity hasn't arisen here yet, in spite of all of the standardized concepts. As a writer, I go through phases. For example, there was a long phase of strong interest in detective novels, but in a more sophisticated manner. Today, I've become interested in short stories and short novels. My most recent book, in a limited edition, is a book of stories, *Mil olhos de uma rosa* [*A Thousand Eyes of a Rose*].

What do you think of globalization?

I'm going to be sincere and tell you that I haven't thought a lot about it. People see things happening around them, but it's all so complex. I think that I haven't yet understood what the word actually means, beyond a superficial or propagandistic sense. There are people who are protesting in Brazil, but this issue hasn't completely come into my universe yet.

Summer in Rio

It could be in London, at the British Museum, pigeons flying around outside and inside, and on the third floor, Kayama Matazô's dazzling screens. Or in some Texas town, in a supermarket full of salads in plastic boxes and a hurricane warning on TV.

But no, none of that. It's pretty much Rio. That's right, Copacabana.

Hidden behind the blinds, I spy with my little binoculars on the neighbor who is checking herself out in front of a mirror. Summer's almost here. It's 10 o'clock in the morning. And the woman (Cornélia? Yes, Cornélia Bingen.) examines her body in front of the mirror in the living room.

Ruthless Heat

I'm trying to discover my weak points. I come to the conclusion: the worst is the fat around my waistline. I have to walk twice as much to get in shape so that I can wear a bikini all day long.

Each year, in November, the same despair and resignation: the entire summer ahead.

Ruthless heat, leaving everybody gasping.

And this followed by the unbearable New Year and Carnival.

These dates, for me, lost their meaning a long time ago.

But it's impossible to ignore what's happening around, while I stay, again and again, locked in my apartment, alone.

I move away from the mirror (is it just my impression or is somebody spying on me from the neighboring window?), I put on my jeans and a T-shirt. I have to go downtown, have to take the diskette to the editor, another free-lance job.

Festive dates, horrible tests that I submit myself to each year.

Will I be able to stand it one more time?

Obviously I'm not planning to commit suicide. It's not that serious, I keep telling myself. Not really.

The thing is that during Christmas everybody's busy trying to please their loved ones. I must be the only person in the world who doesn't have any loved ones. And I don't like to be reminded of this.

When it comes to New Year's Eve, all it means to me is watching the fireworks on TV. There's no way I'd get out of the house the way the streets are that night.

I hate TV but I keep it on all the time during New Year's Eve. What keeps me going is the stupid but nice-sounding voice of the TV announcer.

At midnight, I wish myself all the best, very softly. Yes, I am a Woman That Gave Up a Lot of Things.

Tragic Look

She and her husband separated. She had a daughter who, unexpectedly, chose to live with her father, in a different city. For her, it was a tragedy. The woman whom I'm spying on from my window has a tragic look, even naked.

"Even though it happened many years ago, sometimes I have a feeling that it happened yesterday. I continue to be influenced by my daughter's decision. The feeling of deep sadness. The feeling that I knew a lot f people but they all passed. I ended up alone."

Copacabana

If, at least, I were rich! To be lonely and poor is horrible. At some point in their lives, all women think about it, even those who are apparently the most independent. A commonplace, a cliché. But they do think about it, nevertheless.

All I have is my one-bedroom in Copacabana and an old car. I have no clue whatsoever if I'll ever be able to buy a new car once this one breaks down. The thought is unpalatable.

I catch a cab. Who wants to drive downtown and then end up looking for a place to park? When I tell the driver where to go I can see my face in the mirror.

My serene appearance scares me. Nobody will be able to tell the troubles I have had just from looking at me. For no reason, I ask:

—Excuse me, do you know when the summer schedule begins?

—On the 28th —says the man (I couldn't see his face, just the back of his head). They extended it by 15 days.

In the Mall

I have lunch in the mall, in a restaurant with a salad buffet, then I go back home. One job done, another to be done.

But I decide to give myself a break this afternoon and take advantage of the car, while it's still there. It's not too hot yet, it's OK to go out. And I have enough money to pay for a few things.

I go window-shopping in another mall that is quite far away and that I like a lot, and then I go to the first showing of a movie. All I have to do is to get out of the garage in my building and get into the garage of the Mall — and vice-versa.

I get shivers as I go through the shanties of Vidigal and Rocinha but the view of the ocean and of the mountains is comforting.

I have to admit that like most people I like the malls. I don't usually buy anything, I just go to check things out.

I like to pass invisible through the realities of the rich. Right now I don't notice any sign of rejection by any rich bitch near me.

My clothes are old, I know, but they have a certain class. The sneakers are good, the jeans are good, and so is the shirt. They are quite worn out, but that's all.

I go to a bookstore and, as usual, I keep leafing through illustrated imported books.

I like books that teach arts and crafts, and how to use your hands. The paintings on wood, on fabric, jewelry, this kind of stuff. Or, I leaf through books about exotic oriental cities, that I will never visit. Always expensive books, with colorful illustrations, that I cannot afford.

To escape the attention of vigilant clerks I say: "I'm just looking, I'll call you if I need your help, thank you."

When I get fed up, I leave the bookstore and go for lunch.

I eat vegetarian for lunch. I relish every bite of vegetables, the taste of cheese sauce, and my favorite soft drink: natural guarana.

A Small Private Plane

Later on, I buy a movie ticket. It's a semi-intelligent romantic comedy, with a happy ending, of course. It's exactly what I wanted to see.

The parents of the lead girl died and she, penniless, goes to the country to live with a crazy cousin. Her goal is to write a novel.

At some point, the man she loves arrives in a small private plane and takes her away. They declare their mutual love among the clouds.

As I leave the garage it strikes me, judging by the price of the parking ticket, how much time I spent in the mall.

On Niemeyer Avenue, I decide to stop for a while at the scenic view. I want to see the ocean, the big white waves crashing against the rocks.

The Rain and the Celtic Harps

This is what Cornélia could think in the fall:

Gosh, summer's coming!

Summer with its unforgettable rains. Like the one that started with a huge black cloud above the city.

Minutes after the cloud, the storm came: lightning, winds, hard rain.

Water invaded my kitchen through the outside cracks in the walls and formed a giant puddle.

(The fear was that there might be power shortages. Alone on a high floor, knowing that the staircase was narrow and steep.)

But, in the middle of thunder and rain lashing, I played a CD with Celtic harps. So gentle that I stopped being scared.

Goodbye to a Dark-skinned Friend

This is what Cornélia could remember in the fall:

It was in the summer that I lost touch with my dark-skinned friend. Or in the summer she lost touch with me. Before, we would go out every weekend to see art exhibits.

The dark-skinned friend always smiled. When I met her for the first time — not so long ago (one year? two years?) — I was under the impression that I had known her for a long time.

A short woman, good-looking, in her 50s. When she laughed, her lips, covered with a very red lipstick, displayed very white teeth. The smile of my dark-skinned friend was like bread and earth.

I didn't suspect anything. It never even crossed my mind that her face was just a mask. I didn't suspect anything even when she told me one day: "I am a really good actress."

As time went by, her beautiful smile was becoming yellow. And the dark-skinned friend stopped calling. One day, she finally called and said that she was in a new relationship, he was a painter. And he was married. They were meeting in his studio.

Her dream was to be a great painter herself. For the time being she was a very small painter.

So the verdict came: "With my painter-friend," she declared, "I will be able to take more advantage of going to the exhibits." I noticed in her voice a slight tone of contempt.

Suddenly it became clear to me that the dark-skinned friend was expecting something more from me — and I didn't respond. I remembered the day when she sat real close to me and stayed there still, at the distance of a hand motion. And I didn't do anything.

Beaten to Death?

It could be in London, in the British Museum. Pigeons flying around outside. Or in some Texas town while there is a hurricane warning on TV.

But no, none of that. It's pretty much Rio. That's right, Copacabana.

Hidden behind the blinds, I try, with my little binoculars, to see any sign of my neighbor from across the way.

But it's useless, the windows of her apartment are closed, the blinds are closed. She disappeared. Maybe she went on a trip?

Not so long ago, I got a glimpse of some news on TV that shocked me. It said that while returning from a mall in São Conrado neighborhood (a waitress from a cafeteria identified her) a woman stopped her car at a scenic view on Niemeyer Avenue and was assaulted and beaten to death by a group of youngsters from a shanty. They took her purse and her car.

In the picture the woman who was killed looked like my neighbor.

I'm afraid to ask the doormen in the building across if it was her. No, I couldn't bear to know. This way I can be sure, as long as possible, that I'll keep seeing her going to the beach or checking out her body in front of a mirror in the living room.

It could be in London, or in any town in Texas. But it is Rio. That's right, Copacabana.

— translated by Elzbieta Szoka
with Shanna Lorenz

Esmeralda Ribeiro

Esmeralda Ribeiro

Esmeralda Ribeiro was born in São Paulo. A journalist from the city of São Paulo, she is a member of Quilombhoje Literatura, the literary group responsible for the publication of the series *Cadernos Negros*. She has published more than thirty poems in *Cadernos Negros*, Volumes 5, 7, and 9, and a short story in *Cadernos Negros* 8. She is the author of a short novel *Malungos e Milongas* (1988). Her work was published in the following anthologies: various issues of *Cadernos Negros*; *Pau de sebo-coletânea de poesia negra* (1988); *Moving Beyond Boundries. International Dimension of Black Women's Writing* (1995); *Finally Us. Contemporary Black Brazilian Women Writers* (1995); *Callalo*, vol. 18, number 4 (1995); *Ancestral House* (edited by Charles H. Rowell)(1995).

Esmeralda Ribeiro is the author of several theoretical essays of importance including an essay on children's literature in *Reflexões Sobre a Literatura Afro-Brasileira*. Another significant essay, "A excritora negra e o seu ato de escrever participando," which appeared in *Criação Crioula, Nu Elefante Branco*, examines the role of black Brazilian women writers and the political dimensions of their work. This essay called for black Brazilian women writers to recognize the absence of authentic black feminine images in Brazilian literature in general and challenged them to recognize the significance of self-definition in their works.

What inspired you to become a writer?

Various factors. The first factor that gave me a motivation for writing was my father's death. Our bonds were very strong, although we didn't have a constant dialogue. He died in my arms on a Saturday, and I was very overwhelmed. Then I wrote a prose poem entitled "It Was a Saturday." This poem enabled me to enter a literary contest sponsored by the newspaper of the company where I was working. I won first place in the contest, and the prize was symbolic — it was a pen. For me, however, this contest inspired me to be brave and to enter the Afro-Brazilian literary world. After I discovered that there were other blacks who were writing, that encouraged me even more.

Did your childhood influence your literary creation?

Yes. It was hard, but relatively normal. Among other things, I played on the seesaw a lot, and I enjoyed other pastimes from those days. In the story "Guarde Segredo," [Keep It Quiet], I recreated this intimacy. This text contains ingredients from my childhood. I had the notion of changing the end of the novel *Clara dos Anjos* by Lima Barreto. The story "Guarde Segredo" arose from this dialogue. In the original ending, the principal character, Clara dos Anjos, was abandoned by a young man, Cassi Jones, who seduced her and made her lose her virginity, which was one of the taboos in those times, because women who lost their virginity without being married were destined to be disgraced for the rest of their lives, and that's what happened in Lima Barreto's novel. I changed the ending so that a person whose identity isn't revealed to the reader kills Cassi Jones for having taken her virginity and for casting her out of his life. At the end of my text, the writer Barreto appears in order to celebrate the event, as if he had also wanted this kind of outcome for the famous seducer. I think that my childhood was strongly present in this work. It's also present in the story "A Vinganca de Dona Leia" [Dona Leia's Revenge], where the children of a household servant put vegetables and fruit on the ground at a market. This story draws strongly upon the phase in my childhood where, in order to survive, I was displaying leftover items on the ground at a market close to my home.

Do you think that traveling has any impact upon your creative efforts?

Undoubtedly. There are two types of trips. The first type consists of those where we choose a place to go and where we use the most varied types of transportation for doing it. This undoubtedly brings incomparable rewards, because we learn about places, customs, cultures and people that are so different from our own existence, and, certainly, this is a life experience that we should never be deprived of. Now, there's also the traveling that we do through reading, and perhaps these are the most rewarding trips that a person can take, because they help us to think and to situate our ideas more effectively. A person who reads is many kilometers ahead of other people. A person who reads has a different stance in life. Especially for those of us who are black writers — we need to know our history. Someone who doesn't know his or her own origin is ignorant; someone who doesn't know his or her origin will be deceived by false experts, because sometimes lies are told, and a person can end up believing them. For us, literature enables us to go on maturing as creators. Through our creation, we can include factual elements in our work that refer to mythology, to our origins and to our knowledge. Lastly, travel of both kinds is good, whether it's physical travel or traveling through books. It's excellent when people manage to take both kinds of trips.

Do politics occupy an important role in your life?

Yes, living is a political act. Becoming involved in efforts that guide people toward thinking is a political act. Having an awareness that I'm a person of African descent is a political stance. The decision to have a companion and for a child to be born from my own body is a political act. In terms of party politics, this is somewhat of a challenge in Brazil today, because blacks aren't perceived as people who are capable of contributing to creation of a new nation. For non-blacks, we're just a basis for maneuvering, because, during campaigns, there are speeches on behalf of full citizenship for the Afro-Brazilian community, but, in practical terms, the speakers' actions don't take us into account. So-and-so has a position here, or he receives an adviser's status there, or a coordinating job somewhere else, and there's an impression that issues involving the black population have already been adequately taken into account. The openings are deceptive, and unprepared militants ultimately lack sufficient stability for intelligently combating racism, which is subliminal. I think that militant Afro-Brazilians are also responsible for this chaos, on account of the absence of a black political plan that's capable of deciding upon the number of black politicians that we're going to elect over the long run. Our lack of a political plan and the lack of effective participation in Brazilian politics mean that we accept low-profile positions in municipal, state or federal governments. We satisfy ourselves with crumbs, and we start hunting and pecking when they put some corn in front of us. We destroy one another for crumbs. We don't have a concept of our numbers and our political strength. Having hope is what can make us live and exist as political beings.

Esmeralda Ribeiro

What does being a black woman in Brazil mean for you?

Metaphorically, it means having to kill two lions every day. One because of being black, and the other because of being a black woman. It means using *capoeira* movements so that we don't trip over something. Racism in Brazil is perverse. There are racists disguised as kind people, but, in the end, they're cruel. Their cruelty means that they don't think about professionalism or about a person's character. When they're in power, they have the first and last words. There isn't any dialogue, and there aren't any solutions, and, yes, they do try to burn us alive in the town square. In terms of jobs, people treat us as if we were on the fringes. It's as if we had committed an extremely serious offense, or perhaps our skin color is the offense. For those who most closely resemble Hitler or the Brazilian Ku Klux Klan, power is a potent and lethal weapon that will strike us one way or the other. They want to see us burning or driven through the streets as beggars. From the runway at a show to the gutters of filthy city streets. In my daily life, I try to exercise my right to have a voice and, especially, to have my body respected. Through my literary creation, I'm offering indirect criticism of race relations in Brazil and of relations between men and women. Feminism in Brazil is a struggle where white women go out to fight for their rights while black women stay in the kitchen as household servants. Are we together in this process of demanding our rights, or aren't we? As I go on thinking about these contradictions, I write essays and stories. This is a concern that every woman, black or non-black, should have, and, above all, those of us who are writers.

Is the situation different for men and women writers in Brazil?

A black woman writer in Brazil... It's also a challenge, because there are black female writers who came before me, and it's important for me to know that I'm contributing something, too, that I'm not just following their footsteps… I want to pass on my way of seeing the world and the outlook of the black community in Brazil through my works, without following the same patterns. It's very difficult to find a publisher and a distributor. I belong to the *Quilombhoje* group that was created for solving this situation, instead of standing around weeping. It's even possible that, in the beginning, people were complaining, but, afterward, they took money from their own pockets and they expressed their complaint, and they displayed our creations, and they showed the advances that had occurred. You have to take risks. That's true for any writer in Brazil. It's extremely common for prestigious publishing companies to earn a lot from authors and to produce awful results. A writer needs to distribute, to announce new publications, to buy things and to receive help, but a writer needs this status in order to gain legitimacy as a writer. Very often, no one knows that there's a lot of sacrifice behind this status, or this legitimacy. Prestigious publishing companies chase after certain big names that even receive advances, and the other writers are just the others. In *Quilombhoje*, the costs of publishing are being shared with other writers. Until this road opened, a person had to eat a lot of grass before being successful.

What is the role of the family in your work?

The family is the family, and relatives are serpents, but I also think that they can help, of course. I need a bit of support, because I have a young child. If my sister or my niece isn't there to help me, I have a friend and I always have some support, without which my literary growth would have suffered. So, there are these "invisible" people behind my work, who provide this strength that I need. The concept of family for blacks is very different, but it's important, because it's the foundation, the root. Traditionally, in black families, women have more authority. My adoptive mother was very strong, and she brought me up with that perspective. Because she was adoptive, I could have rebelled against the family, but, in contrast, I managed to forgive my siblings over time. The land is there, and they died. They didn't benefit from it. I had a lot of luck, but I also knew how to change my destiny. I could have been a girl on the streets, I could have been lost and crazy, but I suddenly found another destiny.

Does mysticism play an important part in your life?

It's very important. I believe in *Candomblé*. People have to keep these roots. Brazil is a mixture, and its people are a little bit of everything. *Candomblé* is also a mixture made up of everything. It's not just going to ceremonies, it's also knowing history and practicing it for years and years. Therefore, I can say that I'm just a novice in *Candomblé*. Now that I'm an adult, I've chosen this religion. I'm a daughter of *Oxum*.

Whom do you write for?

Usually, I have a reader out there that I've chosen — a male or a female reader. As soon as I start writing, I become woven into my characters: I'm a character and a narrator. Each character contains a little bit of me and a little bit of someone else. Each one has a male side and a female side. It is created within its own wholeness.

What are your reflections on globalization?

It's a phenomenon that hasn't affected me yet. It's a very slow process. People here in Brazil belong to a whole, but, at the same time, they're somewhat excluded from the whole. It's logical for globalization to have advantages and disadvantages.

We can look at the economic conditions that are affecting us. Today, a hundred *reais* is a lot of money, and tomorrow it's nothing. Imagine how there are people in Brazil who earn 160 *reais* per month... So, globalization is affecting us, but it's going to be something worse in the future. It's either going to be worse, or it will get better. Culturally, however, I think that global exchanging of ideas and styles is very good. Today in São Paulo, which has always been multicultural and cosmopolitan, there are people who do rap with our texts. Disseminating our poetry. I think that's good. Suddenly, people on the periphery, who are people with little access to culture, are paying us back, by commenting upon our work.

In Search of a Black Butterfly

One night, while working at the Humanitarian Center, I went to answer a call. When the phone lines got crossed, I heard the strangest conversation, full of intimate details and emotions, and my life was forever changed.

That night I was the only phone operator on duty. Both the night and the city were asleep. I leafed through a magazine. It was March, only an hour away from the 8th. I should explain that because of the nature of my work, I often heard other peoples' conversations. In my profession, one has to maintain a certain distance from the lives of others. I would never tell this story if it were not such an important one. It would be best for you to call me by my professional name: Operator. But nobody from the Humanitarian Center should know that I have told this story.

That night, somebody called the Center and hung up on me. When I tried to free the line, I heard a woman's voice.

—Please find my black butterfly.

—What? What do you mean Leila?

—I don't know where it went, Baby.

—Leila, it's 11 o'clock at night. I was about to take a bath and wait for Tiago. He is coming back from a trip tonight. Can we talk about your problem tomorrow?

—No. Tomorrow might be too late. I know Tiago. Tell

him that I need your help. He'll understand.

—Leila, how could a black butterfly fly out of your uterus? That is crazy! Am I hearing you wrong? Just wait a minute. I'll turn off the shower.

So I'm thinking… what an absurd story. Leila has called Baby to tell her about a black butterfly that flew out of her uterus…

—Okay, I'm back Leila, you can talk.

—You are my only friend, Baby.

—A friend? I have never really known that much about your life.

—I hope you are ready to listen, Baby. When I went to the doctor to get the results of my pregnancy test, Dr… discovered that I had a black butterfly inside of me. I never told anyone about it, even though I was very happy. It would be a beautiful butterfly, just like the children were.

—Leila, I never wanted kids because it is such a big responsibility. Didn't the butterfly make you uncomfortable?

—Not at all, Baby, I felt as light as a plastic bubble. At moments I had the strong urge to aimlessly walk and walk.

—Leila, I almost forgot to ask you: Can't your hubby, Robert, help you with this?

—Baby, I didn't tell you because it didn't matter. Robert drank himself to death. I didn't even go to the looser's funeral. When we lived together we hardly went out to socialize, and he was too drunk to be any good in bed. But… at least he left me with his pension and this house, where I live with my three kids. But let's not talk any more about him.

—Leila, what about your relatives?

—They hate me. I had lovers even before he died. My relatives were disgusted. Especially when I started going out all the time with that French soldier, Jean. It was tough because, as you remember, he is white and it was very difficult at the beginning of our relationship. We wouldn't hold hands on the street because we were afraid that people would look at us… I wasn't sure what to do with my hair, how to dress. I was also afraid that he was with me because he believed the stereotype that black women are good in bed. On top of everything else, my parents accused me of betraying the family. Even though we still live in different worlds, Jean and I are learning how to deal with it.

—And what about your own family?

—Baby, I don't want anything to do with those people. I try not to bring Jean or other guys over to the house because the neighbors gossip about me. The other day, Marlene, my neighbor, told me that my kids want a different mother. One time some other people from the neighborhood turned me in to the police. I was called in and the judge told me that if there was another complaint, my kids would be taken by the state. Sometimes, when we can't be together, Jean and I have phone sex.

—Leila, how can I help you when you don't even remember where you were?

—On Tuesday I went to a few different places. I spent most of my time at an amusement park, seven blocks away from my street. I went with Jean. I was wearing blue jeans, a red shirt and red sandals with high heels. I was also carrying a red purse, and had a scarf tied around my braids, which was also red. Baby, when we got to the park, I took off my sandals because of the cobblestone. The man turned on the Ferris wheel just for us. We kept going round and round. It was so wonderful. Jean's hand between my legs made my body flutter. I fondled his penis which was hard under his pants. While our bodies were suspended in the air, our tongues entwined our desire. He kept rubbing his hand against my...

...I better get a coffee because this conversation is going to last a while, I said to myself.

—Leila, nobody saw you, right? Not even the guy from

the Ferris wheel?

—No, he was too old. He was having fun watching the birds and the butterflies land on the cobblestones. Besides, who goes to the amusement park on a Monday afternoon. So we began to...

—Leila, you don't have to tell me all the details. Just tell me how the butterfly got out of your uterus?

—It was wonderful... But on one of the passes of the Ferris wheel I saw a boy down below staring at me and shaking his head. Then... I recognized him. He was the son of my worst neighbor. He always reported on everything that he saw back at home. He was his father's dog. Baby, I was so desperate. I told Jean to get me out of there. If my neighbors saw what was going on I would loose my kids. I was so scared! How could I explain all this to Jean. I yelled for the old man to stop that thing. I kept getting more and more desperate as the wheel kept spinning. My head was also spinning and spinning. I closed my eyes. When I opened my eyes, the park was filled with my neighbors. The old man stopped the Ferris wheel and before my feet had even reached the ground I was under attack. They called me a bitch, a whore, a tramp, and yelled: "your kids will go to the state." Baby, they pulled off my clothes and I was naked, naked. The faster Jean and I ran, the more stones they threw at our backs and heads. Jean tried to protect me but it was no use. We tried to get inside bars, but when the owners heard the yelling, they kicked us out. When we got to my street, Jean tried heroically to draw off the crowd, standing alone with his torn clothes while they pelted him with stones. That is when I was able to get away. Baby, I was rushed to a hospital because bloody lumps were running down my legs. When I woke up, the doctor told me I had a miscarriage. He couldn't tell me where my black butterfly had gone. Later, Jean told me, crying into the phone, that the police had saved him from lynching. Baby, I have locked myself up in the house with my kids.

… I think I read about something like this in the newspaper and if I'm not mistaken it happened in Somalia, I said to myself.

—Leila, despite everything that you have told me, how can I go out looking for a black butterfly. Why don't you ask one of your old boyfriends to help you?

—I'm sorry, Baby, but there is no man in the world who would go looking for a black butterfly that had flown out of a woman's uterus and not talk about it later. You know perfectly well that although they say they don't gossip, when they talk among themselves they live to slander us. Do you know why I was almost lynched? Because I always refused the invitations of the neighbor who wanted to screw me, the father of the boy from the amusement park. One day, when we were waiting for the bus and talking about all sorts of things, I made the mistake of telling him that I liked a French soldier. So then he asked me why some women liked to sleep with foreigners. It was so long ago! I just remember that I answered: It doesn't matter. Maybe because they are really different. After that, the entire neighborhood knew about our conversation. I kept going around saying that he would get me one day. Baby, I would be afraid to ask Jean to do such a favor.

—Leila, hold on a minute, let me turn off my radio alarm. It must be broken because it only goes off with music.

"…Passion/Pure enthusiasm/Mystic clan of mermaids/Sand castle/Sharks rage/Illusion…"

… it was good to hear that music I have been trying to get back the Djavan record that I lent to Chris for a while but so far nothing and when she asks me for a favor I always do it. I never say no, I thought.

—Baby, you took so long. Was that song they were playing *Açaí*? I had that record at home but it disappeared.

—Leila, it took me a while because a butterfly flew in

through the window. So how do you feel now that you are not carrying around that butterfly inside of you?

—I feel heavy. I sit around and stare off into space. It's as though the neighbors are watching me through the window and I'm some rare specimen in an aquarium.

—Leila, somebody is at the door. It must be Tiago.

—Baby, answer me, please.

—Leila, wait a minute, I will be right back.

—Listen, we talked about so many things, I almost forgot to describe my butterfly to you. She has bigger wings that the others of her species. During the day she is restless and constantly flaps her wings. I know all this because I felt her moving in my womb. You'll see, she's a big black butterfly. If you find her, bring her home to me. I'll give you the address again…

… why the hell did I write down the address this is none of my business, I thought.

—Baby, are you listening to me?

Then I thought… why doesn't Leila hang up the phone on that rude friend of hers if Baby wanted to help she would have put on a coat and gone right to the amusement-park man I'm cold I'm going to put on my jacket…

—Please, find the butterfl…

So then, Tinair, I got disconnected. I only told you this story because, ever since that day, I can't get much sleep. That conversation mixed me up, I guess. I work at night at the Humanitarian Center, and in the mornings, I go to the amusement park. I go there every day. I sit and watch all the butterfly girls sleeping on the cobblestones. I wonder: what will happen to all of them when they become women?

— translated by Elzbieta Szoka
with Shanna Lorenz

Miriam Alves

Miriam Alves

Miriam Alves was born in São Paulo where she lives and works. She is a social worker, a scholar of Afro-Brazilian literature, and activist in the Quilombroje movement, a poet and short story writer. She has spoken at various international conferences in Austria, the United States and Brazil. She is an author of two collections of poems *Momentos de busca* (1983); *Estrelas no dedo* (1985) and co-author of a play *Terramara*. Her work also appeared in the following anthologies: various issues of *Cadernos Negros*; *A razão da chama — antologia de poetas negros brasileiros* (1986); *Schwartze Poesie — Poesia Negra* (1988); *Poesia negra brasileira* (1992); *Schwartze Prose — Prosa negra* (1993); *Pau de sebo — coletânea de poesia negra* (1988); *Zauber gegen die kalte* (1994); *Moving Beyond Boundries. International Dimension of Black Women's Writing* (1995); *Finally Us. Contemporary Black Brazilian Women's Writing* (1995); *Callaloo*, vol.18, number 4(1995).

Miriam Alves

What led you to become a writer?

I really can't say very well. I only know that I wrote, was always writing. I wrote from the time when I was 10 years old. I had poetry notebooks that I organized. This childhood passion to write has never left me. As time went on, this love became even more pronounced, besides being a secret and clandestine pleasure when at age 20 I encountered the people of the *Cadernos Negros* (*Black Notebooks*). I am 48 years old. When I was in college there were about fifteen black women who were always together; they left school together and sometimes we made weekend plans, but it was always a question of identity: To be together.

One day, one of them received an invitation to a gathering to mark the publication of a book by Cuti, one of the black writers who was known more here than abroad. I had never seen so many blacks together as at that gathering; and it wasn't a samba party. There were more than 150 blacks and that for me was such a great pleasure that it left me totally astounded. They did something called Poetry Round Table. They played drums and recited their poems. I went home full of emotion. I purchased Cuti's book and read it all night. By early morning I wanted to kill Cuti. The poet agitated me, he outraged me, he made me happy, he stirred all of the passionate emotions that were inside me.

At the time I was giving classes in college and I was suffering from all of the standard academic prejudices. One of the instructors, who was helping me because she thought I was an intelligent young woman, said, "Miriam, you are not going to move ahead because you are too suspicious of people." I discovered that I was "too suspicious of people" because I was black and was incapable of handling the pressure of university life. It was a horrible moment in my life. My mother had died and I had broken up with my fiancé, and left the place where I most wanted to be: the classroom. Before I gave classes and now I give talks. I sought out a psychiatrist and at these therapy sessions I was silent for a month; the only thing I did was cry. One day I said to the psychiatist, "Look, Doctor, this happened to me because I am black." And he said, "Now you look, I am not a sociologist. If you want to talk about being black, then go see a sociologist. We are here to discuss personality." I told him to go to hell. It was the most important thing that I did in my month of therapy.

I told myself at that time that there was only one thing that had been steady throughout my entire life and that was my poetry. After that, I got my act together and in 1983 I published my first book. And I entered what I had already done in *Caderno Negro 5* in the *Quilomhoje*. The other member-writers of the *Quilomhoje* accepted me and I was able to express my vision of the world from my place in life and where I currently was.

What was your childhood like and in what way did it influence your work?

I am the daughter of a maid and a tailor. My childhood was a normal one for a little black girl at the time. I was born in São Paulo in the district called *Casa Verde*. It was a district that was fairly new and was a blend of both rural and urban. Where I lived there were *chácaras* [houses with gardens or orchards or poultry] that were mixed in with standard housing. I lived in one of those *chácaras* that had a backyard filled with trees and dense shrubbery. At the time, my parents had bought a small stand at the market where they sold fruit; this was a time of wealth for my family.

My parents were very important to me, and my book *Momentos de busca* [*Times of Search*] is dedicated to both of them. My mother had a first-grade education and today would be called "semi-literate." She was a maid and had begun to work at nine years of age and married when she was 26. The families for whom she worked had libraries, and that is where my mother spent most of her time. The library was always the cleanest place in the house because the vacuum cleaner never stopped running there. With her eyes glued to a book, she would run the vacuum cleaner with one hand and hold the book in the other. The stories that my mother read during her work were told to me and to my siblings, and that was our entertainment. All of the stories that she told us were classics of Brazilian literature: *A Moreninha* [*The Little Brunette*], *O Cortiço* [*The Slum*], *Iracema*. Our mother empowered us with a culture that would become part of our bloodstream, but at the same time because of socio-economic reasons that culture would be out of our reach.

After my mother died at 53, I found among her possessions a little book of poems that she had written. My father discovered that I had inherited my mother's calling. I believed that this was not exactly so. These things are not transmitted by blood; they are transmitted by love. As far as my father is concerned, he is the intellectual of the family. At the time, he had completed the second year of accounting school. My education was important: my mother had the books and my father gave them to me. He gave a doll to my sister, a ball to my brother and a book to me. One day I asked him why he did this and he answered, "Parents know their children." Even today, my sister is a great homemaker. And my brother was the athlete. And since childhood I have been an avid reader. It was a kind of joke to say that in my house the books were always kept in strongboxes as if they were jewels.

Do you enjoy travel? Does travel inspire you?

Travel? What an interesting question. No one ever asks me that question. I love to travel. I always say that I am a ship on a long voyage but I have to stop at a port. I enjoy traveling, but I also enjoy returning to my little corner, to my aromas, to my little dog, to my daughter, to my books. In order for me to be talking in Brazil today, I first had to go abroad. I spent five years traveling abroad. An absurdity. I met my fellow writers in Madison and Miami. I discovered that my country is the most beautiful thing in the world. I would like to travel to all of the parts of Brazil because it is there that my Afro-Brazilian culture has had such an influence. On behalf of *Quilomhoje* and the *Cadernos Negros*, I have traveled a great deal into the interior of São Paulo state and some other Brazilian states. We would carry sixty books on our shoulders and go there for a poetry round table and little lectures. I attended *Congadas* [a kind of song and dance festival reminiscent of the crowning of a king in the Congo] that left me full of emotion in seeing grandparents, parents and children participating; four generations of black people living their culture. I wrote many poems that were inspired by these emotional travel-related experiences. Yes, indeed, I do like to travel.

Do politics play any role in your life?

A political affiliation or relationship is very complicated for me. I am a writer. Politics is very important, but the political partisan is a bird of another feather. On the other hand, the black movement itself, which I joined in 1978, did not feel that poetry was important. My colleagues linked African poetry to the time of independence movement of the African nations and did not connect to the people who are writing here. I never joined any political party. My sympathies lie with the PMDB, the PT and the PCB, but I have a critical attitude when they throw everything into one social bag.

And that social question does not touch upon color and does not touch upon history. The *favela* [a shanty] is about blacks. Oh, yes, there are also whites in the *favelas*, but if there are whites, they are also in a lower percentage. Oh, naturally, the universities have blacks, sure; one black out of 100 whites. I would support the party that shares the viewpoint of the heirs of slavery and slavery-related capitalism, the heirs of the garbage dump; yes, that's who we are. Capitalism is the child of slavery. The blacks were used as part of a system, and later when that system no longer served a purpose, they were tossed out. That is why I haven't any political affiliations and I believe that I never will.

What does it mean for you to be a woman in Brazil?

To be black woman in Brazil is complicated. Black women and white women in Brazil have different lives. When white women talk about independence, they talk about leaving the home to go to work, whereas the black woman has been working for many, many years. After slavery was abolished, there was no employment for black men. The black woman went to work and continued working in the home of the white. For the black woman independence would be *not* to work, unless you mean to work in her very own home.

When feminist ideas arrived in Brazil in the 19th century, we were in the throes of slavery. Which women were talking? White women were doing the talking. The black person did not have any categories: man, woman, child. The black person was just that — black. The women were the "mammies"; the children were the "pickaninnies." It is still like this today: if you're white, then the term is child; if you're black, then the term is nothing.

Miriam Alves

What is the status of the female writer in Brazil?

Once again, let's talk about the black female writer in Brazil. One day a female researcher came to my house and she was absolutely flabbergasted. She was imagining a female writer with an office saying, "Please wait there; I must finish my thoughts." In my house there was everything everywhere — the telephone ringing, my daughter arguing, the dog barking, my neighbor visiting, me cooking dinner — while I am trying to work. Well, as you can see, my house is full of chores, but it is not only that. For me, it is also a place for thought and reflection, and joyous pleasure. If it weren't, I couldn't write. I have a commitment to myself regarding my sensibilities. I am a harp with well-stretched strings, and when the call comes, I play. My antennae are out to the world. If the world is disturbed, so am I. If the world is at peace, so am I.

What role does mysticism play in your life?

A very important one. Mysticism is present in my life. My paternal grandmother was a card reader. My mother was a devout Catholic and by being married to my father, she was influenced by my grandmother. After my grandmother died, my family lost their market, and almost lost the house. My parents had a friend who came from [the state of] Minas Gerais and had immigration problems. Well, my parents helped him as much as were able. One day, my mother became very ill. A friend from Minas Gerais came to visit and said he was in *Umbanda*, and that he had fled Minas Gerais because he didn't want to practice it there. He said had dreamt about working with my mother. She didn't believe him in the beginning, but he did some *Umbanda* rituals and my mother got well and began to pay frequent visits to his *terreiro* [a place of celebration]. I was 15 years old at the time, and lived with that division in my family. In school I learned that *Umbanda* and

Candomblé were religions of ignorant people; mystics, idiots. Anyway, I went to the *terreiro* with my mother, but I quarreled with myself: this was a religion of the ignorance, the religion of blacks. I read a great deal about the religion, despite this division that was imposed by Brazilian culture which my mystical side refused to allow me to set aside. It was a path, a road, a route. Now I am a priestess, and I have my own *terreiro*.

For whom do you write? Have you an imaginary reader?

That all depends. When I write a poem it is because I am filled with passion, with love, or because I am angry, or because I am distressed, or because I am happy. I go through several kinds of emotions and I talk to those emotions, which are not only mine. They pass through me, but are not mine alone. When I am writing, I want to open myself to learn about what you are. And when you read what I have written, you are opening yourself to knowing what I am. The song also passes through all of these emotions, but they are emotions that I am developing with the intent of transmitting various things. And like a recipe for making a cake, emotions are the ingredients, and the type of cake is the intent. When the cake is ready, I cut it and give it to people. Sometimes it's good, and sometimes it's not. Sometimes my inspiration is taken from the recipes of others.

What are your feelings about globalization?

Globalization is a process that concentrates all of the benefits into a few hands and the garbage gets thrown in the neigbor's backyard. And that neighbor is always Africa and Latin America. Well, I'm happy with my last-generation computer, and I'm communicating with everyone, and over there in Timor they are cutting off the arms of people in the public square. And in the countries of Africa there are children dying from hunger in the arms of their mothers, and everyone can see this on television as if it were some big show. The problem is that it's not happening on television, but in reality. Yes, it's all very good to be able to share knowledge and human progress, but will the garbage continue to be thrown in my neighborhood?

Alice Is Dead

I was walking down the hill. Alice kept mumbling in my arms. She was so light, she seemed like a child compared to my huge self. I had carried her home like this other times, but this morning she was very light. It was like she could evaporate at any moment.

She kept saying incoherent, incomprehensible sentences, between which she would repeat the refrain: "No more. No more." Like a broken record: "No more. No more."

I was very patient with Alice. I wasn't madly in love with her, but I couldn't live without her company. We lived in the same project. She invariably needed my help to carry her home. She wasn't handicapped, but she kept getting high on hope which would leave her confused once the drunken stupor was gone. It was funny to watch her walk around like that, tripping over herself outside the project.

I would always watch her before offering to help. Tripping over herself she smoked big ritual cigarettes that permeated everything with a strange, nauseating smell. She kept walking back and forth outside the project. I just kept watching her. It was a ritual of dependency. At a certain point she would slip and fall. Face down, she would give off a weird odor, a mixture of trodden hopes and disillusioned beliefs. That was when it would be my turn to step into the picture. I would hold her gently. I would sing her to sleep, as if she were a black doll made of cloth. I would open the door to her tiny, lonely apartment. I would give her the most tender bath and I would put her to bed. I would wait until she'd fallen asleep and leave quietly. We repeated this ritual of dependency over and over.

One day, Alice and I decided to share an apartment in order to economize. It was pretty weird. I had been separated for years, with a wife and kids all spread out all over God's planet. I treated Alice as a friend. I needed to give someone all of the love and affection that I had stored up. Alice was a perfect partner. She didn't expect anything. However, sharing the same space made life a bit monotonous.

I would observe Alice. Alice would observe me. Once in a blue moon we would sleep together. We were very polite with each other. We needed this routine of dependency. Every now and then a new Alice would pop up. That's when she would get drunk with hope, smoking those strange ritual cigarettes. Once she was over her stupor she would caress me. I would caress her, too, and we'd end up having athletic sex that would make the porn stars in the motel videos jealous. We would do crazy stuff that our senses told us to do. The day after, it was monotony again. It seemed like nothing had ever happened. I'd go to work. She'd go to work. That's all.

Some unnamed thing began to grow between us that sometimes seemed like jealousy. At other times it seemed like fear. Everyday routine, nothing new. Except that the odor of trodden hopes, a mixture of disillusioned beliefs, impregnated our pores and the bricks of the house. And so did the tears. They came out of the faucet and gave birth to red fungi in the kitchen and bathroom sinks. In the beginning the fungi irritated me, but then I came to think that they were responsible for exacerbating the odor. I didn't remove them because I needed somebody or something to blame. As time went by and the odor became stronger, things became more and more strange. The bedroom and kitchen turned red.

One day, to break the routine, we accepted an invitation to a party. We rarely went out, but this time we felt like it.

Alice actually sang in the shower. I went all out, shaving and putting on cologne. Our mutual friends were celebrating their anniversary. We went. We smiled. We danced. And then, in the early hours of the morning, Alice's look told me that she wanted to begin the routine that we had never performed in public. She stared with such intensity that her eyes were about to pop out of their sockets. She opened her mouth wide. She tripped. I went ahead to catch her. I didn't want trouble.

First, I held her in my arms. She mischievously slapped me and slipped away from my embrace. I got annoyed. I could see a scandal coming. I talked to her gently yet firmly. She looked at me with empty eyes. She wanted to go home. She offered me her arms. I put her on my lap. Alice was mumbling in my arms. She was light as a baby. I looked at her face, which was now mixed with the moonlit darkness of the night. She mumbled disconnectedly. She wanted her ritual cigarettes so she could cling to smoky hopes. It seemed that she was going to float away like smoke at any moment.

We were going down the hill toward our shelter. The lines of neon street lights witnessed our dual procession. Alice kept mumbling and weeping. She wanted a life. Did she actually know what it meant? Empty asphalt at dawn. Her mumbling rose to the heavens and echoed against the nothingness. I carried her home, thinking about us.

Living together without much excitement. Me and her in a project, being there for each other. My kids spread out all over the planet. No news from them. Work. Night. Day. Sex. A little bit of crying every now and then. I hated Alice. I blamed her. Reality was unbearable. I looked at the empty street. Thoughts fluttering in my mind. Alice fluttered in my arms. Suddenly I understood: I loved Alice. I loved her. Monotony and the every day. I loved her. I was always close. I strained my memory. I relived her gracious way of taking off her rings. All three of them. One at a time. A ritual she always repeated before we took our pleasure. She'd take them off one by one, putting them at the head of the bed. She had a unique charm. I loved her when I saw that gesture. Whenever boredom and apathy would take charge of our lives, I'd expect that gesture: rings coming off, one by one. A ritual of every day, a sensual one. So sensual that one day, without even touching her, I asked her to take them off and put them back on, over and over again. Alice, who was tired, and not very enthusiastic, began to laugh. Laughing, her bright teeth illuminated her round face. She laughed and laughed. I didn't have to touch her to enjoy it.

Now she was light, like a baby in my arms. She didn't wear those beloved rings. I hated her for it. I was walking down the hill with Alice mumbling in my arms. The empty morning was breaking. Close to home I remembered the place by the river at the bottom of the cliff that was used as a trash dump, where the police got rid of bodies. I went over to the edge of the cliff. It was amazing to see. Alice moved in my arms. I looked at all the waste at the bottom of the cliff. What a dump! Alice mumbled and sobbed. She wanted hope. Our hopes should have been buried a long time ago under that pile of trash. I had nothing to give her.

She began to punch me. She wanted her happiness back. She scratched my face right where my beard would have been. It hurt. It hurt even more that I didn't have what she was asking for. There was nothing even for me. The well was dry. There was enough to keep waking up, sleeping, working and drinking beer on payday. I fought the tears. Hate sprang up. Our hopes buried under a pile of urban waste. I watched the dawn. A new day was coming. Alice was screaming. I sobbed with her. I lifted her to the sky. And then towards the dead-end street. I offered her to Exu, the mysterious trickster of our faith. I shook her to the right and to the left. I greeted Omulu so that he wouldn't curse me with any disease for what I was about to do. In-between sobs, I threw her into the abyss at the bottom of the cliff. It was Monday. She was quiet. The end.

— translated by Elzbieta Szoka
with Shanna Lorenz

Conceição Evaristo

Conceição Evaristo

Conceição Evaristo was born in Belo Horizante in the state of Minas Gerais. She is a professor of Brazilian literature at the Catholic University in Rio de Janeiro (PUC/RJ) and is working on her doctorate in comparative literature. Her work deals with the social factors influencing the family, including the power that women exert in their role as mothers and the consequences of society's failure to provide adequately for its youth. Her work has been published in the following anthologies: various issues of *Cadernos Negros*; *Vozes de Mulheres* (1991); *Schwartze Prose: prosa negra-Afrobrasilianische Erzählungen der Gergenwart* (1993); *Moving Beyond Boundries. International Dimension of Black Women Writing* (1995); *Finally Us. Contemporary Black Brazilian Women Writers* (1995); *Callaloo*, vol. 18 number 4 (1995).

How did you become a writer?

I've been writing since my childhood. I'm from a generation that didn't have a lot of contact with television. I read a lot, and I spent my adolescence reading and writing, too. For me, writing is a form of liberation, a way of creating order for myself and creating disorder. I've always liked to say that, if I could have danced or sung, I wouldn't have started writing.

How did situations and surroundings in your childhood influence your work?

My childhood was very significant. For me, writing was a need for creating order in a very poor, very impoverished childhood. Truly impoverished. I'm from Belo Horizonte. I was born in a large slum in Belo Horizonte, and I grew up in it. I grew up listening to my family telling stories about slavery. All of this oral communication that I received had to spill out in some way, and it began coming out in what I wrote. My writing has a lot to do with my position in Brazilian society, with my position as a woman, as a black person and as a poor person. My writing depends strongly upon me as an individual to a great extent, but it also depends a lot upon my history and upon the history of my community.

Is travel important for you? Does it give you inspiration?

Yes, it does. In order to be able to write, I have a strong
need to examine life, people, and situations. I need to filter all
of these elements, and to be truly attuned. Music also inspires
me a lot, it creates that "immersion"... All of this is material
that I accumulate from day to day. There are specific situations
that I have to write about, because, if I don't write, I'll explode.
I joke around a lot with Miriam Alves from São Paulo, and I'll
say: "Miriam, it's still good that people are writing. Because it's
very hard to keep it entirely to yourself."

In terms of travel in the geographic sense, I went on a trip
that influenced me strongly and that I still haven't written about.
This was a trip to Vienna, where I attended a seminar. It may
be something rather insignificant for other people, but for me,
as someone from a tropical country, seeing snow close up, seeing
people and their differences, seeing windows closed on account
of the cold... Here, the windows are open, and you'll run into
people in the middle of the street. One day in Vienna, we went
out for a walk, and, for two hours, we didn't see anyone on the
street. I've preserved this image in my mind. It was also on this
trip that I was able to figure out Christmas cards. Here in Brazil,
people have difficulty understanding Christmas cards that have
that tree and those hovering birds. I needed to go to Europe to
understand.

What role does politics play in your life?

I believe in the kind of politics that you acquire from your
position, on the basis of your condition as a citizen. I believe
in the role that a person can have in a community. I work with
Afro-Brazilian literature, and I've given a course for teachers.
In my position, I'm capable of having a specific role. My great
dream is to be able to give my texts back to the people who
gave me their life stories. It would be difficult for that to happen

because you're writing in a country were the vast majority is illiterate. In a country like Brazil, I believe that I have a social obligation to return to my origins. I believe in this type of politics, and I think that people need to believe in it.

What does it mean for you to be a woman in Brazil?

I would add to this question "What does it mean to be a black woman who is poor?" "Being a woman in Brazil," — you'd have to think about more than the gender category. You need to think, "What is it that distinguishes certain women?" Beyond the issue of gender it's necessary to analyze what types of encounters these women need to have. For me, being a woman in Brazil today is a bit of being what the women before me were, my great-grandmother, my grandmother, and my mother. It still means being a woman in a male-dominated society, where values are white, or a society where specific social groups and ethnic groups must face problems that other groups don't face. In order to answer your question, a person needs to think about, "What does it mean to be a wealthy woman in Brazil?" "What does it mean to be a poor woman in Brazil?" "What does it mean to be a black woman? Or an Indian woman?" There are still all of these issues. It's necessary not to limit ourselves just to the gender issue.

Does the female writer in Brazil have the same opportunities and the same credibility as the male writer?

They have them and, at the same time, they don't have them. If I'm a female writer or a male writer who has specific social and financial conditions, if I have the media being favorable to me, I have a much greater chance of acceptance than a female or male writer from a particular social level. For those of us who are black female writers, it's much more difficult to break out of a given circle. Brazilian society creates specific roles for women and it creates specific roles for black women. It isn't very common for a black woman to be understood as a writer. It doesn't even enter many people's heads to believe it, or to create pathways for publications of our books.

As a writer are you influenced by other work you do? Your academic work, for example....

It's a two-way street. What I write may influence the academic world. People are experiencing a new era in Brazilian literature. The presence of Afro-Braziliam women writers at the conference in Belo Horizonte was very important because it provided a possibility to begin establishing a dialogue with the academic world. I also think that people will gain from the academic world by reading and discussing theory. I think that this will be a fruitful exchange. I also think that the academic world can gain a lot from our presence, if it's an academic environment that is truly thinking about plurality. I'd like very much for my texts to reach intellectuals and academic readers becauseI have a message for them as well. We bring a new message that other people aren't so familiar with, in spite of good intentions.

Is family important for you?

Very much so. As I said, when I write, I'm reconstructing stories that my family told me. This was a family where women had an extremely vital role. My mother practically raised her children alone. Women possess a far more active role than men. People retain their mother's image much more than their father's image. Many of the women in my family are unmarried women who have raised their children alone. My mother had nine children. She raised her first four daughters without a companion.

I didn't get married for a long time. I have a daughter, and I became a widow 11 years ago. I've ended up leading a life without depending on men. When my husband was alive, he was a man who was struggling and was poor. I struggled alongside him, but I didn't stop working because of the fact that I was married.

The family is extremely important for people because it leads people to develop relationships where one person supports another: mothers, fathers, siblings, aunts and uncles, neighbors... I came to Rio de Janeiro alone. My brothers and sisters are still in Belo Horizonte. It's not typical for someone from a poor family to leave alone and to live so far away. If a person leaves, he or she brings a brother afterwards, and then a cousin. I think that what I did is much more common for bourgeois families. The poorest families are still extremely close families.

What is your relationship with mysticism?

Mysticism is very important for me. However, it is not a contemplative relationship of a passive human being in the presence of a divinity. It is a dynamic relationship of complicity between the human and the *orixás* [Afro-Brazilian deities]. There's no way of denying it. As you know, officially, everyone in Brazil is Catholic. I was born in the Catholic religion, I was baptized in the Catholic religion and I was married in the Catholic religion. After having come to Rio de Janeiro, and discovering black culture, I've had an extremely close relationship with Afro-Brazilian religions. This is a relationship that I've developed according to my own identity. So, worshipping ancestos and believing in the *orixás* is a vital point for us. It's a way for us to affirm our otherness, including our religious otherness, and to have it validated.

Conceição Evaristo

What do you think about globalization?

I don't think that globalization is actually such a new thing. I think that these phenomena merely change names. Globalization represents new forms of imperialism. There was slavery, colonialism, neo-colonialism, post-colonialism, and now we talk about globalization. During all of these periods, some situations were very clearly defined: the haves and the have-nots; those who give orders and those who obey. The power of globalization now may be more dynamic and more severe than in the past. It may affect more people at the same time, but, in my opinion, there aren't many differences in terms of consequences. I think that certain countries and certain people, because they were victims of imperialism, are going to be victims of globalization. And in the same way that those people and those countries created alternative forms of struggle and defense, I also think that, today, the same peoples and countries will look for alternative forms of struggle and defense. It's possible that a significant effect won't occur, but I think that people are trying to break free and to respond.

Ana Davenga

The knocks on the door echoed like a forewarning of samba. It was almost midnight and Ana Davenga's worried heart was a bit more calm. Everything was peaceful now, or at least, relatively peaceful. She jumped out of bed and opened the door. They all came in, except for her man. The men came toward Ana Davenga. Hearing the noise, the women soon came to Anna's shack too. Suddenly the world fit into the tiny space. Ana Davenga recognized the pattern of knocks. She hadn't misheard the signal. Announcing a samba or a macumba ritual, the knocks confirmed that all was well. Things were as peaceful as could be expected. A different pattern of hurried knocks warned that some bad, harmful thing was in the air. The knocks that she heard earlier didn't foretell any disaster. But if this was true, why was her man not there among the others? Where was her man? Why wasn't Davenga back yet?

Davenga wasn't there. The men surrounded Ana carefully, as did the women. Care was needed. Davenga was good. He had God's heart, but when provoked, he turned into the Devil. They had learned to watch Ana Davenga. As they watched her they tried not to notice the life and pleasure that burst from her entire body.

Davenga's shack was the headquarters, and he the general. All the decisions were made there. At first Davenga's companions regarded Anna with jealousy, greed and suspicion.

273

The man had lived alone. It was there that he and the other men invented and plotted all of their schemes. And then all of a sudden, without consulting his mates, he brings home a woman. They thought about getting another boss and finding another place for the headquarters, but they didn't have the courage. After a while, Davenga told the men that the woman would be staying with him for good. She was blind, deaf and mute as far as his dealings were concerned. He had just one other thing to say: he would make sure that anyone who bothered her would bleed like a castrated hog. His friends understood. And when they caught glimpses of her apple-shaped breast and their desire grew, they felt a profound aching in their lower parts. And then the desire would fade, and with it the possibility for erection or pleasure. Ana became like a sister inhabiting the incestuous dreams of Davenga's partners in crime.

Ana Davenga's heart was sore from so much fear. Everybody was there, except for her man. The men stood around Anna. The women stood behind their men, as though they were pairing off to dance. Ana looked at each of them, but discovered no sadness there. What was going on? Were they hiding some deep pain, masking their suffering so that she would not suffer in turn? Was this one of Davenga's practical jokes? Was he hiding somewhere? No! He was not that kind of man! He did like to joke around, but only with his buddies. A kind of roughhousing. Punches, kicks, slaps, you sons of bitches, you…It looked more like fighting. Where was Davenga? Did he get mixed up in some sort of trouble? Her man was big, but he was like a child. He did things that she preferred not to think about. Sometimes he would spend days and days, even months, on the run, and when she would least expect it, she would find him at home. Yes, Davenga seemed to have the power to make himself invisible. She would go out for a bit, to retrieve the laundry hanging in the back or to talk with her girlfriends, and when she came back, she would find him lying in bed. Naked. He was so beautiful dressed only in the skin that God had given him. Black, firm, soft, shiny. She would push the door closed and open herself up to her man. Davenga, Davenga! And then something would happen that she didn't understand. Davenga, who was so big and so strong, and such a child, took his pleasure while washed in tears. He cried like a child, sobbed, leaving her wet all over. Her face and body were wet with Davenga's tears. Afterwards, still naked, they would lie together as she wiped his tears. There was such sweetness, such pleasure, such pain. One day she refused him so that she wouldn't have to see him cry. But he kept asking, chasing, insisting. There was nothing else to do but to wipe up the pleasure-cry of her man.

They all stood there watching Ana Davenga. She remembered that not so long ago, none of these people were her friends. They were almost enemies. They hated Ana. For her part, she neither loved them nor hated them. She had no idea what role they played in Davenga's life. And once she found out, she could not remain indifferent. She had to either love them or to hate them. So she decided to love them. They didn't like her. None of them liked having her at the headquarters, knowing all their secrets. The were afraid that she wouldn't fit in and would get them in trouble. But Davenga was madly in love with the woman.

When Davenga met her at a samba party she was pretty and danced smoothly. Davenga liked the way that her body moved. She moved her butt in a beautiful, nimble way. She was so intent upon the dance that she didn't even notice Davenga watching her insistently. In those days he was always afraid. He had to be careful. Men were after him. A bank had been robbed, and the cashier had given a profile that fit his description. The police had already come to his shack several times. The worst thing was that he was not even mixed up in that shit. Did they think he was stupid enough to rob a bank in a neighborhood so close to his home? He worked farther from home, and on top of that, he didn't like robbing banks.

He had done a few bank jobs, but he thought it was lousy work. You couldn't even see the victims' faces. And what he liked was to see the fear, the dread, the terror, in their faces and gestures. The stronger the guy, the better. He loved to see bigwigs scared shitless, like the politician that he mugged one day. It was hilarious. He hung out by the guy's house. When he arrived and got out of the car, Davenga approached.

—You know how it is, sir, life isn't easy. It is a good thing there are guys like you on top, defending poor people like me. —It was a lie. —I voted for you, sir.—That was also a lie. — And I have never regretted it. Did you visit your family? I am also going to visit mine and I want to bring them presents. I would like to show up well dressed, like you, sir.

The guy was no trouble at all. He was afraid of the gun that Davenga hadn't even pulled out yet. And by the time he did, the politician had already done the work of handing everything over. Davenga looked back at the street. It was lonely and dark. A cold daybreak. He told the guy to open the car and turn over his keys. The deputy was trembling while the keys jingled in his hand. Davenga bit his lip, trying not to laugh. He looked deep into the politician's eyes and asked him to take off his cloths, and then picked them up.

—No, sir, not your underwear. I don't need your underwear! You might have some disease or you might have a dirty ass!

When he had collected everything, Davenga pushed the man into the car. He looked at him, swung the keys and waved goodbye to the politician, who waved back. Davenga's heart was bursting with laughter but he didn't laugh. He began to walk fast; he had to cut it short. It was about 3:15 in the morning. Soon the cops would be patrolling the street. Days earlier he had studied the neighborhood.

It was about that time that Davenga met Ana. He had some cash from selling the watch, in addition to what was in the wallet. And with an easy mind, he decided to go to the samba with some friends. However, he knew that he had to keep watch.

And he did indeed keep watch. He watched the movements and the dancing of the woman. She reminded him of a naked dancer, like the one he had seen on TV one day. The woman danced exuberantly at some festival in an African village. It was only when the drum stopped playing that Ana stopped dancing and went to the bathroom with her friends. Davenga watched it all. On her way back she came close to him, looked at him and gave him a long smile. He tried to get up his courage. It took courage to get close to a woman. He went over to her and invited her to a beer. She thanked him. She was thirsty and wanted some water, and gave him an even bigger smile. Davenga got emotional. He thought about his mother, his sisters, his aunts, his cousins and even about his grandmother, Isolina. He thought of all of these women, women he hadn't seen since he had left to make his way in the world. It would be so good if this woman wanted to stay with him, live with him, belong to him. But how? He only wanted one woman, just one. He was tired of not having a secure place to rest. And that woman, who reminded him of an African dancer, had touched something deep inside of him. She had made him long for the peaceful childhood he had known in the state of Minas. He was going to try, he was going to try… Ana, the dancer from his memories, drank water while the madly-in-love Davenga drank his beer without tasting the flavor. When he finished, he took her by the hand and left. Davenga's friend saw him fearlessly cross the dance floor, walking with his new lover's hand in his, and go outside without any thought of danger that might await him. Since that day Ana had lived in the shack and was a part of Davenga's life. She didn't ask him how he made a living. He always brought home money and things. When he was away, his friends made sure that their women brought her what she needed. She didn't need anything. Davenga often asked her to take money and things to his friends' women. They would accept them and ask when and if their men were coming home. Ana knew very well what her man was up to. She knew the risk that she took by staying with him. But she also knew that any life was a risk and that the biggest risk was not even to try to live. On the first night, in the shack of Davenga, when it was all over, and they were calm, and Davenga's tears had been dried — he had let out many tears in his pleasure-cry — they talked and Ana decided to take his name. She decided that from then on her name would be Ana Davenga. She wanted his mark in her body and in her name.

Davenga loved Ana at first sight, and would love her forever. He gave both his name and himself to her. With her he began to discover and to think about the meaning of his life. With her he began to think of the women he had known before her. He felt remorse when he though of one of these women. He had ordered the death of Maria Agony.

He met her while visiting a friend in jail. The friend had picked a fight and it hadn't turned out well. Prison must be horrible. He would get frightened and desperate just thinking about it. If the day came that he was arrested and couldn't escape, he would kill himself. And it was during his only visit that he met Maria Agony. She spent her time speaking of the agony of life without the Lord's protection. That day, when they left the jail, she talked with Davenga. She was pretty wearing a long dress, with her hair pulled back. Her calm voice matched her tranquil movements. Davenga liked to hear Maria Agony's words. They decided to meet the following Sunday at church. When he arrived, the preacher was talking, and she was there with an open Bible in her hands. She looked up and met Davenga's gaze for a brief moment before he lowered his eyes piously. He left and walked over to the bar on the other side of the street. After the prayer meeting was over, she walked outside with the rest of the people, and when she passed in front of him, she gave him a signal. He followed a few paces behind. When the others had left, she told him that she wanted to be with him. She wanted to find someplace to be alone with him. They went and made love for a long time. He cried, as always. They would have many, many encounters. First the church, the prayer, the faith. Then everything in silence, in secret, hidden. One day he got fed up with it. He asked her to come home with him for good. To share the danger with him. To leave the Bible, to leave it all. She resisted. Did he really think that she, a believer and the educated daughter of a pastor would leave everything to live with an outsider, with a criminal? Davenga raged. —Oh! Was that so? Just fun? Just pleasure? Just rolling around in the bed? Once she left it was back to the Bible?— He told her to get dressed. She was still saying no. She wanted more. She needed the pleasure that only he could give her. They left the hotel together, and like always, he got out of the car first and continued walking alone. He wouldn't have to do a thing. He had someone who would do the job for him. Days later the following headline would appear in the papers: PREACHERS DAUGHTER FOUND NAKED AND TORN BY BULLETS. She had a Bible at her side. The young woman was known for bringing the word of God to prisoners.

As hard as Ana Davenga tried, she could not understand why her man wasn't there. All the others were there. Which meant that wherever Davenga was at that moment, he was alone. And it wasn't common, during times of war like that one, for them to go around unaccompanied. Davenga must be in danger, in some kind of fix. Her mind was alive with the stories and deeds of Davenga. In one of these stories was a woman, like her, who was now dead. She had never been afraid of her man, not even of the day that Davenga, with his head lowered, told her this story. She searched the faces of the other women. They were calm. Was it because their men were there? No, that wasn't it. Why were they so calm, and so distant?

When knocks were again heard at the door they no longer forewarned a samba. The samba had arrived. Ana wanted to break through the circle of people around her and open the door. The men closed the circle even more tightly while the women began to sway their bodies. Where was Davenga, where was her Davenga, oh Lord?! What was going on? It was a party! She heard the little voices of the children who had now arrived. Ana Davenga stroked her stomach. Inside was her own small child who was still a dream. The children, from near or far, would learn about their parents' occupations. Some would follow in their footsteps. Some might even find different paths. And what path would her and Davenga's baby travel? Anyway, that was for the future to tell. Except that the future came quickly in those parts. Children grew up quickly. Killing and dying also came quickly. And Davenga's child? Lord, where is Davenga?

Davenga breaks into the circle. Happy, playful, dreamy, spaced out. He hugs his woman. She could feel both his body and his gun pressing up against her.

—Davenga, what's this party for? What's it all about?

—Woman, have you gone crazy? Have you been drinking? Have you forgotten about life? Have you forgotten about yourself?

No, Ana Davenga hadn't forgotten, but she didn't know what she was supposed to remember. It was the first time in her life she had been given a birthday party.

Ana Davenga's shack, like her heart, was full of people and happiness. Some people hung out at Ana's small place. Others squeezed into the neighbor's places, where beer, liquor and many other things flowed. When dawn broke, Davenga told everyone to leave, warning his friends to stay alert.

Ana was happy. Only Davenga would have done that. And she, addicted as she was to suffering, had found pain in the moments that preceded such great joy. Davenga was in bed, wearing only the black, shiny, soft skin that God had given him. She was also naked. It felt so good to just touch each other first. Then came his sobs, so deep, so full of pain, that she delayed his pleasure-cry. They were about to explode inside each other when the door burst open and two armed policeman entered. They told Davenga to get dressed quickly and not to try any tricks because the shack was surrounded. Another policeman pushed open the window from the outside. A machine gun pointed toward the inside of the house, toward the bed, toward Ana and Davenga. She huddled up, covering her stomach with her hand to protect the baby, her little seed, still a dream.

Davenga slowly pulled on his pants. He knew when he had been beaten. What good was life? What good was his death? Prison, never! His gun was right there under the shirt that he was about to pick up. He could grab both of them at the same time. He know that this move would mean his death. If Ana survived the battle, perhaps she would have another destiny.

With his head lowered, and without looking at the two policeman in front of him, Davenga picked up a shirt, a gesture which led to a flurry of shots.

The news reported that a policeman had regrettably died in the line of duty. In the shanty town, Davenga's friends cried for their dead boss and for Ana, who had been killed in bed by machine-gun fire, while protecting the life inside of her with her hands. In an old beer bottle filled with water, the rosebud that Davenga had given her at the first birthday party that she had ever been given, at 27 years of age, was opening.

— translated by Elzbieta Szoka
with Shanna Lorenz

Renata Pallottini

Renata Pallottini

Renata Pallottini was born in São Paulo where she lives and works. She holds degrees in law and philosophy from the University of São Paulo (USP). After working as a lawyer for a few years she decided to dedicate herself to writing and research. She is a faculty member in the department of Arts and Communications at the University of São Paulo where she teaches dramaturgy and history of drama. She has been a visiting scholar at universities in Cuba, Peru, Spain and Italy. Her most important publications include: Poetry: *A casa* (1958); *Livro de sonetos* (1961); *Antologia póetica* (1968); *Os arcos da memória* (1971); *Coração americano* (1976); *Noite afora* (1980); *Ao inventor das aves* (1985); *Esse vinho vadio* (1988); Prose: *Mate e a cor da viuvez* (1975); *Introdução a dramaturgia* (1983); *Colônia Cecília* (play) (1987; 2001); *Nosotros. Romance bolero* (1994); *Um calafrio diário.* Her play *Enquanto se vai morrer* was revived in July 2002. Her work appeared in numerous anthologies in Brazil and abroad. She is also a recipient of prestigious literary awards.

Renata Pallottini

How did you become a writer?

It must have been something very early in my life. Something that started very early. I suppose that I had a certain sense of solitude because I was an only child and didn't have any other children nearby with whom I could share all of my feelings every day, or my sentiments and emotions. Moreover, I was a girl who lost her father very early. I was 3 years old, and that influenced my upbringing and my need to communicate with someone one way or another, and to share with someone this feeling of unexplainable loss, because death doesn't yet have a meaning for a child who is 3 years old. Moreover, I'm also convinced, even though I can't explain why, that people are born with a specific inclination for certain things. It's innate. People are born to communicate in certain ways, to write, or to create music, and others are born to make shoes, and I think that it's marvelous and wonderful that way.

How did your childhood influence your career? What was the role of your family?

My childhood was rather odd because I was born to very young parents. When I was born, my father was 20, and my mother was 18. It was somewhat of a Romeo and Juliet love story, in opposition to the wishes of their parents, who wanted them to wait a while longer. My parents married, but they only had four years of life together because my father died. This loss greatly influenced my childhood, along with the fact that I was an only child. I suddenly became the only daughter of a mother who was a widow when she was 23. It's obvious that my mother had to recreate her life, and I was the child with whom she had to share this restructured life. After two years, she remarried. Then I had a stepfather who was a marvelous man. He was exceptionally refined, gentle and polite. When I hear of children who are abused I think about how I was fortunate to have a stepfather who was a flawless man. He was truly a gentleman. This considerably influenced my life, helping me a lot. I can remember that he told me not to worry about survival, that I should only think about getting an education and about the things that would work for me in the future. I'm indebted to him for this opportunity to study and to do what I wanted. That's something very rare in Brazil. It's for privileged people, and I had this privilege.

Apart from these good things, there were also unhappy aspects: the unexplainable longing that I felt for my father, the envy that I felt in relation to my mother was also something unexplainable for a 5-year-old girl, as well as the fact of being alone. Therefore, I regarded school as an ideal place. I adored school. As we know school is something that many children hate. So, I had a very unusual and different childhood, but it wasn't a sad childhood. I was happy. I can remember my childhood with nostalgia and tenderness. There were many amusements, and I had cousins with whom I shared my life, and who are still my friends today. Mainly boys; more boys than girls. I played soccer with my cousins. It was a free and healthy childhood, but it was marked by this loss. Behind everything, there was still the sadness from my loss.

The role of my family was very important, because I'm clearly a descendant of Italians in everything that I do and in my way of being. In my own way, all of the time, in my creations, in my worldview, in my pleasures, I feel the presence of Italy and Europe very intensely. I have gone there several times looking for the places where my grandparents had been, and I've found very distant relatives in various places. Just the other day, I found an extremely distant cousin in Ancona. Most of my family is from Rome, but, originally, they came from Ancona. There's a small part of my family that's from Puglia, in the southern part of the country. For me, my family was and is important, even though I haven't created a family. My way of being, my personal life and my behavior are extremely private for me. I strongly protect my intimacy and my way of leading my personal life, and, fortunately, my family respects me. Therefore, I can approach them, and I can spend time with them. When I'm lonely, I can call my aunt and say "I'll come and eat macaroni with you," and people will open their doors for me.

I've written about my family many times. My theatrical works include three plays about Italians: *Colonia Cecilia* [*Cecilia Colony*], *O pais do sol* [*The Land of the Sun*], and *Tarantela*. It's possible that I'll still be writing more about my origins and my family. My family has remained a bit behind me because I haven't created a family ahead of me. My friends are my family ahead. There are a few, but I've chosen them very carefully. I care a lot for the friends that I have, including some who aren't in Brazil. One friend in New York, another friend in Rome, a close friend in Paris, a close friend in Madrid, another in Barcelona and another in Portugal. I maintain this family that's ahead through letters and trips.

You have been traveling a lot. Which of these travels means the most to you?

The first long trip that I took was in Brazil. Brazil is so large that it's possible to take many long trips. I traveled by ship. It was an odd thing; a German ship that came here during the First World War. I don't know why Brazil inherited this ship, but it made short trips along the coast of Brazil. My stepfather, my mother and I sailed from Rio de Janeiro to Recife, and we stopped at various ports. It was my first contact with the sea and with other places. This was a big adventure for a 14-year old. Another big trip was during the 1950s, when I went to Europe as a tourist. I was fascinated, and I've always tried to return. I spent a year studying in Madrid. I've had a strong fascination for Europe and Latin America. Today, my favorite countries in Latin America are Cuba, which is the country that I know best, Peru and Mexico which also fascinate me, and I consider Paraguay a very alluring country. The people of Paraguay are fascinating, and they're very gentle people. This must be the Guarani character that they've maintained.

Do politics play an important role in your life?

Without a doubt. When I was in law school, I ended up entering the Academic Center, which was the school's democratic center. That's where my participation or my struggle began. First against the dictatorship of Getulio Vargas, when people we to the streets in order to demonstrate. "The oil is ours!" and all of those things. When the harsh dictatorship came, after the 1964 coup, I was already writing, and I began to write texts against the regime. I wrote plays that were prohibited and haven't even been performed today, because, at the time, they couldn't be performed, and now things have changed and they no longer have the same appeal.

One of these plays, *Enquanto se vai morrer* [*When One Dies*], was written in 1972 during the height of the dictatorship, and it was going to be performed in 1973, but it was totally prohibited. This was very harmful to my career as a playwright. This was a play about my life in the law school and mainly about torture. Torture at that time had reached its most intense level because of the dictatorship. I spoke about a person whom we had studied in law school in the criminal-law course, Cesare Beccaria. During the 18th century, he had written a book entitled *Dos delitos e das penas* [*On Crimes and Punishments*] where he expressed ideas in opposition to torture as a way of determining the truth. Even today, torturers say that they use torture in order to obtain the truth about organizations and people. Obviously the play also included my personal recollections, it included love stories, and situations from those early years in the law school.

There was a time when we recited poetry in the street. Various friends would come together in front of a bookstore, and we would read poetry. The police made us show them the texts beforehand. Many were indicted, too. So, I carried out my struggle against the dictatorship inside the country. Many people left or were forced to leave. I pursued my struggle with my writings, inside the country. Both with my plays and with my poetry for 20 years, from 1964 to 1984. Now, I'm continuing to write about this situation. I'm very disappointed with Brazil's current situation, with the poverty and violence that trouble us today. Violence is a worldwide phenomenon, but in Brazil it is propelled by poverty.

What does it mean to you to be a woman in Brazil?

It means taking part in a struggle to obtain respect for women, as well as dignity and an increasingly fairer position in society because our situation in Brazil isn't fair at all. It's obvious that, for people who have money, things are easier, as they always have been. For poor women who often have to take care of their children alone, which means being a mother and a father at the same time, life is constantly more difficult. They encounter discrimination, and they are mistreated. I'm also thinking about older women today. I wrote a poem, "Mulher longeva" ["Long-lived Woman"]. "Mulher longeva" is an expression that the president of the republic used a long time ago, when he was saying that retired women faced many difficulties in surviving, but that, with the increase in life expectancy, women were becoming more long-lived every day.

I thought that this was an absurd expression. It seemed that he was complaining that women live longer. Therefore, I wrote a poem, *"Mulher longeva,"* which is very much my viewpoint in relation to this matter. Women should be cared for, precisely in the sense that being long-lived is something that everyone wants. Life expectancy is increasing throughout the world. Why should the president of the republic regret the fact that people are living longer?

What about being a woman writer in Brazil?

It means having the same problems as all writers, in general. We don't have editors, and if a person isn't successful, then there's no space in print. Publishers can't be concerned with being selective. They select certain male or female writers who have large numbers of readers and have been successful. They don't attempt to select male or female writers who, even though they haven't been successful, haven't created commotion and don't have marketing, are still people who it is worthwhile to investigate, and worthwhile to notice. The status of writers is divided into those who sell and those who don't sell. Writers who don't sell encounter enormous difficulty in continuing to write and because they don't have publishers, because bookstores won't reserve any space for them; and because Brazil has few bookstores and few readers in relative terms, everything becomes much more difficult, but I don't believe that there's a difference between a female writer's difficulty and that of a male writer. I think that it's more or less the same thing. The credibility that female and male writers have is also the same thing today. Before, there was a time when women who wrote were considered to be either frivolous creatures who were coddled by male companions or, in the words of today's men, a skag that couldn't get laid and was completely unloved. They believed that these women were writing because they didn't have men.

Renata Pallottini

Besides writing you have also worked as a lawyer and an academic. Is there any relationship between these three worlds?

Certainly. My first occupation was as a lawyer. If you look at my creations, either in poetry or for the theater, you'll often find the theme of justice. I have a play that's entitled, *O exercicio da justica* [*Practicing Justice*], and another play that is entitled *O crime da cabra* [*Goat's Crime*], which is a comedy about what crime is and what property is. I also have this play *Enquanto se vai morrer* that takes place in the Law School, and I have another play called *Serenata cantada aos companheiros* [*Serenade for Friends*] that takes place on the 10th anniversary of a graduating class from law school.

The theme of justice often appears in my poetry. Hence, my law school and my work as an attorney initially helped me to learn about a lot of people, because an attorney has to be a psychologist and a priest. A lawyer has to take the oath of professional confidentiality and needs to be trained in that area, and, for a woman, it's a difficult thing to do, without any preconceptions, because women have less of an inclination to keep secrets. We like to share the things that we know with one another. But I learned that, too. I tried to understand people who came to my office by the way they looked, by what they didn't say and by the feelings that were visible. I helped a lot of women who were being abused by their husbands, who wanted to know what they should do. A lot of divorces. All of these experiences prepared me better for knowing human beings.

In that way, my work at the university did the same thing. Perhaps even more, because it was longer. I worked as an attorney for 10 years, and the rest of my life, I have worked as a professor. As a professor, you're always obligated to be up-to-date. You're obligated to study all the time, and you always have contact with young people, with the generations that come after you who make you re-examine your viewpoints and reject frozen things that a typical elerly person doesn't want to see change. The typical elderly person only sees the world with an elderly person's eyes. I don't; I have to enter the worlds of different people and different ages. Being a professor has been very good, it has kept me studying all the time, and it continues to challenge me even today. Right now, I've been reading a thesis about Brecht. All of this has helped me considerably with being alive, with rearranging things, updating myself, looking at other people and thinking about their emotions in comparison with mine, and I think that all of this has been very good for my work.

Does mysticism play a role in your life?

I don't think that I'm a mystical person. However, I have my own beliefs and I could never be a materialist. I believe in God, and I call upon him when I need to. I feel weak, I feel linked to other things, and I always feel that I'm searching for an absolute, that I don't know what it is, but I'm drawn to it, and I call upon it through many names. I'm drawn to entering any church. Any church. When I go to a *Santeria* ceremony in Cuba, where the saints are African gods, I feel moved by the faith of simple people, by the hope that they put in the Savior, in someone who will help them. All of this affects me, but I can't say that I'm a person with mystical tendencies, or that this is expressed in my work.

Whom do you write for?

For everyone. I speak to myself first, however. The first critic and the first listener is me. So much so that, if I don't like what I've done and someone comes and says "This is very good!" it doesn't affect me, and I'll throw it away. I've thrown away many things because they didn't satisfy me, and then they no longer interested me. After myself, I want everyone to read me and to see my work. Without any limits. It's a necessity. I'd like to be able to reach the simplest people who don't have access to anything, and who don't even have access to books or theaters. Therefore, I've done television, too, because television is much more popular, and it affects you much more.

One day, I was asked to recite my poetry on television. Without being modest, I can say that I can recite poetry. That's very rare among poets. I learned in the drama school. The program was very good. It was shown again many times. I think that it would be very good if Brazilian television, which is generally of poor quality, would have more programs of this kind, where poets or actors could read poetry, so that they could reach more people from time to time, for five or 10 minutes. That way, people could gradually learn to understand poetry. It would be a good exercise and even another pleasure in life.

What do you think about globalization?

About globalization done by the Globo network, or globaliztiona in general? I think that it's an inevitability. The world is constantly shrinking in terms of distances. Everything is very fast. If people decide something now, tomorrow they'll be in Europe or China. The world is shrinking a lot not only in terms of physical distances, but also through media. If I go on the Internet, I can find out what's happening in various parts of the world. If I put my text on the Internet, they can be seen throughout the world. On the other hand, it's a shame that globalization is managing to allow the most powerful to oppress, and to control, and to dominate the less powerful. It's also a problem in the sense that the less powerful countries that are called "underdeveloped" or "emerging" nations end up losing their most fundamental, most genuine and most authentic characteristics. Each mountain dweller in Bolivia is constantly becoming less of a Bolivian mountain dweller. I'm afraid that globalization will make everything the same. Everything will be affected by the power that money wields. In Brazil today, you hear a lot of North American pop music. I hardly hear any French music, and no Ecuadorian or Peruvian music. On the political level, this makes us increasingly dependent upon a debt that has been multiplying to such a point that it's no longer payable. We are trapped as a result.

O grito

Se ao menos esta dor servisse
se ela batesse nas paredes
abrisse portas
falasse
se ela cantasse e despenteasse os cabelos

se ao menos esta dor se visse
se ela saltasse fora da garganta como um grito
caisse da janela fizesse barulho
morresse

se a dor fosse um pedaço de pão duro
que a gente pudesse engolir com força
depois cuspir a saliva fora
sujar a rua os carros o espaço o outro
esse outro escuro que passe indiferente
e que não sofre tem o direito de não sofrer

se a dor fosse só a carne do dedo
que se esfrega na parede de pedra
para doer penalizante
doer com lágrimas

se ao meos esta dor sangrasse

The Cry

If at least this pain were useful
if it could beat on walls
could open doors
could talk
if it could sing and uncomb hair

if at least this pain could be seen
if it could jump out of my throat like a cry
could fall out of a window with a crash
could die

if this pain were a bit of stale bread
that you had to swallow hard
then spit out the saliva
soiling the street the cars the space the others
that dark other who passes indifferently
and doesn't suffer has the right not to suffer

if this pain were only the flesh of my finger
that rubs on the stone wall
to hurt hurt hurt watching it
penalizing pain
tearful pain

if at least this pain could bleed

Vivadeus

A Zecarlos Andrdae e Chico Medeiros

Deus é morto. Viva Deus.
Sangre Deus; que Deus se desfaça;
que Deus surja de onde se esconde.
Que ele estoure da História,
ou da Igreja, se ali esteja.
De Marx, se ali ele jaz,
de Freud, se é que pode.
Viva Deus, que Deus renasça
disfarçado como possa,
sem mácula e sem jaça
ou poluído, ou sujo, ou isso.
Quebre-se Deus, que ele se parta
qual os cristais das portas
fechadas, sempre fechadas;
abra-as Deus, alvo e meta.
Possa Deus até ser calvo,
não seja belo nem branco
seja ele a linha reta
que em nossas mãos entortamos
seja Deus ensanguentado,
feminino, semeado,
púbere, fértil, materno,
abeterno, eterno, interno.
Deus é morto. Adeus. A vinda
nova de Deus é saudada,
a vinda de Deus será linda
com a lindeza da Liberdade,
a contra lindeza da saudade,
a antilindeza da nostalgia,
a safadeza da alegria;
e todos os adeuses a todos os deuses
da tortura e da tirania.

Long Live God

God is dead. Long live God.
Bleeding God; may God be undone;
may he gain rebirth, if he can,
may God come out from where he is hiding.
May he burst from History,
or from the Church, if that's where he is,
from Marx, if that's where he lies,
from Freud, if he thinks he can.
LoveliveGod, may God be reborn
as disguised as possible
without a stain or fault
or pollution, or dirt, or anything.
May God break, let him shatter
like the crystal of doors
closed, always closed;
open them God, purpose and measure.
May God even be bald,
not be beautiful or white
let him be a straight line
that we twist in our hands
may God be bloody,
feminine, broadcast as seed,
pubescent, fertile, maternal,
noneternal, eternal, internal.
God is dead. Adieu. The new
coming of God will be beautiful
with the lovely lines of liberty,
the counter-beauty of longing
the anti-beauty of nostalgia
the deception of happiness;
and all the go-with-gods to all the gods
of torture and tyranny.

Declaração de última vontade

Quando eu estiver pra morrer
levem-me depressa a Madri,
avisem Juan Carlos e Sofia
e preparem o Teatro Real.
Flores verhelhas e amarelas,
tapetes pendurados nas janelas
e os reis — tão acertados, tão repousantes.
Tanto, a essa altura, já será vitoriosa
a revolução socialista...
Por que não posso morrer monárquica?
Por que não posso me enterrar antiga?
É um velho desejo, um conflito
insopitado. . .

Levem-me para a Praça Isabel Segunda
(antes, Praça da Ópera)
e deixem que o povo venha vender
      castanhas no meu enterro
Este povo, para sempre dividido
entre a revolta e o amor ibérico às bandeiras.

Mas se alguém me quiser ainda viva
pra responder por malfeitos
ou retribuir um beijo
bastará que ordene à banda pra atacar *La Revoltosa*.
Em dez segundo estarei de pé
com um cravo na orleha
e um touro vivo no coração.

Declaration of Last Will

When I am about to die
carry me quickly to Madrid
advise Juan Carlos and Sofia
and prepare the Royal Theatre.
Red and yellow flowers,
carpets hung from the windows
and the kings — so correct, so reposed.
By that time the socialist revolution
will be so victorious…
Why can't I die like a monarch?
Why can't I be buried in the ancient ways?
It's an old wish, a restless conflict…

Carry me to Isabel the Second Square
(formerly, Opera Square)
and let the people come to sell chestnuts at my funeral
That people forever divided
between revolt and the Iberian love of flags.

But if someone wants me still alive
to answer for evildoers
or to respond to a kiss
I'll just order the band to strike up *La Revoltosa*.
In ten seconds I will be standing tall
with a carnation by my ear
and a live bull in my heart.

Os travestis do Hilton

São os travestis do Hilton,
são tão alegres rapazes!
Ah, confessa! Alguma vez
já correste de salto alto?
Podes rir, em ti não dói.
Sabes lá o que é ser dois?
Quem faz barba de manhã:
Joãozinho ou Vivian?
Quem vai ao enterro da mãe?
Podes rir não te faz rugas...
Quem é que empreende a fuga
guardando a dignidade?
De quem é a identidade,
quem apanha dos milicos
e quem paga o silicone?
Quem atende o telefone?
E quem tem os faniquitos?

É aquela esquizofrenia.
Quem se autodefiniria
antes que um outro o defina?

São tão bonitas meninas!
sim: podemos ser felizes.
Ou: não façamos o gueto.
Queremos ser objetos?
Onde estão nossas raízes?

Que o cílio não se desfaça,
que o dente não apareça,
que a barba espessa não cresça!
Há mil porradas na praça,

The Transvestites From the Hilton

They're the transvestites from the Hilton,
they're such happy boys!
Ah, confess it! Have you ever
run in high heels?
You can laugh, it doesn't hurt you.
Do you know what it means to be two?
Who is it who shaves in the morning:
Johnny or Vivian?
Who goes to Mother's funeral?
You can laugh and not get wrinkles…
Who is it who starts to flee
in a dignified way?
Whose identity is it?
Who gets hit by the soldiers
and who pays for the silicone?
Who answers the telephone?
And who has the little fan club?

It's that schizophrenia.
Who dares define the self
before another defines it?

They're such pretty girls!
Yes: we can be gay.
Or: let's not get down in the dirt.
Do we want to be objects?
Will our roots have to pay?

May our eyelashes not come undone,
may our teeth not show,
may our thick beards not grow!
There are a thousand beatings waiting on the Square,

há mil gringos de avidez.
Quem sou eu? Quem são vocês?

Somos travestis do Hilton,
tão alegres contumazes,
tão loucos e tão felizes
(ou quase).

Se eu sei?

Se eu sei
que algum dia   uma tarde
sozinha sentindo a minha vida esvaziada
terei uma saudade exata deste preciso instante
Se eu sei
que este cheiro de café recém-coado e a
        voz de minha mãe
cantando uma velha canção sem palavras
        velhas até mesmo para ela
estão proibidos de voltar sob nenhum disfarce
Por que não interrompo a voz com um grito
não digo — minha mãe me dá um copo de água
não impeço o momento de ser tão soberanamente
com seus perfumes seus sabores
sua carnação de tempo
se eu sei?

a thousand avid gringos,
Who am I? Who are you?

We are the transvestites from the Hilton,
so joyfully contemptuous
so crazy and so contented
                              (or almost).

If I Know?

If I know
that some day   one afternoon
alone feeling my life emptied
I will feel an exact longing for that precise instant
If I know
that the smell of this just-filtered coffee and my
          mother's voice
singing an old wordless song, old even for her,
are prohibited from returning under any guise
Why do I not interrupt her voice with a cry
why not say — Mother give me a glass of water
why not stop the moment of such sovereign being
with its perfumes its flavors
its time made flesh
If I know?

Vizinha

Vizinha
me dá um pouco da tua sopa
me deixa partilhar o azeite
e as batatas da tua ceia
estou tão triste.

A esta hora da noite
sois ao redor da mesa
uma família
e o vapor da terrina embaça os óculos do homem
e as crianças riem.

Sei muito bem das vossas dificuldades
Que o dinheiro é pouco e a paixão já se acabou

porém
vizinha
tua sopa cheira bem, teus filhos estão crescendo
tens um canário e rosas
e não sabes de nada;
abre porta, vizinha, e me admite no seio
dessa coisa que um dia eu supus acabada
que detesto e desejo,
e não compreendo.
Por favor, por favor,
deixa-me entrar, vizinha.
Estou tão triste.

Neighbor

Neighbor
Give me a little of your soup
Let me divide the oil
And the potatoes from your dinner
I'm so sad.

At this hour of the night
You sit all around the table
A family
And the vapor of the terrine fogs the mens' glasses
And the children laugh.

I well understand your difficulties
That there isn't enough money and no more passion

However
Neighbor
Your soup smells good, your kids are growing
You have a canary and roses
And you don't understand anything;
Open the door, neighbor, and let me into the body
Of that thing that one day I supposed was finished
That I detest and desire,
And don't understand.
Please, please
Let me come in, neighbor.
I'm so sad.

Fica Combinado Assim

À memória do Thomas

Olha garoto fica cominado assim:
não me importa se foi por transfusão
se te picaste com mais vinte ou o quê.

Só o que importa garoto foi o espaço que
                                    deixaste
lugar vazio, palavra falta, pensamento
brilho do teu trabalho, criação
sonhos que nós sonhamos os dois, viagens

tão esguio e sutil eras garoto
tão pouco falamos e me deste um presente
ninguém sabe o que vale e está na minha sala

ninguém sabia talvez garoto o que valias
não me importa que digam foi ou não transfusão
em tudo isso existe um grande e ignóbil preconceito

no teu sangue nadavam peixes de ouro
estás entre os soldados do melhor exército
todos nus e deitados ao sol ouvindo música

garoto meu amado
ouvindo música e sorrindo ao contrabaixo
escrevendo de leve ironias terríveis
e sempre terno

não não foste o meu filho não te choro por isso
choro as mães que nem sabem por que choram
choro as mães que se escondem pra chorar

Renata Pallottini

Then it's all set

To the memory of Thomas

Look, kid, then it's all set:
I don't care if it was by transfusion
If you stuck yourself with more than twenty or what.

The only thing that matters kid was the space that you
abandoned
Empty place, without words, thoughts
The shine of your work, creation
Dreams that we two dreamed, trips

So thin and subtle you were kid
So little did we speak and you gave me a present
No one knows what it's worth and it's in my room

Perhaps no one knows kid what you were worth
I don't care if they say it was a transfusion or what
All that is just a big and ignoble prejudice

Golden fish swam in your blood
You're among the soldiers of the best army
All naked and lying in the sun listening to music

Kid my love
Listening to music and smiling at the double bass
Jotting down terrible ironies
And always kind

No no you weren't my son I don't cry for you over that
I cry for mothers who don't even know why they cry
I cry for mothers who hide away to cry

olha garoto fica combinado assim:
perdemos só esta batalha e não a guerra.
Onde estás brotam flores, é irremediável
teres morrido é irremediável
mas só isso.

Isso não foi o fim de tudo.

Isso

Esse moinho — o poeta —
que em solidão tritura
e amargo grão esmaga

esse operário
que em pó fino transforma
o que lhe dão de carga

essa pedra que mói o que lhe dói

Isso conheço eu que a volta dou à vida
girando e ouvindo o ruído
da pá do tempo a me ganir no ouvido

isso carrego eu
que escavo e esculpo a pedra
com a faca já dita
e que tanto erra

eu que amontôo o grão porque não sei
sepultá-lo na terra

Renata Pallottini

Look kid then it's all set:
We've lost this battle but not the war.
Wherever you are flowers will bloom, it's incurable
Your having died, it's incurable
But only that.

> That wasn't the end of everything.

That

That mill — the poet —
who grinds in solitude
the bitter smashed grain

That worker
who transforms in fine powder
what they give him in goods

That stone that grinds up his pain

I know all that, I who go around life
spinning and hearing the noise
of time's shovel scraping in my ear

That I carry
to excavate and sculpt the stone
with the aforementioned knife
that so often slips

I who collect the grain because I don't know
how to bury it in the ground.

— translated by K. David and
Elizabeth A. Jackson